W9-ACB-842

WITHDRAWN

How Theater Managers Manage

Tess Collins

The Scarecrow Press, Inc.
Lanham, Maryland, and Oxford
2003

SCARECROW PRESS, INC.

Published in the United States of America
by Scarecrow Press, Inc.
A Member of the Rowman & Littlefield Publishing Group
4501 Forbes Boulevard, Suite 200
Lanham, Maryland 20706
www.scarecrowpress.com

PO Box 317
Oxford
OX2 9RU, UK

British Cataloging in Publication Information Available

Library of Congress Cataloging-in-Publication Data

Collins, Theresa.
  How theater managers manage / Tess Collins.
    p. cm.
  Includes bibliographical references and index.
  ISBN 0-8108-4683-7 (pbk. : alk. paper)
  1. Theater management. I. Title.
PN2053 .C615 2003
792'.023—dc21

2002153432

Printed in the United States of America

∞™ The paper used in this publication meets the minimum requirements
of American National Standard for Information Sciences—Permanence of
Paper for Printed Library Materials, ANSI/NISO Z39.48-1992.
Manufactured in the United States of America.

Contents

Acknowledgments

There are so many people to thank and acknowledge for making this book possible: not only those who have contributed directly through interviews and anecdotal submissions, but also the many hundreds—possibly thousands—of people I have worked with during my twenty-plus years in theater, many of whom have become friends as well as colleagues. Each one of them, in their own way, has also contributed to my learning. While I can't possibly name each of these people, I thank them all anyway. My heartfelt thanks also go to the following people: Mark Andrews, Maria Anderson, John Anderson, Robert Atkins, Peter Botto, Mitch Brower, Paul Buller, Isa Campbell, Veronica Claypool, F. X. Crowley, David Cushing, Caron Dawson, Ben Davis, Chris Delucci, Gordon Forbes, Jim Friedman, James N. Frey, Bob George, Michael Gilmore, Ray Gin, Martin Gold, Carole Shorenstein-Hays, Tim Hilyard, Ann Jones, Ginny Kolmar, Hanns Kolmar, Robert Lazzara, Loren Lewis, Louis Ligouri, Bob MacDonald, Margot McFedries, Sherry Eve Penn, Harry Nederlander, James M. Nederlander, Scott Nederlander, Carol Neilson, Edward C. Powell, H. Anthony Reilly III, Mel Rodnon, Howard Rogut, Arthur Rubin, Michael Sanfilippo, Walter Shorenstein, Maria Somma, Debra Stockton, Jim Stoye, Joseph Traina, Jose Vega, Alan Wasser, Herschel Waxman, Alan Williams, Waimea Williams, and Bill Woody.

Finally, a special acknowledgment must be accorded to the Shorenstein and the Nederlander families, who took broken-down buildings and turned them into palaces where theater comes alive. Thanks for giving me my first job in theater.

Since writing the first draft of this book, it is no surprise that many of the people interviewed have gone on to even more exciting work. After an amazing five-year run with the San Francisco company of *The Phantom of the Opera*, Bob MacDonald served as theater manager for San Francisco's prestigious American Conservatory Theater and is currently the company manager of Cirque Du Solie's new production at New York New York in Las Vegas. Joe Traina is the general manager of two off-Broadway theaters, the Gramercy Theatre and Playhouse 91, and will soon produce his first show, Anthony Clarvoe's *Ctrl+Alt+Delete*. Mitch Brower finished a thirteen-year stint at the New York State Theater at the Lincoln Center for the Performing Arts and is now putting his years of experience to work consulting for the National Executive Service Corps on numerous not-for-profit theater projects.

Sadly, Hanns Kolmar passed away after working five decades as a press agent and publicist. He was an example to follow, a rock to depend on, and an inspiration like so many who have lived and worked their lives in theater. It is to these fine people in the theatrical industry that this book is dedicated.

Introduction

It was like any other night in the theater. On November 29, 1933, several customers arrived early to purchase tickets to the operetta *Show Boat*. Twenty-five-year-old Hewlett Tarr checked his watch after selling tickets to a tuxedoed man and his fur-coated companion. As soon as the show started he planned to call his mother and tell her he was on his way home. She was preparing a special Thanksgiving dinner for him and his girlfriend Dorothy Reed. In only a few more weeks Dorothy would become his wife.

The producer, Howard Lang, and the show manager, Lee Parvin, stood behind him engaged in conversation, causing Tarr to lean forward in order to talk to the next customer. He liked this time of night: with less than an hour before the show began at San Francisco's Curran Theater, it was like the beginning of a fairy tale . . . "Once upon a time." For the audience, it was magic. For him, it was a job. Maybe there was a little bit of magic, and he knew the next evening it would all start again.

Tarr looked up at the deep mahogany-colored ceiling which gave the lobby a rich, warm feeling. Built in 1922, the Geary Street theater was an intimate playhouse designed by Homer Curran, San Francisco's theater impresario. Suddenly, a slender dark-haired man with a pencil-thin mustache pushed to the front of the ticket line. A sharp crack sounded. "What was that?" Tarr called out. "My God! I've been shot!" He stumbled backward, fell down a small flight of steps, and collapsed. By the time the first person reached him, he was dead.

Edward Anderson ran from the Curran lobby and hopped a cab to Geary and 18th Avenue, where he robbed the Koffee Kup restaurant of sixty dollars. Several weeks later, he held up the Bank of America at Geary and Jones, stole $1,951, and wounded a policeman in a shoot-out. Once in custody, the twenty-five-year-old, fourteen-dollar-a-week electrician claimed his obsession with a new girlfriend was the reason for his life of crime. "I couldn't do much on fourteen dollars a week," Anderson said. "So I quit my job and started hoisting [heisting]."

Anderson was tried and convicted in record time. The *San Francisco Chronicle* headlines boldly read: CURRAN KILLER MUST HANG! By December 30, 1933, he faced a death sentence for the murder of Hewlett Tarr, and was incarcerated at San Quentin Prison until hanged on February 15, 1935. He lies buried in the infamous Boot Hill cemetery.

In 1933, the *San Francisco Chronicle* printed the killer's story, in his own words. The focus of other articles from that time are on Anderson's love life, his unfortunate friendship with a cohort who encouraged his life of crime, and his own pitiful pleas that the shooting was an accident. After the initial reports of the tragedy, Hewlett Tarr is rarely referenced.

The *Marin Independent Journal's* 1986 article about the unfortunates buried in Boot Hill mentioned Tarr, but it is Anderson's picture printed along with a photo of the cemetery. The killer was the star. Tarr was noted only as a name—even mistakenly identified as an usher, as a person shot by an automatic pistol from the distance of two feet—a footnote. His life and work were unexplored, and after so many years, are forgotten (Allen 1986; "Crowds" 1933; "Jury" 1933; "Slayer of" 1933; "Slayer Tells" 1933).

Unfortunately, for most people who work in theater, the breadth of their work is unknown. Their names go down in history only when they take a bullet. Luckily, most of these bullets are not literal. Working in theater can be fraught with other kinds of bullets—customers, bosses, coworkers, show personnel, or the changing nature of the work itself. Sometimes the bullet is a simple misunderstanding of intent, an ignorance of the way things work, or merely stepping into a situation of which you know nothing.

This was the situation I found myself in over twenty years ago when I accepted a job as the assistant manager of San Francisco's Golden Gate Theater. While recognizing the opportunity presented to me—and at age twenty-two it was a significant one that I might never have again—I knew little about theater management. Much of my learning was trial and error, and at first more error than trial. But, as is often the case, one learns more from mistakes than successes.

I also found another truism—my situation was not unique. Others who worked in theater tell of similar experiences, being thrown into a job and told to do it. Somehow, despite the lack of a theater management background, they figured out how. Marty Bell (1993, xii) notes that, "Even in the best of times, working in the theatre is an irrational occupational choice." And yet, not only do many people still seek to work in theater, they remain involved in some aspect of this industry throughout their lives.

While this book cannot offer the level of personal involvement gained from mentorship, it is intended to be a stepping-stone. Just as having a map makes a journey easier, I hope this information makes it possible for anyone beginning a career in theater management to walk into the theater and have a foundation on which to build, as well as a reference to turn to when in doubt. While my experience is in commercial theater, and much of the information here addresses this type of venue, many of the ideas put forth can be applied to not-for-profit theater and facility management. While this book is from the perspective of the theater manager, I want to acknowledge that there are many people working in the theater building. There are theater employees and the show's personnel, and each of these people could write their own book about how a theater and a show come together to create a theatrical experience.

I have included some experiences, memories, and ideas of other people who have worked in theater. One of the reasons I decided to do this project was that as a theater manager I was always in one place. Shows came to me. There is some advantage to being in the stability of a theater environment where you see many type of shows and observe many different show management styles. At the beginning of my career in my early twenties, the show managers that came to my theater were older. They had been in the profession for many years. As I got to know many of them, they told me stories and shared their experiences and opinions of the industry. After I had been working for about ten years, there was a shift, as many of them retired or became general managers and producers. The traveling company managers were younger than me and I ended up being the person with stories to tell. It is my hope to pass on some of them to theater managers who do not have the opportunity to travel or visit other theaters. It is unfortunate that outside of one's own city, theater managers rarely communicate with others in the profession in the same way that the show's managers tend to talk to each other about the theater and city where they will next visit.

In this book I have brought together the stories, beliefs, and experiences of some seasoned theater managers. Through these, a portrait and a concept will emerge depicting what they have unknowingly practiced throughout their careers. Theater is often known for its ability to "turn on the dime"—that is, to put out its product at the available budget. Yet, cost is only one slice of the pie that forms the whole of theater. The way work is accomplished and problems are solved is through some of the most imaginative and ingenious methods that exist in business management. It is what I call managerial imagination.

In the story of the ticket-seller, the facts are simple. Shortly before the show began, Edward Anderson entered the theater lobby and shot and killed Hewlett Tarr. The reason I have such a special interest in this incident is that in 1982, forty-nine years after the death of Hewlett Tarr, I became the manager of San Francisco's Curran Theater. Work skills can be taught but we start with the people. Each of us has our story.

Part I

THEATER: THE WAY IT WAS, THE WAY IT IS, AND THE WAY IT IS BECOMING

Chapter 1

Theater and Theater Managers

Theater is said to have its origins in the myths and rituals of the world's most primitive people. "Perceiving an apparent connection between certain actions performed by the group (or its shamans) and the results it desires, the group repeats, refines, and formalizes those actions into fixed ceremonies, or rituals" (Brockett 1995, 1–2). While anthropologists can only speculate on the transition from rites to entertainment, that these events were conceptualized confirms that the ancients were the forerunners of organization.

Fifth-century Greek theater is cited as having what might be termed the first theater building. No one knows what sort of management existed for these huge arenas, which held as many as 13,000 people. Did all 13,000 show up on time? Was there a policy for latecomers? Who dealt with two people fighting over the same seat? If a society matron's hair obstructed the view of the stage, did anyone demand satisfaction? We know officials and priests sat in a special place, the Proedria—the front seats, of course, but did the multitudes resent this privilege? (Karayannakos 2002). While much is written about the artistic value of theater's origins, little is known about who managed the facility or how it operated.

Better documented is the role of the actor-manager of the nineteenth and early twentieth centuries. As both artistic and business manager of a theater, these people were the sole "authority" of the organization. The fortunes of the acting company members were dependent on this one individual. This theatrical venture was often a family affair with relatives assigned acting roles (Harris 1994, 3).

While men were the main staple of theater management, it was one of the few nineteenth-century vocations in which a woman competed with equal success and failure. In her book *Nineteenth-Century American Woman Theatre Managers*, Jane Kathleen Curry counts at least twenty theater managers who started or inherited theater companies in the 1700s, long before their better-known counterparts, Laura Keen and Mrs. John Drew, in the 1850s.

Curry (1994, 20–28) documents how these women booked tours across the country or managed their own theaters. She details how some like Mary Elizabeth Maywood did not make enough money to pay her creditors or actors, while more flamboyant characters such as Matilda Clarendon horsewhipped the theater landlord in an incident that might have been a publicity stunt. Madame De Marguerittes lead a police charge to regain possession of her theater when a former manager, Mr. Henry W. Preston, upset by the idea of a female manager, took control of the building with a gang of thugs. While many of these women were actresses who built their seasons around themselves, they also were charged with "holding leadership positions, supervising male employees, and concerning themselves with the practical and business aspects of the theatre" (Curry 1994, 29).

As venues changed from artistic homes for acting companies to becoming real estate for rent and shows became an artistic product of a producer, the theater manager became an employee of the landlord. Inevitably, the area in which theater and production engage each other is mostly a business arena, but in intention they are part of an aesthetic realm and support an artistic vision. The theater manager will walk the line between business and art as they respond to the expectations of their employer and the needs of the show.

The theater manager, sometimes called the house manager, has been defined as the person "responsible for supervising all the other front-of-house employees who are also contracted by the landlord" (Langley 1990, 534). This person is "responsible for the safety of the public, their comfort, and creating the right conditions for their enjoyment of the production" (Menear and Hawkins 1989, 116). When I contrast my own experience of being a theater manager against these definitions, I find them rather generalized. While front-of-house supervision, safety, and audience comfort are important elements of what I do, they are only one part of a complete picture. This is perhaps due to the nature of the company operating the Curran Theater, which allowed its managers more authority than seems to be the prevailing norm. The Curran Theater does not have a resident acting company, and therefore serves as space for traveling productions to perform. In the business, this type of theater is called a roadhouse.

While a theater manager's job can include a variety of tasks, management in general is filled with individuals who misperceive their own roles. "If you ask managers what they do, they will most likely tell you that they plan, organize, coordinate, and control. Then watch what they do. Don't be surprised if you can't relate what you see to these words" (Mintzberg 1990, 163). Former theater manager Bob MacDonald, who also served as the company manager of San Francisco's *Phantom of the Opera*, believes in "a steady, calm approach to the work at all times," and that "common sense" is what serves a manager best. Eighteen-year-manager Joe Traina, who has managed the Belasco Theatre on Broadway, cites being "responsible to the public" as one of the most important duties of a house manager. "We are the face of the industry and need to try our best to present an understanding philosophy. Not always easy, but no other position is as conspicuous to the theatergoer as that of house manager."

A West Coast manager reminds everyone:

> How many of us have the fortitude and the necessary authority to stop a performance in order to prevent injury? This duty is not for the faint of heart, and must always be uppermost in mind and action. Indeed, all activities of a house manager are in preparation for the ever-possible and always awful moment when life-threatening decisions must be made. Your carriage, bearing, dress, and manner must always convey authority, even in the smallest of details. For when the time comes to stop a show in midperformance and clear an auditorium of thousands of people, your authority must not be questioned.

This same manager recounted a situation in which a show's concession salesperson continued to block exits despite dozens of warnings. "I did not hesitate to invite a fire marshal into the house to discuss what I knew to be illegal placement of merchandise stands in the path of egress. His response was quick: if he found an egress blocked, he would issue citations and close us down." While the generalization of being responsible for safety and comfort sounds easy to do, the implementation often leads to circumstances that are not so easy, as these managers pointed out. As Mintzberg (1990, 168) acknowledges,

> the pressures of a manager's job are becoming worse. When before managers needed to respond only to owners and directors, now they find that subordinates with democratic norms continually reduce their freedom to issue unexplained orders, and a growing number of outside influences (consumer groups, government agencies, and so on) demand attention.

Some of the more select responsibilities Traina includes in his job description are to prepare the weekly payrolls of the theater staff, calculate a weekly settlement of expenses for the company and theater owner; prepare various monthly reports on union welfare; house maintenance, and "anticipate any work, improvements, or alterations that might be necessary to the production or the public." While many of these more financial duties can be taught, MacDonald notes that theater is "a 'hands on' business. One must learn it. Mostly it cannot be taught. New people coming out of colleges today think you must go by the book—it is a business of making it happen as it happens. We do not have guidelines, but common sense comes into play."

From the variety of tasks and traits described by these managers, it is easy to see why the duties of house manager are so difficult to confine in a simple definition.

Generally, there are three kinds of theater managers. One is a head usher-manager who sees to the seating of the audience and may try to resolve simple complaints. Duties may include the supervision of other employees such as ushers, ticket-takers, and janitors. This manager may also count tickets stubs, make sure that the public areas of the theater are clean and well stocked with supplies, and handle the opening and locking of the theater premises.

A second kind of theater manager has similar supervisory responsibilities to those of the head usher and ushering staff. In addition to signing a box office statement that accounts for tickets sales for each performance, this would extend as well to a weekly settlement of expenses. Sometimes these managers must explain the expenses to the visiting show's manager, while others send the settlement on to a main office where an administrator or the theater's CEO is the primary negotiator. A more typical scenario is that the settlement procedure is split by having the house manager discuss most issues with the show's manager. Anything they could not agree on would be forwarded to their respective general managers for a final decision.

A third type of manager performs general management duties. This individual is in charge of all theater personnel, both front-of-house and backstage. Department heads for the box office, ushering staff, stagehands, musicians, and wardrobe report to her. She, in turn, reports to the general manager or owner. The physical management of the facility also falls under her domain. She checks the box office statement, puts together a weekly settlement, aids her employer with budgeting and negotiating show and union contracts, and facilitates the show moving into the theater. In addition, she handles any situations that arise with the show itself, as well as with customers and employees. The duties of these three types of managers often intermingle and the lines of responsibility blur depending on the segment of theater and kind of venue for which they work.

The two major divisions of theater are commercial and not-for-profit. Commercial or legitimate theater is epitomized by what plays on Broadway. Marty Bell (1993, xi), in his book *Broadway Stories*, calls Broadway a small town within the big city of New York. Extending from there are road

People You Will Meet
Tim Hilyard, head usher

One of the most interesting people that I have dealt with as a head usher was an elderly woman by the name of Ruth. I was called to assist a patron who had made it halfway to the balcony only to find that she could not make it the rest of the way. After checking with the box office for a relocation, I climbed the stairs to find her sitting out of the way on a stoop and wearing a big smile.

The relocation seat was for the orchestra level. I explained that we had a great seat for her downstairs and that I would help her get to the seat. The next five minutes that it took to assist her down the stairs, I will remember always. In a strong southern accent and a "couldn't be happier" tone, she told me her name was Ruth and that she was from Alabama. After asking my name, she very excitedly explained that we both had biblical names and that the meaning of my biblical name was "to serve God." Though I had heard this before, it sounded much more true coming from Ruth. She further explained that she had traveled all the way from Alabama and little things like seating problems didn't worry her because she had traveled all this way with God.

At first I didn't take this as a literal statement but as she continued I realized that she was very serious. She said, "Whenever God and I go to the theatre, I never purchase *her* a ticket. She always manages to get the seat next to me." I explained to Ruth that the show was well sold and that I could only get her a single seat at the rear of the orchestra but she maintained that "God would find a seat."

At intermission I checked on Ruth to see how she liked her new location and found that the seat next to her, though it had been sold, was empty. She gestured at the empty seat and said, "God and I thank you for your assistance." Before the end of intermission I had informed most of the staff to "Be on your best behavior, God is in the house."

After the performance, Ruth said that both she and God truly enjoyed the show and wanted to know how to get to the cable car because they were going to Ghirardelli for some chocolate. Before leaving the theatre, Ruth stated that she was thankful to be a liberated southern woman who could still travel, and after a quick kiss on the cheek, informed me that my biblical name suited me and that I was invited to Alabama anytime for lemonade.

companies of Broadway or pre-Broadway productions that play major city venues. These tours fall in two categories: first-class and bus-and-truck productions. The first-class tour often includes performers from the New York production or actors who have marquee value. A first-class tour, including the megamusicals in which the show itself is the star, are also defined as "a regular evening bill in a 'first-class' theatre in a 'first-class' manner with a 'first-class' cast and a 'first-class' director" (Farber

1993, 9). Generally, these tours are more closely supervised by the originating production team. While bus-and-truck tours can play major city and first-class venues, they typically are on a small town circuit that might include university and colleges for one-night stands or split weeks (Farber 1993, 10).

Not-for-profit theater includes repertory companies, many of which include or are part of a school; regional theaters, which may operate during summer months or for a specific season; and urban theaters whose productions are charged with a particular goal or mission statement. "A nonprofit or not-for-profit organization is created for the purpose of serving the public. . . . These organizations must be engaged in performing educational, scientific or related public benefit, and may not be privately owned by anyone or created for the purpose of merely serving a particular constituency" (DuBoff 1996, 170).

According to MacDonald, the significant difference between commercial and not-for-profit theater is in "how the money is spent." He also notes that unions make a big difference in how the two segments of theater operate and that "commercial theatre tends to be more exciting." Another West Coast manager has a more cynical view of this difference and states:

> Non-profit folks have their heads in the clouds, while the holes in their pockets bleed cash. Commercial folks make a dive bomb to the bottom line: do it quick, fast, and cheap. Commercial is the way the world works; non-profit (or no profit) is the way heaven would work if there was such a thing and there isn't! Commercial is the $70,000.00-a-year manager out in the lobby hanging posters. Non-profit is the $100,000.00-a-year publicity director calling a meeting next week to discuss which poster to hang.

Regardless of intent and friendly competition, both segments still have buildings to manage. While the management approach may be formed by the interest or agenda of the theater company, the operation of the theater does not vary significantly.

What often does vary is the employer's expectations and your understanding of your job. While the technical, legal, and ethical responsibility of a theater manager toward the building, the customers, and the show is immense, it is often underestimated and unacknowledged by those you work for, serve, or assist. Higher management will often regard union employees as an expense, not an asset; their concern is the bottom line, how much profit the theater will make. This attitude, especially when disparagement of employees is a covert company policy, gives rise to a bitterness and an us-against-them mentality. Managers who can stay above this fray have an opportunity to add to their own experience, even if they might feel their paychecks do not begin to cover their responsibilities.

Traina, who oversaw an ongoing restoration project at the Richard Rodgers Theater, says, "I will probably never have an opportunity such as that again as a house manager, and maybe it's just as well. The owner reaps the benefit of such work and it certainly doesn't ensure your position in any way whatsoever. On the brighter side though, it was a great experience for me and made me a better manager because of it." Traina believes that house managers face

> the same plights as much of middle management across America. There is a growing movement among most upper management that continues to diminish our responsibilities and reduce the importance of the position. It is highly unlikely that anyone not in the field working in the theater building night after night could possess the same insight as the house manager, and yet most of us are underutilized.

San Francisco's Orpheum Theater manager, Robert Lazzara, who counts his normal work week at about fifty hours, and load-in and load-out weeks between sixty and seventy hours, points out: "The hours are long, but I treat myself well. Good food at breaks, I take walks outside to clear my mind, and I enjoy the time-honored theatrical tradition of gossip as a way to let off steam and have a good laugh."

Despite the hours and workload the position of theater manager can be a very fulfilling and diverse job for self-directed individuals who like being captains of their ships. Through my twenty years of managing I have been referred to in the range of "Mom" to "Captain Janeway," though there might have been a few other names behind my back. Theater is one of a few industries where a younger person can move through the ranks quickly. Through hard work and proving themselves able to do the job, ambitious young people can accumulate an enormous amount of responsibility. The same kind of career in the corporate world might take a decade or two.

When I first arrived in San Francisco, I was twenty—not even old enough to buy a drink. I was hired with six other people at a local theater to work in the administrative office. Within the year, all of them had quit, except for me. I soon became the general manager's assistant and was later promoted to assistant house manager of the Golden Gate Theater. After four years, and at the young age of twenty-five, I signed a contract to manage the Curran Theater. Becoming the theater manager gave me experiences, both work and personal, which not only created a career for me but were instrumental in my growth. Through these, I became an adult.

The Association of Theatrical Press Agents and Managers (ATPAM) is the union that represents legitimate theater managers in the United States and Canada. Their jurisdiction covers managers at Broadway theaters, off-Broadway venues, major New York auditoriums, and venues in seven major U.S. cities: Boston, Baltimore, Chicago, Los Angeles, San Francisco, Philadelphia, and Washington, D.C. Their membership also includes show or company managers and press agents. Officially named ATPAM in 1946, its origins can be traced to as early as the 1920s when a group of press agents formed the Theatrical Press Representatives of America (Greenberg 1993, 2).

The positions of house manager, press agent, and company manager cover different but essential areas of theater. While aspects of their jobs are adversarial, it behooves all to get along or at least be professional in their disagreements. Much of this discord will make itself noticeable during the first days that a show moves into the theater, and empathy for the problems of others can smooth ruffled feathers. Do not be surprised that aspects of these jobs overlap, such as when a house manager ends up handling an opening night television crew, or a press agent quells a star's tantrum, or a company manager deals with a disgruntled customer. It is at these times, as MacDonald says, a manager's most valuable assets are his/her ability to: "Stay relaxed and calm at all times. Always be on the lookout. Observe!" Traina notes that the house manager's job is about people. "If you can get along with a great number of very diverse personalities and really like to be around people, that is the best asset you bring to the job."

Many times managers are thrown into the position with little or no training. This difficult situation has the benefit of approaching a complex job with "no preconceived notions of what is expected of you" says a West Coast manager who was in these circumstances. "I started with a fresh slate, a willingness to learn and lots of energy. I tried to be fair to all, never asked someone to do something I wouldn't do myself, and I treated everyone with dignity and respect no matter how small their roles in the operation of the theatre." This same person, after years of experience, believes that moral authority is a manager's most valuable asset. "Managers are the captain[s] of the ship. If they don't look and act the role, and they are not respected and liked, then they will fail. This is not to say a manager should be a pushover; you can still be firm, know right from wrong and stick by your guns, and still be admired and well respected."

While you will hear many of the interviewees in this book state that the house manager's job is to help, this too often becomes a catchword for "dumping ground." This is especially true for situations that cannot be easily fixed, if at all. The house manager must guard against becoming a kind of kindergarten teacher or a repository for everyone's problems. When this perception becomes institutionalized, an odd logic then comes into play that the cause of the problem is the house manager.[1]

Traina points out that

above all else a house manager needs to be understanding of other's needs and points of view. You may not personally agree with the wants and desires of the public, show or employers, but you need to be flexible enough to try to accommodate those needs whenever possible. I also think it's helpful to realize that there's lots of hypocrisy in the theater business in general. Jobs in the theater are not especially skill motivated, I have found, and you need to do the best you can with the people you're surrounded by. If you can enlighten the public and show personnel as to how you're trying to cope with old facilities or special show-related circumstances, in an honest manner, then most of the time you'll be all right.

The job of theater manager is made up of disparate roles. On one hand we are counted on to be hard-nosed negotiators with company personnel; sharp-as-a-tack detectives to ferret out box office theft, payroll inconsistencies, and employee abuses; and nitpickers who give upkeep of the building the white glove test. On the other hand, we are expected to drop our hard edge and give compassionate, beyond-the-call-of-duty customer service to patrons who do not hesitate to scream, lie, and steal. These dual roles are not exactly consistent. Some managers are better at one type of work than the other. The results of these job pressures are best described as driving a manager to "take on too much work, encourage interruption, respond quickly to every stimulus, seek the tangible and avoid the abstract, make decisions in small increments, and do everything abruptly" (Mintzberg 1990, 174).

Mintzberg (1990, 168–72) continues to describe managers in general as moving back and forth between a series of ten roles. Interpersonal roles vary from being a figurehead who represents the company in ceremonial duties or functions—such as going to lunch with customers or vendors; to a leader who directs staff and is responsible for their work; and a liaison between subordinates and superiors. Informational roles are being a monitor who surveys both the environment and staff for important information and trends; a disseminator who keeps necessary information flowing at the appropriate time; and a spokesperson who may represent the company outside the organization. Decisional roles consist of being an entrepreneur who takes personal responsibility to improve their own unit; a disturbance handler who addresses long- and short-term problems; a resource allocator who determines how work is accomplished; and a negotiator who mediates issues from contracts to problems and grievances.

Integrating these roles becomes a job in itself. As I examine a theater manager's responsibilities, these various roles show themselves in different degrees. Within each is a notch of managerial imagination—an ability to look at issues from unusual perspectives and discover solutions that range from common sense to creative management. It can also consist of techniques or management tips learned by experience or from others. Managerial imagination can also come into play when there is no precedent. You have to decide what to do and build a model without having any previous example on which to model it on or a situation to compare it against.

As the person in charge, all the other employees will look to you to know what to do. But, unfortunately, sometimes you will not know what to do. Often managers practice a version of faking it. Pretend that you know what to do, then make the best decision you possibly can. Traina found himself in just such a situation when *A Christmas Carol* played at his theater and a customer in the front orchestra began snapping pictures.

> I was summoned back to the lead actor's dressing room (a frequent occurrence with this actor) and he demanded the film from the patron's camera. I went down into the front of the orchestra section and asked for the film but no one would confess to having been the culprit. I then sent the theater engineer next door to a film shop and instructed him to purchase the cheapest roll of film they had. I pulled the film out of the canister and presented this to the actor right before he went on for act 2. He thanked me and proceeded with the rest of the performance. I, of course, had to pray that the people would not continue to snap his photo for the rest of the show.

Even when we make the best decision possible for the time and circumstances, our judgment is still likely to upset someone. Customers who arrive late can be incensed if you will not seat them immediately. After all, they explain, they paid a lot of money for those tickets and do not care who you have to disturb to get them seated. After yelling at the usher, the security guard, the box office, and you, they demand to be seated this instant. Even when you force them to wait for the appropriate time, the seated patrons now complain that you have disturbed their enjoyment of the show by late-seating the tardy family. And god forbid that some other customers have taken the opportunity to sit in those empty seats. These kinds of situations will pop up daily and everyone will be upset with you, the manager whom they hold responsible for their circumstances. Traina says, "A wise man in the theater once told me to try to stay as close to the truth *as possible* in all things, and I have found this to be a valuable quality in performing my duties."

A West Coast manager thinks that an occasional "crisis" can be just the thing to "free your creative juices." He recalls,

> I managed a theater that had ventilation problems. Seats down front by the stage were always cold. When we turned on the heat, seats in the back under the balcony overhang became too hot. During a cold snap, we had to turn on

the heat. One night the house was full, and seats in the back quickly became overheated. A woman fainted during the first act. At intermission, a man passed out and fell to the floor of the lobby. I bent over to assist him, but he got up too quickly and passed out again. I caught him before he hit the floor, and held him until we could lay him out to revive him. The next day, frustrated with the owner's inability to fix the problem (too expensive they said), and with the memory of the man unconscious in my arms, I dug up the old theater blueprints and stared at the layout of the auditorium, balcony, basement plenum, and the air ducts. The curve of the balcony rail kept getting my attention. This curve made me think: What if we built a wall in the basement [that] followed the balcony curve? This wall would allow us to heat the front of the house, but not send any heat to the back of the house. To my surprise, the owners agreed to the minimal cost. The work was done, and the problem solved. The first night of operation after the wall was done, a man came up to me at the start of the show and complained he was cold in the rear seats, and I knew we were successful!

Taking the time to research, think, imagine, and create led this manager to a solution that no one else had time to conceive. He used his managerial imagination to the fullest.

Now that we are familiar with the kinds of facilities theater managers can work in, the types of theater managers, and the sorts of professional problems theater managers can face, let us meet the people a theater manager works around. I affectionately call them the cast of characters.

NOTE

1. I have often heard press agents express the same frustration. When a show does not sell well, a producer will blame them, when often it is the show that is a flop.

Chapter 2

The Cast of Characters

To meet our cast, let us enter the realm of make believe, with you, the house manager, as a leading character. The Renaissance Theater, located in Midtown, USA, is a 2,500-seat house rented primarily to touring Broadway productions. It is owned by Joshua Jones, a local restaurateur who purchased the property as a run-down, vaudeville-turned-movie-house building, and refurbished it to its 1930s glory. A touring musical production of *The Time of My Life*, starring Broadway great Dan Dandy, and TV soap opera actress, Gina Gem, has contracted to rent the theater for four weeks.

Josh Jones has worked hard, enjoys seeing live shows, meeting stars, and having opening night benefits for local charities. He has reached that time in life when he leaves the details to someone else. And in that pursuit, he hired Eric Edwards as a general manager (GM). The GM is the person the house manager reports to, and will be the person the manager hears from when the show has been booked.

Regarding the GM, San Francisco's *Phantom of the Opera* manager, Bob MacDonald, points out that "keeping this individual informed at all times" is important, "but too much information will burden and get you nowhere. I always look for the right time to get the information in place. Know the general manager is human and not always willing to talk or deal."

The Renaissance Theater GM, Mr. Edwards, is currently negotiating with the show's producer[1] to nail down dates and a contract. The producer wants the show guaranteed $550,000 a week and Mr. Edwards has asked you, the theater manager, to calculate the theater's expenses.

The producer has provided a technical sheet that summarizes the needs of the show. After retiring to your office, you read over the material and then make copies of it for the backstage department heads: the head carpenter, master electrician, master property man, master soundman, and wardrobe supervisor (while these positions are typically designated "man" and often are men, any of them can be staffed by a woman). Each should look at the show's technical requirements for their department and tell you if they have any areas of concern. While they are doing that, you find the crew requirements and begin calculating the cost of presenting this show at the Renaissance. You also estimate cost for box office, ushers, janitors, teamsters, and any other expenses you might incur because of the show. Without knowing what Mr. Edwards has in mind for advertising, how early he might want to put tickets on sale, or how well the show might sell, many of these estimates are merely guesses based on your experience with shows like this one.

If ticket prices have not been set, Mr. Edwards may also ask you to do some gross potentials—an estimate of how much money this show could make based on the ticket price. You will want to make sure you give him a variety of options to choose from and that the prices selected cover all expenses. (Budgeting and gross potentials will be presented more in depth in chapters 8 and 9.)

After completing a budget and several gross potentials, you send them to the GM and wait to hear about a contract. A week later Mr. Edwards sends you a copy of a deal memo outlining the show dates, contract terms, and prices. You, in turn, write a separate memo to the theater's box office treasurer, Sally Smith, giving her the ticket prices, and the tentatively agreed upon percentages for group sales, credit cards, and discounts. Sometimes a GM may do this or have one to several assistants funnel this information to the right person. But, for our purposes, let us keep the house manager involved. Ms. Smith will order the tickets from a ticket printer if the Renaissance is not computerized. Major cities usually have computerized box offices. The treasurer gives the dates and ticket prices to an account representative of the ticketing agency, who then enters it into a computer system for the theater.

Ms. Smith meets with you and Mr. Edwards about box office hours, and is told that the box office will open one week prior to the show's first performance. You are relieved since you budgeted a two-week preliminary sale—so far, you are under budget. Mr. Edwards will reserve newspaper ad space for two weeks prior to opening and the ticketing agency can begin telephone sales when the first ad appears.

The situation I have described above is an ideal one, but rarely do all the events progress so smoothly or even in chronological order. The head carpenter may inform you the theater loading door is two inches too small for the sets, requiring you or him to call show personnel to confirm whether or not the measurements are correct. Often tech sheets have preliminary estimates made well in advance of any set being built and the final numbers may be different. If this is the case, does the set get cut down to size, does the door get widened, or does the show get canceled?

Suppose the show wants to come in on a guarantee, but Mr. Edwards insists on a "four-wall deal" where the show guarantees his expenses. A four-wall deal is a contract term that specifies that the show is taking over the theater wall-to-wall. Basically it means that the show guarantees the theater's expenses. On a four-wall deal, much of the preliminary activities such as calculating gross potentials, arranging for advertising, and setting the box office opening date could be done by the show's management rather than the local theater staff. The producer and GM may not agree on a contract until after the show opens, and in extreme cases, closes. As the house manager rides these waves, he often discovers that ironing out details is an ongoing process.

Now let us jump to two weeks prior to the show's opening. Based on the budget provided to the treasurer, Ms. Smith will hire ticket sellers and prepare the box office for the first day of sales. Carol Neilson, who has worked as the head treasurer at San Francisco's Golden Gate and Orpheum Theaters, lists some of her presale duties as putting "all house, company seats,[2] press and sound kills[3] on hold, preparing the house seat book, the performance back-up file, will-call file, and information sheets for the ticket-sellers." She also talks to the company manager about their company seat release policy, VIPs, and anyone she should be aware of for special treatment.

Orpheum manager Robert Lazzara itemizes his preshow work:

> type and distribute the show schedule; arrange parking signs so the trucks can unload; review the show contract, do preliminary outline of settlement, run settlement issues past the GM; review ushering and box office schedule; touch base with the show's company manager and stage manager; review the show's technical rider and verify that all local requirements are met; review supplies (office and janitorial) and order if needed; inspect the theatre for safety and comfort problems.

There are four other theater department heads that you will notify of the basic show information: the musician contractor, security, stagedoor person, and the head usher.

If the show is a musical, the show's conductor or musical director will contact the theater's musician contractor directly to find out about rehearsal spaces, local conditions, and hiring the best players. As a rather intimate community they may already know each other, or find one another rather easily though the Musician's Union. The American Federation of Musicians boasts over 424 local affiliates, representing 45,000 musicians throughout North America (www.afm.org 1998). As a last resort, the house manager may receive a phone call asking for the musician contractor's phone number. The house manager does not become involved in the hiring of the musicians. The contractor, who is hired by the theater, will acquire them from the Musician's Union based on the instrumentation required by the show. At this point, these musicians become employees of the theater but will work under the direction of the show's conductor.

The head of security schedules guards to be available for the load-in and load-out of the set, and to aid the trucks in parking and watching over the loading area to ensure no one walks away with equipment, props, or set pieces. During performances, security typically works more in the front-of-house area, watching for purse snatchers, pickpockets, and annoying or abusive panhandlers. They may be called on to help intervene with out-of-control customers or problem employees. The physical setup of the building determines the need for security in different areas. A theater situated directly on a city street may require more security than one located in a complex where access and sophisticated surveillance equipment discourage criminals. Since Dan Dandy and Gina Gem are fairly well-known performers, they may require additional protection. The show's manager will alert you to any known problem fans or stalkers.

Security can be a delicate area. While guards work at the direction of the manager, there may be times when their law enforcement expertise supersedes the manager's experience. This can especially be the case when the theater employs off-duty police officers or those who have more than basic security guard training. A West Coast manager relates this story:

> [A] drug-crazed young woman attending a rock concert at the theatre next door . . . crashed into our lobby and entered the balcony during a show. She climbed over patrons, grabbed people and thrashed about. We called guards to the balcony, where they attempted to subdue her. It was only when a guard got a hold of the woman's hair and yanked it hard that she calmed down. They began dragging her out of the theatre by her hair. Her strength was almost superhuman, but I didn't realize this. I told the guard to stop dragging her by the hair, and he just looked at me and said, 'Do you want to do this?' 'No!' was my answer! On the street, the guards flagged down a patrol car where an officer came to arrest the woman. While he was holding her, she jumped up and struck his head with her chin, causing a sharp crack in his skull! I will never doubt a security guard again when they are dealing with a problem like this.

The stagedoor person has a position that is part security, part public relations, and part clerical. Usually stationed at the door to the backstage

---

People You Will Meet

Martin Gold, production stage manager

After a show has officially opened, the key element in my work as a stage manager is to maintain the concept of the creative aspects of the show. This includes making sure that the actors maintain their performances, that the understudies are prepared to go on at a moment's notice and that they blend into the production in a natural and nondisruptive fashion. When a director returns to look at his show after not seeing it for a good length of time, and after it has gone through a series of replacements, it is a source of great pride to the stage managers if the director is pleased with what he sees and finds that the performance is fresh and vital. Rightfully, the stage manager can take a good part of the credit for the show's condition. It follows that he has fulfilled one of his most important job functions.

---

area, he must quickly get to know the show personnel and know whom to allow access. He will accept packages, take messages, and announce the arrival of company members' guests. Those showing up at the stage-door can range from family and friends, to fans wanting autographs, to admirers and even stalkers. The general philosophy of the stagedoor person is that no one gets backstage—no one. This is usually the best and safest approach to visitors.

A company member expecting guests should be summoned to the stagedoor where he is responsible for identifying his guest, and escorting the person in and out of the theater. If a star performer is not in a position to come to the stagedoor, an assistant, wardrobe dresser, or stage manager will accompany the guest to the dressing room. Under no circumstances should the stagedoor employee allow a stranger into the theater and say that the dressing room is down the hall and to the right. Even the most upright individual may be unable to resist wandering out onto the stage and taking a prop as a souvenir. Additionally, backstage areas are fraught with trapdoors, electric equipment that should not be touched, and delicate costumes that could be jeopardized by someone picking them up. Show personnel who reset their departments for the next day might miss the fact that a visitor had unwittingly moved a costume to a different rack and out of its proper order.

In the front-of-house the head usher supervises the ushers and ticket-takers, whose primary responsibility is seating the audience. The head usher will also keep count of the programs, inform the house manager of shortages, and assign duties to the ushering staff. These may include stuffing programs, lobby and bathroom cleanup after the walk-in and intermission, and dealing with customer emergencies such as illness or accidents. The head usher should work closely with the house manager to train ushering staff in both customer service and theater safety. Based on the available information, a memo to department heads can look something like this:

Date: January 1, 2003
To: All Department Heads
From: Tess Collins, house manager
Re: Tentative* Schedule, *The Time of My Life*
Performance dates: June 2, 2003 to June 29, 2003
Box Office opens: May 24, 2003
Load-in: May 31, 2003
Rehearsal: June 1, 2003
First preview: June 2, 2003, 2 P.M. and 8 P.M.
Opening: June 3, 2003 8 P.M.
Final Performance: June 29, 2003, 3 P.M.
Load-out: after the show, June 29
Regular performance schedule:
    Tuesday: 8 P.M.
    Wednesday: 2 P.M. and 8 P.M.
    Thursday: 8 P.M.
    Friday: 8:30 P.M.
    Saturday: 2:30 P.M. and 8:30 P.M.
    Sunday: 2 P.M.

---

* Always use the word "tentative" on these preliminary schedules. Things change very quickly in this industry and a show booked one week can be canceled the next. Some unions require an authorization to hire, which should be a date as close as possible to the show's opening. Still, you will need to get preliminary information out sooner and do not want anyone to use your tentative information as an authorization to hire, because once hired, union employees usually have some minimum contractual salary.

Another memo would go to the box office detailing their hours (see page 21).

The more information given to the treasurer about advertising allows Ms. Smith better opportunity to prepare for sales. It could be that more people will buy tickets when television commercials run than after the second or third print ad, so the more details the better.

In addition to the departments inside the theater, there may also be a theater administration with employees that deal with subscriptions, group sales, accounting, publicity, and marketing. The people in these offices will be working on the show in the weeks, and sometimes months, before the show arrives to town.

Date: January 1, 2003
To: Sally Smith, treasurer
From: Tess Collins, manager
Re: Box Office Hours, *The Time of My Life*
First print ad/telephone sales: May 23, 2003
First TV ad: May 25, 2003
Box opens: May 24, 2003
Hours: Monday–Saturday: 10 A.M. to 6 P.M.
     Sunday: 12 to 6 P.M.
Performance hours:
     Monday: 10 A.M. to 6 P.M.
     Tuesday–Saturday: 10 A.M. to 9 P.M.
     Sunday: 12 to 6 P.M.

The subscription department may have been busy selling the show long before the house manager becomes involved. If the theater has a subscription season, several shows may have been put on sale to the public, perhaps months prior to any show arriving. Subscriptions are known as the bread-and-butter of theater. By providing a presold audience, producers know they have a cushion should single sales not be up to expectations. Subscriptions often have a discounted price that will affect the gross potential. The subscription manager will supply these prices to the box office treasurer and a subscription percentage is charged on the box office statement. This percentage is retained by the theater as its subscription fee. The perk for subscribing is that the patron receives priority seating in advance of single sales. Longtime subscribers often have the advantage of sitting in the same seats season after season.

The group sales department maintains a list of regular groups they sell to; it also takes orders from a onetime group interested only in a specific show. The number of tickets that constitutes a group is decided by the producer and the GM. For a large order, a group sometimes gets a discounted ticket price at an amount set through agreement between producer and theater. A commission is charged on the box office statement as a fee for the group sales department.

Press agents may be employed by the theater, but with road productions, they are more likely connected with the show. A theater that has a press agent will usually put him in charge of maintaining local press lists and relationships with the town's major critics. He would be responsible for gathering marquee artwork, the publicity budget, press releases, ad copy, reserving ad space, TV, and radio time, and securing approval for all of these. Familiarity with the local press is an asset in getting publicity for the shows and in booking performers as guests on television for publicity and advertisement.

In review, we have seen that the setup of a theater begins with a GM. Underneath him is a series of department heads that include the house manager, subscription manager, group sales, and press agent. Inside the theater the house manager supervises the backstage departments: carpenters, electricians, props, sound, wardrobe, and stagedoor. In the front-of-house this supervision covers the head usher, security, and box office treasurer.

Now that you have a sense of who operates the theater, let us move on to the show personnel and the engagement.

NOTES

1. As you will see in the next chapter, this sample show also has a GM who may be the one to negotiate on behalf of the show. However, to avoid overuse and confusion of the title "general manager," I have designated the show's representative as the producer. In cases where the show's GM is the main contact, the producer's role can range from raising capital to artistic development.

2. House and company seats are tickets, usually in prime locations, which are set aside for guests of the show and theater to purchase.

3. Press and sound kills are seats that are taken off sale. Press seats are held for nights when reviewers and critics are invited to see the show; these tickets are usually complementary. Sound kills are seats that will not be used at all because the show equipment, usually the soundboard, will be placed in this location. These tickets are subtracted from the theater's potential sales.

Chapter 3

The Show Must Go On

Within weeks of *The Time of My Life* moving into the Renaissance, the schedule of your day will take on a quality of a roller coaster, a speeding bulletlike projectile moving toward opening night. There are three people from the show with whom the house manager may have the first contact: the show carpenter, stage manager, or company manager. Let me make clear that we are observing the people in these positions from the perspective of the house manager's dealings with them. Each has a complex, comprehensive job, and certainly could have a book written from their point of view about the rigorous work they perform. Orpheum manager Robert Lazzara says that the touring company's manager usually calls several weeks prior to opening. "We discuss all aspects of the show—from money matters to temperamental actors." About a week before the show, the stage manager calls and "discussions are focused on the load-in, rental equipment, expendables (if any), running times, and the late seating policy." Other questions about stage or production personnel depend on the size of the show. "A big musical might have a production supervisor or specific needs, like pyro, in which case we would discuss the . . . [particular] needs of the show which must be obtained locally."

Depending on how the show is set up, one of these people—company manager, stage manager, or carpenter—will contact you to get the theater's technical information. This packet, detailed in chapter 5, contains stage blueprints, measurements, dressing room configurations, and front-of-house information.

The carpenter will be more interested in stage measurements; the stage manager in dressing rooms, offices, phones, and rehearsal space; the company manager in box office, housing, physician's lists, and local transportation. In some companies the stage manager and company manager share certain responsibilities, or at times their company members will pester them with the same questions. So, it is likely you will be asked for information several times.

The company manager is for the show what the house manager is for the theater. When company manager Helen Harman calls you to touch base, she has reviewed your information packet on the Renaissance Theater and has some questions about housing. Some company managers who have worked extensively on the road may have their own records on each city and theater they have played. If this is Ms. Harman's first time in your town, she is as much a stranger to it as a tourist. She will be busy arranging housing and transportation for her company, and at the same time, needing information about company seats, how sales are going, requesting sales reports for her general manager (GM), and facilitating the move out of the city where the show is currently playing. At this point providing information to her is your primary function. As much data as you can get into your packet will cut down on the number of phone calls.

The stage manager is responsible for "everything that happens onstage and backstage" (Farber 1993, 72). You may or may not hear from him prior to the show's arrival. The key information you will want to get is the running time of the show, the late seating policy, rehearsal schedule, and any specialties or exceptions. For instance, if the show has extensive pyrotechnics, this may require a visit from a fire department inspector to view the production and license its safety. If the pyro is as simple as smoking a cigarette or lighting a candle, then depending on your city, it is possible that only a permit is necessary. Since the show is coming to you from out of town and their staff likely knows nothing about your local and state fire laws, it is up to you to inform them of any regulations, keep required permits up-to-date, and maintain a relationship with local officials so that last minute details do not derail the show's schedule.

Most companies employ three stage managers. The highest rank is the production stage manager (PSM). The PSM is often considered the on-site director who keeps the show fresh and in top form. He can "call rehearsals, do replacement casting, and direct the rehearsals" (Farber 1993, 72). He is "in command of stage, performers and crew during performances throughout the run of the show" (Langley 1990, 44). Under him are the first assistant stage manager and the second assistant stage manager. Their duties can include acting as an understudy, helping out at rehearsals, checking the stage prior to performance, and miscellaneous duties assigned by the PSM. These positions are represented by Actors' Equity. It is rare for a roadhouse to have an on-site stage manager, though some may employ a technical director who would coordinate with the show's crew.

The show carpenter may communicate directly with your house carpenter rather than calling you. His main concern will be loading the show into the theater. Any problems will probably be communicated to you via the house carpenter. You will discuss these problems with the company manager or your own GM rather than talking directly to the show's carpenter. In any preliminary discussions, the key information you will want to get is the day and time of the load-in.[1] You will need this information to schedule security and stagedoor personnel, as well as to adjust your budgets.

Some time during the day of the load-in you will meet the rest of the show's crew, though there are instances of house managers never having to interact with backstage personnel. Typically, these visiting department heads will need to order supplies on your local accounts, and check sightlines with you and the treasurer in case some seats need to be taken off sale. If this includes locations already sold, the people holding those tickets will need to be reseated. Other items to discuss would include safety, especially if elements of the set, such as speakers, lighting instruments, soundboards, or even an extension of the stage, protrude into the house.

The show supervisors will mirror the house department heads:

- carpenter
- electrician
- props
- sound
- wardrobe

And at times will also include:

- pyrotechnics
- makeup artist
- conductor
- automation
- dance captain
- hairdresser

The press agent Brian Barnes may have already been to your city in the preceding weeks. At that time, he will have set up press interviews for the two stars, publicity for the show, and looked at a few apartments for Ms. Gem and Mr. Dandy on behalf of the company manager. Most show's press agents are located in New York, but often they will work with a local press agent who knows the market and has the contacts necessary to promote the show. The house manager's main interaction with the press agent early on will be regarding marquee, front-of-house publicity shots, and special events that might take place in the building and on opening night. Press agents can be invaluable for dealing with difficult performers and personalities. Press agent Harvey Sabinson is said to have acted as a cushion between one of the industries more difficult producers, David Merrick, and the rest of the world. "Sabinson was . . . gracious where his boss was gruff, congenial where his boss was contentious" (Kissel 1993, 309).

If Brian chooses not to use the box office to dispense opening night tickets to reviewers and special guests, then an area needs to be set up for him. The press agent will accompany television crews and photographers invited to tape and photograph parts of the show for publicity purposes, and insure they only record approved portions. Once you have found out what type of press is coming, you will need to inform your department heads that these individuals will be filming according to established guidelines, set aside a place for them, secure a sound feed from the show, and provide electricity. Most crews are self-contained, but sometimes something needs to be plugged in.[2]

Just as the theater has an administrative office, the show will have its own parent company that manages the show for the producers. The person heading this operation is also called a general manager. He may manage several shows for a variety of producers, while others work with one very successful producer or producing company. For most road shows, this office is located in New York, but can be located anywhere. Producers such as the Really Useful Company and Cameron Macintosh, Inc. are located in England and funnel their foreign business through a New York GM's office, while some may open a satellite office close to Broadway.

The GM's office might include a production manager, production personnel, a group sales division, press associates, and various assistants. If these people are not on staff, they are often outside vendors whom the GM hires. The show's GM will negotiate contracts on behalf of the production. These contracts can include the terms with the venue, the actors, show crew, equipment rentals, and production contracts.

Depending on their relationship, the GM will either hire a design team or consult with the show's producers about assembling a team and make recommendations about which vendors or individuals to use. This can go the other way around as well if the producer is without a GM. In this case production designers can recommend a GM they have worked with successfully in the past. Once the show is touring many of the daily duties are transferred to the company manager who works under the GM's authority.

In commercial theater, the producer is usually the person who discovers the show, though in some cases a GM or other person brings a product to a producer or producing organization. After rights are secured, capital is raised, and staff hired, a producer's involvement varies. Some limit their presence to opening night and reviewing their royalties and profit/loss statements; others take a more active role in airing their opinions of the production. In total, while the producer may be a nebulous figure around the theater whose presence is rarely felt, her contribution and ultimate authority should not be underestimated. The bottom line, after all, rests with her. "The primary goal . . . is to make as much profit as possible. If, however, there is no profit, and there are outstanding debts after all the capital has been spent, then the producer is personally liable" (Langley 1990, 28). Many shows are now organized as limited partnerships, or another type of business entity, for liability reasons. Yet, whether the producer is at the theater or sitting in an office 3,000 miles away, covering expenses and profit are on this person's mind, and because some of those expenses are generated by the theater, it is prudent to be mindful that the theater manager's work may be called in question.

The show is designed by a production team that, depending on how long the show has been touring, may come to put it into the theater. If the production has been traveling for some time, the crew that travels with it will install the set. In an originating city where a new production is being created, a production manager supervises the project. The design team is made up of the people who put the show together. They include a scenic designer, costume designer, lighting designer, sound designer, occasionally a pyrotechnic or special effects designer, and makeup designers, as well as assistants and staff who work under each of them. Often the design team will stay through the opening night, and occasionally until reviews are out, in case changes are needed.

People You Will Meet
Mel Rodnon, production musical contractor

From their inceptions I have hired the orchestras and done management/ union liaison and worse for: *Cats, Starlight Express, Aspects of Love, Song and Dance, The Phantom of the Opera, Sunset Boulevard*, and others for Andrew Lloyd Webber; in addition, *Les Miserables, Miss Saigon*, the original *Chicago, Chess, My One and Only, On the 20th Century, Singin' in the Rain, Pippin*, and many others including the Royal Shakespeare Company's *Nicholas Nickleby*. To give some idea of the amount of people involved, for [a show like] *The Phantom of the Opera*, both on Broadway and on tour, I reckon that I engaged something like 1,500 musicians alone. Over the years the theatre music business has gone through some serious changes. Years ago someone like myself had rather a lot of power due to inadequate contracts and lack of cohesion from the musicians themselves. That has all changed . . . there are Musician's Committees galore to advise the union for their needs and wants. Some of it is a bit over the top but that's the way of the world now. The theatre music business is much more structured and the music is more difficult to play, bringing a generally higher caliber of musician to the theatre than before. You have only to compare the scores of *Hello Dolly* and *The Phantom of the Opera* to see what I mean. One other reason for the influx of top musicians in the theatre is the collapse of the recording and jingle industries in the major cities, mostly due to the use of the synthesizer and the nature of today's music.

Because most shows are put together in New York and travel out from there, the house manager will probably never meet the design team. Long-running shows such as *Les Miserables* and *Phantom of the Opera*, whose stays in a theater may last longer than a year, will have members of the design team come out periodically to view the show and make adjustments and improvements. Rarely does the theater manager become involved in these areas unless there is a direct impact on the show. One example of how a house manager and designer might interact would be that of lighting. Nearly every lighting designer who crossed the threshold of the Curran wanted the exit lights dimmed and the aisle lights eliminated. Obviously, the fire department would have closed us down had we granted this request. But, often there are compromises, such as darkening the gels over the exit lights so they are still bright enough for the audience in the event of an emergency and dim enough to please the eye of the designer. Remember that any changes you make in an area that might affect audience safety must be considered carefully and should have the approval of the fire department or designated government agency.

And finally, the last people through the door are those who bring the product to life, the performers. They may be stars, singers, actors, dancers, principal performers, or chorus members. Contrast the empty hull that the show carpenter walks into at 8 A.M. on the morning of load-in with the prepared dressing room, arranged costumes, and set stage that the actor sees at the next day's rehearsal. This often gives an actor the reputation of being privileged, in contrast to a stagehand who uses his physical labor to install the set, the wardrobe people who dress others with dexterity and quickness, box office personnel who supply their computer skills, and ushers with their knowledge of the theater building. The actor, on the other hand, uses himself, his physicality, his talent, his essence, to do his job. Despite enormous sets, spectacular pyrotechnics, and full orchestra, it is the actors who must create the fictive dream; it is they whom the audience comes to see create magic onstage. "When the work of these artists is placed before an audience, the dramatic illusion is created. . . . Each audience member selects out of this experience—this movable feast—that which he needs, that which is meaningful and relevant and nourishing to him personally" (Pickering 1975, 22). Herein lies one of the most concise reasons for theaters to exist—the audience.

THE LOAD-IN DAY

Now, it is 7:30 A.M. on the day of the load-in. On your way to the theater you stop and get a strong cup of coffee. Theater people are usually night owls so it is good that load-ins only happen once a show. In front of the theater, two forty-five-foot trucks are parked back to back and a number of stagehands and teamsters meander around talking, drinking coffee, and filling out employment papers. You check in with your head carpenter and find out that all is on schedule, but that the show's carpenter foresees some problems fitting a set piece into the odd angle of the theater's back wall. This might require staying late to rebuild it.

At 8 A.M. the teamsters begin unloading road boxes from the trucks. They take the crates to the stagedoor where the local stagehands, under the direction of the show's department heads, unpack them and begin installing the set. All during the morning your department heads call you about various show- or theater-related items. The electrician needs to restock the show's inventory of duct tape, light bulbs, and gels. You okay the order and remind the electrician to give you the packing slip. Once you have this invoice, mark it as an item to be charged to the show. The propman has found a leak underneath the sink in a star's dressing room. He has wrapped it with duct tape and put a bucket underneath, but that will only hold for a few hours. You call the plumber and insist on service that day.

At 10 A.M. you inform your GM about the potential problem with the set. If this cost is incurred, he will have to discuss responsibility for the expense with the show's GM. This is one of the gray areas in theater/show contracts. The question becomes, is it the show's fault the set does not fit on the stage or the theater's fault? The theater will argue that the building comes "as is" and any changes to it must be restored to the original condition before the show leaves. The show will argue that they sent their tech requirements out months ago, so it is not their problem if the set does not fit. The resolution is usually dependent on negotiating skills or relationships.

Around noon, Helen Harman, the company manager, arrives after spending the morning getting her cast and company members into hotels, arranging transportation, and a hundred other details of moving seventy people from one city to the next. After introductions you will take her down to meet the treasurer so they can conduct any business relating to company seats and opening night tickets. Helen checks out keys to her office and proceeds to set it up from a workbox taken off the third truck. You and she may talk several times during the day about items she needs to arrange, such as a veterinarian for Gina Gem's Pekinese. Your specs did not have one listed. Point made, the more information, no matter how unlikely it might seem, the better. She also tells you that the two stars will be arriving nightly in two separate limousines. You take down the information to give to your security guards, who will allow the cars to park near the stagedoor.

At 1 P.M. the wardrobe crew arrive and unpack the costume crates. They will spend the day setting up the costumes in dressing rooms; learning the sequence of dressing the performer they are assigned to; and getting work assignments from the show's wardrobe supervisor about costume cleaning, repairs, and maintenance. Around 3 P.M. the trucks are completely unloaded and the teamsters repack the empty crates and take them to storage.

PREPARING FOR THE PERFORMANCE

Brian Barnes stops by to look at the marquee and front-of-house display cases, speaks to the treasurer about his opening night tickets, and checks in with the company manager. Knowing that the first performances are only half sold, Brian and Helen call you about dressing the house. Sometimes referred to as "papering" or "comping," it means to fill the house with people to make it look better. This usually happens on a preview performance or on opening nights in order to elicit a robust audience response when critics are reviewing the show. Bob MacDonald tries to "collect lists of local groups—drama groups or students" to fill out performances which need comping. Joe Traina adds that it is a good idea to "give the tickets to the people who are most likely to turn out in the greatest numbers and who will talk about the show." A West Coast manager advises that the decision to paper an audience be made "early enough to make calls and send out the tickets. Actors can be the best audience, so try the local equity offices or acting schools. Other theaters can offer tickets to staff members who enjoy shows. Keep a list of past invitees who were good audiences and invite them again."

People You Will Meet
Hanns Kolmar, press agent

My former job (I'm now retired after more than fifty years of writing press releases, setting up interviews, making up ad schedules, and baby-sitting stars and featured players) not only consisted of publicizing shows and personalities, but also (in special cases), keeping personal things and offstage "adventures" of the star entrusted to our care *out* of the papers and *off* the TV screens. But the job also brought with it many perks. For example, when I toured with *Give 'em Hell, Harry*, starring James Whitmore . . . I was given personal tours of the Truman Library in Independence, Missouri, and the White House in Washington, D.C. And I'll never forget the day in the 1940s when I took the great but much maligned Paul Robeson for an interview at the *Oakland Tribune*, then owned by the wonderful actor-singer's chief malinger, Senator William Knowland—and the whole staff applauded Robeson. At age eighty-six, I have plenty of memories; maybe I'll write a book or do a one-man show.

After conferring with the treasurer, your company will give out 300 tickets for the two performances and Brian and Helen will distribute another 200. Since the first performance is a preview, a similar amount will also be distributed for the show's opening. An enthusiastic crowd is important on opening night. Most theaters maintain a complementary ticket file or comp list—a slate of organizations that provide audiences for shows. Sometimes the house manager will distribute complimentary tickets. Other times this is done from the administrative offices, with the house manager receiving tickets for her staff.

Comping by a house manager is best started with the people who have worked on the show. Even those who are working the performance and will not be able to see it love to have their families come to watch what they are a part of. From there, the comp list spans out to include other theaters and their staffs, other shows if they have a night off, group sales leaders and hotel concierges as an incentive to purchase tickets, and nearby merchants who might have been inconvenienced by the load-in. Lastly are groups which are used strictly as fillers—bodies in the seats. These include senior groups, charities, programs for the disadvantaged, and student groups.

CLOSING OUT THE DAY

At 4 P.M., the house carpenter calls you to say the set fit with some minor adjustments and they will not have to stay late. At 5 P.M., everyone is leaving the theater for the day. A technical rehearsal is called for 8 A.M. the next morning, with performers arriving at 1 P.M. for a run-through. The musicians are already rehearsing at a rental hall down the street, and tomorrow they will be in the orchestra pit by 12:30 P.M. for a brushup before the stage rehearsal. By 6 P.M. you are walking out of the building as well.

A good way to describe what the house manager is doing while all of the above is going on is simply "keeping track." That is—getting a sense of what is going on and anticipating responses. Troubleshooting might be another way of saying it. If there is trouble, just being available, listening, and exerting a presence is the unassuming way of looking at your job. Checking in with key department heads throughout the day, touching base with the treasurer, passing out comp tickets and making sure that the crew who worked on the load-in receive some of those tickets before they leave for the day are all ways to avert trouble.

While working as manager of San Francisco's Golden Gate Theater, Lazzara describes his nightmare load-in when *A Midsummer Night's Dream* opened its American tour.

The tech rider, hanging plots, and set plans came to us from the UK in metric sizes. We, in turn, had sent our stage area plan prior to the set being built. Our measurements were in feet and inches. Before the load-in, we had to cut two large traps in our deck; we sweated our conversion from metric, crossed our fingers and did the work. The set arrived from the UK and the crew began putting it together. It consisted of an enormous racked deck, with openings for two large door frames that sprang up from the newly cut traps. Once the set was assembled and the surrounding deck laid, the awful truth became known: the traps were about two inches off from the holes cut in the set. The solution: all work on the load-in stopped. The surrounding show deck was pulled up, and then every available stagehand lifted up the show set (at this point an enormous, several thousand pound wedge-shaped object), and moved it back and forth and back and forth until the theater traps lined up with the opening in the show set. Finally the show deck was cut and re-laid, and the traps worked perfectly.

By the end of this day, many people will have made a tremendous number of things happen. Mere labor is not the only commodity needed throughout this process; relationships also play their part. A manager who has developed a good working relationship with the local fire department can smooth the way for a show in filing the proper paperwork. Being considerate of neighboring businesses might prevent an ugly scene when large road boxes and set pieces block the public sidewalks. So while most of the workers are applying their physical labor during the load-in, the manager has also made a lot happen or kept potential problems from snowballing. Everyone can be proud of their contributions, and still, there is much more to do.

THE FIRST PERFORMANCE

After a morning of teching and an afternoon of rehearsal, you begin to sense a tiredness in the air. During late afternoon the coffee gets stronger. It is from now until the curtain goes up on this first performance, which is usually a preview, that tempers can grow short. As smoothly as some load-ins go, there is always preshow nervousness. Load-ins fraught by problems with props that do not work, inadequate wing space, or costumes that do not arrive can be full of tensions that can lead to an opening night ranging from distressing to hysterical. I typically do not put a lot of stock in the unpleasant words I may have with anyone on this day. Everybody is under stress and it is easier to let outbursts be bygones.

Keeping perspective will be essential during this time through to the opening night. Remember that on most shows this is a two to three day process; as soon as the reviews are out, everyone will calm down. Overwork and no sleep is often as much a part of the problem as the deadline to get the show up and running. I have had a stage manager scream because exit lights distracted the actors; a company manager who refused to work until her workbox was found amid the six trucks yet to unload; and a wardrobe supervisor who intimidated workers to tears. A good night's sleep sometimes eases the tension. On the other hand, I have seen a producer screaming at press agents about his preview seat location not because the location was bad, but because it appeared to be what he believed a producer was supposed to do.

Around 5 P.M., the front-of-house staff start to arrive and instill a fresh energy as they begin to sort programs, set up concession stands, and arrange the lobby for customers. This is the beginning of their day and also a good opportunity for you to catch a nap, if you have time.

On this first day, the load-in of the show will not be the only arena of potential explosions, as the theater staff for San Francisco's Yerba Buena Center for the Arts found out. At their grand opening, 700 people were still standing in the lobby at show time waiting for their tickets. "Advised by a fire inspector to clear the jammed lobby, theater officials told the crowd to forget about the tickets—which in classic opening-night style, arrived just about curtain time—and simply grab a seat" (Hamlin 1993).

As 7 P.M. approaches, patrons walk through the front door. Ticket-takers tear tickets and tell customers which direction to proceed. Inside the auditorium ushers show them to their seats. As theater manager, you should walk to each level of the theater, checking on how the lobbies look, if the auditorium temperature is comfortable, and if the ushers are suitably dressed. A quick tour backstage to check in with the department heads results in no major catastrophes. So, at 7:30 P.M. you go to the box office.

The window sellers are in a flurry of giving out will-call[3] and comp tickets, selling to people who walk up to the window at the last minute, looking up the records of those who never received their tickets by mail. They may also have to refund tickets of customers who buy balcony tickets and discover they have a fear of heights or patrons who decide to bring their newborn infant to the show.

At the Curran we have had people smuggle their babies inside in backpacks. One set of parents was so upset they threatened to sue the theater for violating the infant's civil rights. They left after making quite a scene, which upset their child more than anything. Lying about a child's age is another humorous antic of customers who try to get children in who are simply too young to attend an adult event. After assuring me their child is seven, a parent will often be embarrassed when I ask the child how old they are and they proudly hold up four fingers.

At 8:05 P.M. the curtain goes up and, for the first time in hours, the day slows down—for the front-of-house. Activity is now centered on stage

and backstage. Around 8:30 P.M. the treasurer calls to say that the box office statement is ready. You and Helen meet at the treasurer's office. The
statement is computerized, so after checking the relevant numbers, you
add your signature, along with the treasurer's, showing your agreement
that the ticket sales are as this document indicates. Helen checks the statement and finds that the subscription percentage is not what she was told
by her GM. She insists that you change the statement. Your GM has given
you a deal memo signed months before by the show's producer that out-
lines the terms under which the show will play, including box office deductions. You find the memo and see that it clearly states the percentage
as shown, so this is a conversation the two GMs will have to settle, and
you do not change the statement. For this reason, Helen signs "under
protest" until the discrepancy is cleared up.

MacDonald explains that signing "under protest" means "he or she objects, or has a question about the actions of either the treasurer or house
manager, or a mistake on the statement cannot be corrected at that time."
Joe Traina finds it "rare when the charges are reversed or the company
confronts the theater owner about comp tickets that shouldn't be there,"
but he encourages company managers to "assert themselves whenever
possible, and if they want to sign 'under protest' it's okay with [him]." At
times a company manager will not sign the statement at all until the discrepancy is cleared up. One show manager signed under protest so much
that Lazzara told him "I'll get you [an] 'under protest' stamp to make
your job easier."

It is relatively quiet during the first act until the stage manager comes
to the front-of-house to say some ushers seated customers in the mezzanine during Mr. Dandy's show-stopper. The head usher immediately
proceeds to that area to find out what happened and insure that the ushering staff has the proper information. She returns a few minutes later
and tells you that no ushers were seating, but some customers had gotten up to go to the bathroom. Since there is seldom a way an usher can
prevent that, she assures the stage manager that she posted staff at the
auditorium entrances so that those who exit are not reseated until an appropriate moment.

You spend the first few minutes of intermission in your office. This is
where it will be easiest to reach you if there are problems backstage.
About five minutes later, you go to the main lobby to watch as customers
buy drinks, souvenirs, and talk. The head usher brings over two couples
who are unhappy with their seats and you arrange an upgrade to the orchestra. One couple is willing to pay the increased price but the other is
not. The head usher also says people are complaining about the heat in
the balcony. Because you are still talking to the couple who refuse to pay
for the upgrade, you ask the head usher to call the building engineer to

adjust the air conditioning for the balcony level. You notice the stage manager waving frantically to get your attention. It seems at the end of the act, a camera flash went off several times in the mezzanine. You assure him you will have an usher posted close by to try to catch anyone illegally taking pictures.

The dissatisfied couple decides to return to their original seats after telling you that you have been most unhelpful and they will be writing a letter to your boss to request a refund even though they will stay and watch the rest of the show in the most uncomfortable seats in the world. Near the end of intermission two toilets overflow making them unusable to the long line of women outside the ladies' room. And, the second act is set to begin. You quickly close off the flooded areas and divert the women to the nearby men's room which empties out much faster. A few straggling men do not like going up a floor to another restroom, but grudgingly make the detour and do not complain. At long last, the overture to the second act begins and what remains of the audience files back to their seats.

As stressful as intermission can sometimes be, with many different people coming at you from many directions, the good news is that it only lasts about twenty minutes. After the second act begins, another realm of quiet sets in.

This is just one scenario for the first performance. As filled with activity as it might be, it could also go smoothly with no distractions. Premiers, shows with stars, or products created by well-known writers or directors generate their own excitement. Something special is being created that might be big, might be great, might go down in history. The theater becomes filled with a magic that you have helped to make happen. Time passes too slowly as everyone waits impatiently for opening night.

OPENING NIGHT

After one or a number of preview performances comes the official opening night. This is the night that press, invited guests of the owners and producers, and all sorts of "important people" attend. Oddly enough, many of the things that go wrong on a preview night either work themselves out by the opening, or anyone who was upset is too tired to complain. Early the next morning, you call the GM, Mr. Edwards, to inform him about the possible problem with the box office statement. He is meeting with the show's GM later that day to sign the contract and will discuss it then. Since this producer has brought other shows to the Renaissance, the GM asks you to look up what subscription percentage was charged the last time and get back to him ASAP.

As you are looking back through files for that information, you receive a phone call from the plumber who will have to install a new sink drain in the star's dressing room. You ask him to look at the two flooded front-of-house toilets when he comes and to let you know if there is a costly problem. Otherwise, you ask him to just fix it. Prioritizing will be important now because of the tight schedule. Any other time, you might have gotten bids on repairing the plumbing. Now, it simply has to be done.

Word of mouth from the show's preview is good and box office traffic and phone and Internet sales are picking up. Helen calls from her hotel room asking if you know of a good Esalen masseuse for Ms. Gem, since the one listed in your specs only specializes in Shiatsu and Swedish. Since Esalen has never been requested before, all you can recommend is that she check the phone book.

I have found that the afternoon of opening night is always strangely quiet. This is a good time to get away from the theater for an hour or so because tonight will be as hectic as the previous nights. If you find yourself running short of energy or patience, remember that you have gotten this far and have accomplished much. The next few hours are going to be like the sprint at the end of the race. Not only are the show's producers arriving and wandering around the theater, but your GM, the theater's owner, and a couple hundred of his friends are coming to opening night. This is in addition to the critics and television crews. With so many important people in the building, just walking around and noticing details in the same way as they would is a good idea.

After several phone conversations with your GM, a contract is signed with the show's producer and a copy is faxed to you. Just as the night before, the theater begins springing to life like the slow motion opening of a budding flower. However, there are some additional activities. The owner's assistant has fifty guest tickets to hand out. You set up a special table for her needs. Brian Barnes, the press agent, is also distributing press seats. Another place needs to be set aside for him. You inform the treasurer and head ushers of these locations in the event that guests come to them looking for their tickets. They, in turn, tell their staffs. Brian will be watching for the TV crews and photographers. Either he or you can escort them to their designated areas, but once the show begins either Brian or one of his assistants should be with the media at all times to insure that established guidelines are followed.

Opening nights have their own unique ambiance that is unlike any other performance. Even with the simplest of shows, the opening nights are what you remember. Lazzara remembers the American tour premier of *La Cage Aux Folles:*

> A huge production, enormous set, major Broadway director, big stars, every important production person in the Broadway universe there to rehearse the set and its complicated moves. Because of the theme of the show, the opening night

was a benefit for an enormous gay group. Hundreds of bare-chested "Dykes on Bikes" paraded in front of the theatre prior to the curtain. The famous Broadway director assembled the entire cast and crew in the mezzanine lobby and gave notes. It was thrilling to hear his years of wisdom boiled down to hard truths: "You lead the audience; don't let them lead you with their response. No matter what happens, keep playing." The opening sequence was a breathtaking combination of spectacle, song and costume. The audience went wild. During the middle of this opening, without warning, the set for the next scene, which was suppose to "wipe" the first set away from stage right to stage left, suddenly began its advance right into a dozen chorus dancers in the middle of a big production number. As the set made its way across the stage, the chorus was pushed aside and into one another. They kept dancing and singing. Half way across the stage, the set stopped and reversed itself. The audience, thinking this was part of the show, howled with laughter and screamed in delight. The applause was thunderous at the end of the scene. I watched all of this silently from the back of the house, amazed at the courage and hard work of theatre people, and happy to be a part of the wondrous community of live theatre.

MacDonald remembers the opening night of the original New York production of *A Chorus Line:* "Everyone, but everyone, knew it was a big, big hit. Electric. You felt honored to be part of it."

Sooner than you think, opening night is over. Tomorrow is a regular show and at 8 P.M., the curtain rises, and the magic begins again.

THE ENGAGEMENT

Once a show has opened, the flurries of frantic activity and packs of producers, designers, press agents, and all their assistants who have wandered through the theater prodding, poking, and commenting like doctors diagnosing a patient, will suddenly disappear. You may never see them again. This is not to say that their work is finished or that you will not feel the effect of their influence. Their responsibilities have simply been transferred to their home office. The next time period is one of waiting for the reviews. Depending on the opening date, these can be in print as soon as the next day and certainly within a few days.

If reviews are good, watch to see if box office traffic picks up. If so, this may warrant an increase in the sales staff and the ushers. Likewise, if reviews are mediocre to bad, staff may have to be cut in order to keep expenses down. Producers react differently to disappointing reviews. Some will depart quickly, leaving the show to languish with mediocre sales. Others will try to overcome the reviews with media campaigns, appearances by the stars, or publicity gimmicks, all of which have varying degrees of success. MacDonald had the experience of a producer closing the show on opening night at intermission! "He hated it so much. Lost so much of his own money. He told the audience the show was having technical problems."

People You Will Meet
Anonymous, company manager

Egos, egos, everywhere . . . but it makes a manager's job much easier if they refrain from having one. . . . [H]ere's a little tale: Producer swoops down on the out-of-town production, touring with the original cast (super egos) for a quick look-see. . . . Disappointed with one of the five [stars'] performances, he insists that the manager send flowers to the other four stars conspicuously leaving star number 5 out. Well, you can imagine the fury backstage come the next performance on Tuesday evening. On Wednesday, a half hour before the matinee the largest arrangement of flowers imaginable arrives for star number 5, with an apology note from the producer about the oversight and singing the star's praises. Manager called producer to ask what the heck is going on . . . he didn't send it! It turns out the star sent them to herself but who would dare to prove it!

Either the company manager or the press agent will inform you of events that will require media-related use of the theater. Try to remind both of them that it is a good idea to inform you well in advance. A TV appearance can increase walk-up ticket purchases at the box office and you will want to make certain you are properly staffed. There is not much point in having a line of people ready to buy tickets with no one to sell them. It only irritates customers and can cause them to walk away and go to a movie instead.

There may also be union requirements if costumes are taken from the theater for press events. Often those workers traveling with shows will not have, or take, the time to study the work rules of every single union contract. You can save them money if you know their intention. Shows that are not doing well financially might forego their original plans for taking costumes to a TV appearance if they know in advance that it will cost them a four-hour call for a theater wardrobe person to accompany the costume to the press event.

Of course, at times, inexperienced personnel traveling with a show will forge their own path, despite your best efforts to advise them. In these cases, regardless of their screaming and yelling afterward that no one informed them, they sometimes have to pay for their mistakes.

CLOSING OR RUNNING

Closing

If the worst happens and the producers decide that the reviews are so bad they simply cannot keep the show open, then the theater manager might be asked to quickly calculate the costs the theater has incurred because of closing the show. Looking at the settlement expense sheet in chapter 12 will help you do this. Upon closing (whether early or at the end of the engagement), Lazzara advises:

> [D]ouble check the contract to make certain nothing has been missed in the settlements. Are the company bills paid up? Are you holding enough to cover any bills to come? Inspect the theatre, especially backstage, to discover any damage. Make certain no trash or hazardous materials are left in the theatre. Make certain no theatre belongings are taken on a show truck. Make sure you get all the keys back.

For closing before the posted date, all the preliminary expenses, payroll costs of removing the show from the theater, and other bills incurred will be compiled into one package. At this point, whatever early closing terms were specified in the contract come into effect. If there is a huge loss, expect some haggling between the producers and the theater's GM. Almost no one wins in a situation such as this. At times the theater's costs are not covered. Some producers simply write a check and say better luck next show. Others plead poverty and ask for some relief from the theater owner. This is often the reason why theater owners are very insistent that box office receipts are maintained in venue accounts, and that shows on guarantees do not receive payment until after the performances have played out. Of course, this can also go the other direction, when presenters do not pay guarantees because of lack of sales, and off to court they both go.

Running

When the show has received a rave or simply passable review, and plans on playing out its four-week engagement, I call this situation a wave. The first week is hectic, almost frantic; the second is busy addressing everyone's concerns and disagreements about the first week. The third is slow, like coasting on the crest of the wave and everyone seems to be resting. The fourth brings back some of the first week's bustle, aided by the familiarity of the players knowing each other much better by now. MacDonald says that a typical pattern with shows is that after the whirl of opening week "usually everyone gets sick." Another manager experiences a "big let down where janitorial problems, nasty customers, horrifying actors—the real stuff—kicks in."

Throughout this run there are rehearsals, work calls, perhaps special events such as benefits for the Actors' Fund,[4] charity drives for Broadway Cares/Equity Fights AIDS,[5] private benefits, and the occasional disaster, such as earthquakes, fires, floods, and riots. All of these have at one time or another affected the Curran.

On October 20, 1991, a small brush fire caused the "worst urban disaster in U.S. history" in the Oakland, California, hills. The fire resulted in $2 billion worth of damage (www.nasa.gov 1998). In January 1997, forty-two California counties were declared "major disaster areas because of flooding" (www.fema.gov/home 1998). For several days the North Bay of San Francisco had communities awash in mud, washed out roads, and disrupted communications. In another instance, protests against the verdict of the policemen charged in the Rodney King beating erupted into full-blown riots in Los Angeles and smaller confrontations and vandalism in San Francisco and other cities. While the press reported that the Curran sustained property damage, broken windows, and vandalism, we actually had none.

Once aware of neighborhood activity and knowing we had to cancel the evening's performance and perhaps several others until order was restored, I asked stagehands to bring 6' × 6' boards to the front lobby and lean them against the inside of the glass doors. This was a preventative measure in case protesters decided to vent their fury on the building as they passed by. While the hotel next door received a broken window, the Curran did not, but reporters saw our blocked out windows and assumed the worst without investigating further.

The Loma Prieta earthquake (7.1 on the Richter scale) began at 5:04 P.M. on Tuesday, October 17, 1989, and lasted approximately fifteen seconds. It occurred during rehearsals of *Les Miserables*, which was making its San Francisco debut. Since moving to San Francisco in 1978, I had experienced several earthquakes, some as strong as 6.1 on the Richter scale. As I sat in my office that day working on some preliminary budgets, the day's rehearsal had just broken for dinner. When the slight shaking began, I thought to myself, "Oh, an earthquake." Like the others I had experienced I expected it to end in a few seconds. This one did not.

The shaking grew stronger to the point that I thought it would be a good idea to hit "save" on the computer and make my way to the nearest door frame, still expecting the vibration to cease. It did not. The walls swayed with a force I can only describe as violent, as if someone had taken me by the arms and was jerking me back and forth. My eyes searched the office in a way they never had before. The only thought that went through my mind was, how can I get out of here if the building starts to fall? I fully expected the walls to crumble at any second. "Come on, stop," I said as if my voice could command it. The windows beside me and the door behind me were possible escape routes. If I had to, I could jump from my second-story office. Then the shaking started to slow, became even slower, and finally stopped.

For a moment, it seemed as if the entire world paused. A cloud of dust blew past the window. I raced downstairs to see if everyone was okay. The box office personnel were fine. Inside the auditorium, several production people were upset but okay. The stage was intact, the set, recently installed in the past weeks, still stood. Most of the actors had just left for their dinner break. Everyone in my building was safe. One of the stagehands summoned me outside. The reservoir tower on top of the building was spewing water, flooding the alley. Dave Costa, a stagehand, began stacking sand bags strategically so that the water would not flood into the building. There was nothing else that could be done until the tower emptied. Glen Chadwick, the house carpenter, took the precaution of throwing the main electrical switch to shut off all the electricity to the theater. Within minutes there would be no electricity in our entire area of the city.

As I stood in the outer lobby, several people from the offices of American Conservatory Theater ran from across the street to the Geary Theater next door to the Curran. Someone told me their auditorium had collapsed. I found out later that only the first five rows of seats were covered with debris from the fallen ceiling. It was five o'clock in the afternoon and not one of us could help but imagine if this had happened three hours later with an audience sitting in those seats. The image sent shivers through us all. No one likes to dwell on the thought.

Before long, a stagehand had hardwired a television set to a battery. We found out then that part of the Bay Bridge had fallen and apartment buildings in the Marina District had collapsed and were burning. After staff members contacted their families to ensure that they were all right, Marie Barrett, the *Les Miserables* production manager, had each department head assess their area for damage. The theater department heads made the same assessment for the building. Within a day, the real estate company that leased the theater had hired engineers to tour the property. They pronounced it structurally sound and we realized how lucky we had been.

The Geary Theater was closed for many years; several freeways to the city were closed indefinitely; the Bay Bridge was months in repair and the collapsed Cypress Freeway had claimed too many lives. The historical record cites 68 deaths, 3,757 injuries, 3,530 businesses damaged, 366 businesses destroyed, and total loss estimated at $6 to $7 billion (www.kron.com/specials/89 1998). The city would never be the same.

Eventually tourists returned, tentative at first, as if the earthquake had never happened or were some interesting facet of the city's distant history. Geologists reported that this was not the "big one." Citizens either moved out of the state or nervously stayed, playing their chances like they lived on a Las Vegas roulette wheel.

Though our vendors and staff did a nearly impossible job of repairing the building in time to make the originally scheduled opening night performance, it still took about six months for earthquake problems to work themselves out. Sludge in the water pipes constantly backed up drains; water pressure varied from too much to barely there; aftershocks kept staff in a steady state of trauma; and the emergency system often went off for no reason an electrician could discover.

Even though the day of the emergency had long passed, the effects of the earthquake were with us for nearly a year. When *Les Miserables* closed at the Curran a year and half later, the Gulf War began giving this production the distinction of being the show that came with an earthquake and left with a war.

All of these events—earthquake, fire, flood, civil disturbance—caused sales to drop, as well as kept subscribers and advance purchasers, who had been directly affected or were afraid to leave their homes, from attending the theater. In such cases a policy must be developed to accommodate these people. Usually it is in combination with the show's wishes, but if a hard-nosed producer says "too bad," it is in the theater's best interest to recognize that these ticket holders are your customers, not necessarily the show's. Not to accommodate them under extreme circumstances may cost you a theatergoer for life. Most producers understand this concept. To antagonize a customer for the sake of one show may mean that the next show's sales will suffer, and, sooner or later, the next show will have the same management team. Other producers simply do not think that far ahead.

Luckily for the Curran, both the earthquake and the North Bay floods happened during the productions of *Les Miserables* and *The Phantom of the Opera*. Both shows, represented by GM Alan Wasser, approved a system of addressing customers who held past-dated tickets and had missed their performances for reasons that were beyond their control.

Usually a program of getting people into performances that are not sold out will address the situation. The theater can be of help should a show have to close before the customers are taken care of. Remember those complimentary tickets for previews? The next show will have a preview as well. If people are unable to attend the show for which they bought tickets, then perhaps an upcoming show's previews will work just as well.

If a customer is simply not able to come back to the theater, it is often best to simply refund ticket money rather than earn the reputation of a company that stands by its "no refund, no exchange" policy, even in the event of an emergency or natural disaster. There is little point in breaking one's back to ensure the show must go on if there is no one willing to buy a ticket.

In April of every year, there is a gathering on Market Street to honor those who lost their lives in the 1906 San Francisco earthquake. In recent years around a dozen survivors have attended. These few people have the original story to tell. The 1989 earthquake is now one of my stories. It is not really the tale of a disaster. It is the story of how many people worked together to make an event happen. The opening of a show might not seem as if it is a necessary bandage for a traumatized community. But I believe in a way, it was. With all that the city had been through, restoring stability was a step toward healing. The show must go on, and it did.

NOTES

1. Larger shows often send production personnel to the theater weeks or months prior to the show's arrival to scout out the location. Many of these questions can be answered at this time.

2. Different union locals may have varying guidelines regarding press and publicity filming and photographs, so you'll want to know what they are and inform the company manager and the press agent of these rules in advance.

3. This is a designation for tickets to be picked up at the box office. Usually they are ordered by phone or mail, and the customer is told to get them before the performance at the will-call window.

4. The Actors' Fund provides services for those who have worked in the entertainment industry and are ill or unemployed. Some of those services include the AIDS Initiative Program, Chemical Dependency Services, Mental Health Services, Services to Employable Persons, Elder and Disabled Care Services, and Retirement and Nursing Homes (Actors' Fund).

5. Broadway Cares/Equity Fights AIDS gives grants to "AIDS Service Organizations" across the country as well as "direct assistance" to individuals (www.beefa.org/about/index.htm 1998).

Chapter 4

Front-of-House: It's Not a Dress Rehearsal

When a play or musical is in rehearsal, the actors stumble until they learn their part bit by bit. The director gives them instructions, the conductor tweaks performances, and the dance captain aligns the clumsy people with the surefooted. All the players fall back on their training and before long the production emerges.

Opening the front-of-house is not so different. It happens every night the same as a performance. It is the same production and yet, it is different, because just like a live performance anything can happen. The front-of-house staff will need to fall back on their training just as surely as an actor.

The box office and ushers are the first contact a customer has with your theater. To say that this first impression may mark the rest of their evening is obvious. Many customers feel that in paying for a ticket, they have also paid in advance for a perfect evening, unmarred by disturbance. "In the United States, the basic objective of our market-directed economic system has been to satisfy consumer needs as they—the consumer—see them" (McCarthy and Perreault 1993, 638). While procedural training is a matter of repetition—computer skills to sell a ticket, correct a seating error, late seating, insurance accident forms—customer service and life safety are more a matter of judgment.

The interaction between staff and patron is a satisfying one when expectations are met and problems are resolved. It is a complex one when they are not. Every employee starts out to perform a job well and be of service. Unfortunately, customer service is what the patron perceives, which may differ from the employee's perception. From this inequity can grow a resentment and bitterness toward the customers. The interaction can develop into "uneven exchanges, to be treated with disrespect or anger by a client, all the while closeting into fantasy the anger one would like to respond with. Where the customer is king, unequal exchanges are normal, and from the beginning customer and client assume different rights to feeling and display. The ledger is supposedly evened by a wage" (Hochschild 1983, 85–86).

Joe Traina once had a customer during a performance of *A Doll's House* who was "very drunk" and created a scene in the lobby. "She actually tried to throw the rest of her drink at me. Her date fled the scene from embarrassment and I scolded the patron, driving her from the theater by loudly proclaiming that I knew children who behaved better." Bob MacDonald's irate customer story occurred because the woman was late. Being told to watch the show on a TV monitor was not acceptable. She was abusive until MacDonald explained that the director, Mike Nichols, made the seating hold decision. This name impressed and calmed her down, though "she later wrote a letter of complaint."

One West Coast manager approaches these kinds of situations with what he calls his "power arsenal: refund cash, security guards, my own power (voice, control, authoritative experience)." Believing it important to extract the existing front-of-house staff from the situation, this manager intervenes by

> introducing myself with security behind me, informing the customer politely to cease their actions, as I am there to help them, but making it clear they will be removed from the theater if they do not calm down. If this does not stop them, I will place refund cash in their pocket, order them to leave, and if they do not, have security remove them. This is done only in the worst cases where the continual presence of the patron will interrupt the performance or cause harm to the staff or other patrons.

As a house manager, it is easy to spout the cliché that the customer is always right. It may be more realistic to admit that they are usually wrong and you still have to deal with their perception of being right. Should an employee who becomes hostile with a customer be given some leeway to react, considering the abuse that has just been heaped upon them? Traina is one of those managers who does not think the customer is always right:

> If there is a dispute, I usually hear both sides and make a determination. . . . Certainly if a customer cannot behave or is abusive, I phone security and we may request that they leave the premises. I have even called the police on certain occasions when necessary. If a refund does not satisfy a customer, or an invitation to return another time, I refer them to the owners for their assistance.

MacDonald says he would "step in immediately" if situations get out of control between house staff and customers. "Tell the front-of-house person that [you] will deal with this—kindly. Tell the customer who you are—ask what is the problem. Apologize for any misunderstanding and try to deal with it as best you can. If the customer is unreasonable—it stops there. Don't bend too far."

One of the stranger incidents that happened to Traina occurred during the ninety-minute play *Honour*.

Apparently an older woman was seated behind a younger man and woman, and was bothering them throughout the performance. At the end of the show a heated argument began after which the younger woman slapped the older one. Security and the police were called and both women failed to calm down. The husband disappeared. The older woman later broke away from the policeman questioning her and attacked the younger woman, who had found her husband by this time. The police then handcuffed the older woman, who was not right in the head, as we learned after she asked me to take a photo of her in handcuffs.

A West Coast manager had an unfortunate experience with an elderly woman who had lost her group sale ticket and could not be satisfied no matter how the staff tried to accommodate her.

She lost control and accused the staff of stealing her ticket. She didn't know where her group was, and was not happy with an empty seat offered to her. She began screaming that she would march onto the stage and stop the show once it started. The staff got her out of the auditorium and to the lobby. I introduced myself, and she began shouting at me in the loudest voice I have ever heard a human being use. I spoke quietly to her, but she shouted "Don't you use that soft tone of voice on me!" at the top of her lungs. I got a location pass and attempted one more time to seat her. As I walked her to the seat, she began screaming how filthy the theatre and show was, and at this point, I realized my mistake, did an about-face and ordered the woman out of the theater. She refused to leave and began screaming. I ordered a security guard to pick her up and carry her to the street. She dug her fingernails into the guard's hands and drew blood. The staff applauded as she was carried out.

At times these episodes can be humorous. With the passage of time, even the horrible ones can be retold as "remember that crazy person?" These events become our stories to tell, our legends. No matter how many times I think I have seen and heard everything, every year brings a new incident and there is a new yarn to add to my repertoire. These stories can also be instructive in training those who come after us.

Staff training includes knowledge of emergency procedures. These may involve fire and bomb drills, instructions on how to operate fire extinguishers and pull stations, and proper conduct in the event of an actual emergency or a false alarm. "I try to address these matters on a fairly regular basis," says Traina. "I do this training as needed for the box office (usually when there's a security issue) . . . and [for] the ushers . . . to [know] how they should respond in case of fire, accidents, patron problems."

Fire is one of the most feared emergency situations in the theater. It destroyed Shakespeare's Globe Theatre in 1613 when the shot from a stage cannon ignited a thatched roof. The Drury Lane burned down in 1672 and 1809. The fire at Covent Garden in 1808 cost the lives of twenty-three firemen, only to burn again in 1856; 186 people died in the fire at the Theatre Royal at Exeter. In America, 300 people, including two actors, died in the 1876 Brooklyn Theatre fire. The Richmond Theater fire in Virginia claimed seventy-one lives in 1811, and 600 people died in Chicago's Iroquois Theater in 1903 while actor Eddie Foy tried to calm the desperate audience from the stage. In 1942, a fire at Boston's Cocoanut Grove nightclub killed 491 people. The Ringling Brothers Canvas Big Top fire in 1944 left 168 dead. In other theater fires, 800 people died in 1837 in St. Petersburg, Russia; another 800 in 1847 in Karlsruhe, Germany; and the worst loss of life from a theater fire was in 1845 in China, which resulted in the deaths of 1,670 people (Law et al. 1994, 172; Wilmeth 1993, 182).

Nowadays, life safety has become more complex, ranging from fires to bomb and terrorist threats. The theater manager will want to maintain security procedures as well as policies for emergency evacuation.

A false alarm can cause as much panic as an actual emergency. Life safety systems typically installed in theaters are usually those designed for high-rise buildings, though the similarity between these two structures is questionable. In a high-rise, the lights are on and business is being conducted. In a theater, as many as 2,500 people are sitting in the dark. The loud siren and strobe lights that signal the alarm and result in the clearing of an office building can easily cause panic and terror among those watching a show in a dark auditorium. A stampede toward an exit in a theater could easily cause more harm and possible loss of life to patrons than a rush of people hurrying down a high-rise staircase.[1] Ushers and security personnel need to be trained to handle a false alarm as if it were an emergency because it could easily become one. How to write a manual for these emergency and security procedures is covered in chapter 5, and additional information on customers and their safety is covered in chapter 7.

In one instance I learned that opening the front-of-house can merge with the attraction in a dramatic way. I was managing a special event, a one-night engagement of a broadcast of the Mike Tyson–Leon Spinx fight. The theater was not usually rented out for this kind of an event, but since it was seldom booked with a legitimate show during these days, any kind of income was welcome. The 3,000-seat theater was filled to capacity, mostly men. Prior to the start of the fight, I had noticed several policemen hanging around outside on the street. The area was known as a high-crime and drug area, so I was relieved to see them and did not say anything as they slowly meandered toward the door and came into the theater without paying. While the presenter did have their own security on site, I thought it was smart to have policemen in the building just in case anyone got out of hand. Just prior to the start of the fight, I walked up to the balcony, checking on each level as was my custom. From the mezzanine level overlooking the main lobby, I saw the policemen running out the front door. A massive groan emerged from the auditorium. One of the presenter's security came out of the auditorium. Her eyes were wide, mouth dropped open, head shaking in disbelief. "It's over," she said. "I can't believe it. It's over." She looked at me, then ran down the stairs toward the front of the building. I walked into the back of the mezzanine. On the large screen was a victorious Mike Tyson dancing around a fallen Leon Sphinx. And there I was with 2,500 angry men who had just paid thirty-five dollars to see a fifteen-second fight. I grew up in the 1970s when the feminist philosophies were well entrenched. But that night, I learned the value of a baby-doll dress and a strand of pearls.

NOTE

1. High-rise life safety systems have been a thorn in the side of theater managers who have to deal with them. Many question why life safety experts have not designed a more adaptable auditorium system.

Chapter 5

The Theater Building: You Work for a Theater but I Work for a Theatre

Whether your venue is named after the British "theatre" or the Americanized "theater," do not be surprised to find that the building has as many quirks as the personality of a retired vaudevillian. While the older structures may have more color, the newer ones quickly begin to establish their own particular legends. A narrow staircase leads to a set of offices above San Francisco's Orpheum Theater. It is rumored that theater impresario Alexander Pantages used this route to sneak chorus girls to his suite. Daniel Frohman, the owner of Broadway's Lyceum Theater, which was built in 1903, had a peephole in his office wall, from where he could watch the stage while continuing to conduct business. New York's Virginia Theatre, built by the Theater Guild in the 1920s, was a financial disaster. Structural decisions, made by the designers, rendered the theater practically unusable. "The stage was made so large that there was little room left for dressing rooms or even audience space. 'We made the ghastly mistake,' [Guild founder, Lawrence Langner] wrote, 'of providing a theatre with all the stage space necessary for a repertory of plays without enough seating capacity to provide the income necessary to support the repertory.' The theatre had 914 seats" (Atkinson 1985, 42; Botto 1984, 158).[1]

A theater building can be looked at as two individual components—the front-of-house and backstage. These two areas are separated by the edge of the stage. The front-of-house includes the audience areas—lobbies, seating, lavatories, box office, theater manager's office, and changing room for ushers. Backstage consists of the dressing rooms, wardrobe, shop, stage, and wing space. Often the front-of-house is ornate and decorative, with attention spent on the appearance of the public areas, though in the 1800s theater balconies in general had a reputation for prostitution. Theater managers ignored this activity rather than lose the revenue it provided (Curry 1994, 83–84). Backstage areas can be gloomy in comparison, with the exception of star dressing rooms. Other areas can resemble apartments in a perpetual state of having tenants moving in and out.

While some theaters, such as a repertory company or a city-owned facility, may produce their own product, many times the show is a separate business entity. This is usually the case in roadhouses; this type of theater is owned by an individual or organization that may or may not also produce plays or musicals. The show is a product of a producer who may be the sole investor, but more frequently the production is set up as a limited partnership. This partnership signs a contract or a license agreement with the theater that usually spells out the terms of use for the facility.

Management of the building can be handled by the house manager, a facility manager, or some combination of various staff members. If you are lucky enough to have an operations manual, this may specify who is responsible for various areas. If not, then you will want to be aware of certain system operations.

As a house manager you will probably not know in detail the workings of the life safety system, how to inspect a rigging system, an electrical system, or know if a plumbing problem is caused by a sump pump or city water pressure. What you can do as you learn more about your building is note where vital equipment is located and what vendor or department head services it. A simple list of locations can be especially helpful to others when you are not around. This would include information such as where to turn off building electricity, the location of the fire alarm panel, pull stations, fire extinguishers, water cutoffs, breaker panels, fire pump, and a list of monitoring service phone numbers. If 8" × 11" blueprints or even hand drawings are available, these should be consolidated into a packet for the use of the department heads in an emergency. Someone in your organization will be responsible for checking emergency systems. Typically this is an engineer, house electrician, carpenter, or a combination of several people. They should maintain records of having performed the checks and note any unusual conditions they found and any action they took.

These records can be of use in ways that might not always be obvious. After a slip-and-fall accident at the Curran, we submitted a completed light check form to attorneys in pretrial discovery. It showed that the head electrician had checked the lighting in that area on the evening of the accident and that all lights were in working order. This form, kept in the file for over a year, eliminated the opportunity for the litigant to argue that the theater was at fault because of inadequate lighting.

One West Coast theater manager considers understanding the life safety system to be essential. "No one else will care about it, and it is the manager's legal responsibility to know how to operate and maintain it." Joe Traina, who has managed a number of Broadway theaters, believes that "the inquisitive and best-informed managers ask a lot of questions of both the house crew and the theater owner's department heads to determine which systems require management attention and knowledge." He has managed buildings that range from the ninety-one-year-old Belasco Theater to venues with modern burglar alarms, fire safety systems, and HVAC systems, and he recommends that "the best way to learn about [the systems] is to ask the folks who either [were] on the scene or came before you."

THEATER BUILDING AND STAGE SPECS

Theater specs are the advance information provided to the show prior to its moving into a theater. Traina notices that many professionals use *STAGE SPECS*, a publication of the League of American Theatres, which gives technical information to shows about individual theaters. "This information is becoming more accurate year after year because it is revised annually." Another manager describes theater specs as having the "full stage measurements and blueprints," as well as a wide range of other important details:

> stage access, house curtain and counterweight system information; rental equipment, drapes and sound equipment available in house; information about electrical service, sound and light console location; backstage information such as mail, visitors, pets, phones, hazardous materials, storage, layout of the dressing rooms and work rooms; local union contracts; orchestra pit information; front-of-house seating plans; theater cross sections with spot booth, box boom and rail positions; photos of the theater inside and out, and local information such as hotels, restaurants and doctors.

While specs may contain some of the same material as the operation manual, the difference is that the specs are oriented toward providing information to the show or producers considering renting your venue. They will contain more exact measurements that are pertinent for a production moving into the theater. I divide the theater specs into two separate sections: one relating to backstage for the stage manager and show's carpenter, and another for general or advance information which will be of more use to the company manager.

The advance information portion contains lists of staff and their titles and phone numbers; capacity of the house broken down into seating sections; banking information; union addresses and business agents; city, county, and state ordinances regarding the employment of minors, taxes, and government contacts; vendors for local transportation, hair salons, child care, dry ice, oxygen, computer rentals, and gyms; lists of physicians; available housing along with maps of the city and state; and theater policies specific to your venue.

The backstage specs must be prepared with the assistance of the department heads, who will take measurements and provide information about the stage's technical systems. All stage measurements should be exact and accompany information on rigging, electrics, grid, loading door, and blueprints relating to the areas in question. The orchestra pit should also be measured with a list of available equipment, music stands, and chairs. Dressing rooms should be itemized in terms of star, principal, or chorus rooms, and detailed as to whether they have sinks, lavatories, and telephones.

If offices are backstage, their dimensions, amount of electrical outlets, phone lines, and numbers should be listed. The electrical service should outline available power, location of the house board, the hanging positions in the house, box booms, spotlight positions, sound system, number of available circuits, and the various distances from the hanging positions. Theatrical vendors and suppliers can be listed in this section, along with either a contact or a request that orders be placed through the theater if the show intends on using theater accounts. Blueprints should accompany this material, or at the least, a roughed-out drawing indicating measurements, which is better than nothing. An example of a specs packet containing advance information and backstage specs is in appendix A.

EMERGENCY PROCEDURES

Instruction in emergency and security procedures should be as close to common sense as possible. This ensures that the information is easy to remember for most employees, and instills them with a sense of confidence for unexpected situations. For more rule-oriented conduct, periodic training sessions, fire drills, and life safety classes may be necessary. Employees are just as likely to panic as customers in an emergency situation. Repetition of procedures can help them automatically respond in a professional way.

I separate emergency procedures from security procedures. Each covers some of the same ground, and this ensures that employees read it twice. I also conduct a life safety class as many times a year as needed. When there are a number of new employees, this is an opportunity for everyone else to repeat the class. Traina has regular meetings with his front-of-house staff. "In the event of any kind of medical emergency, the staff is instructed to contact the manager immediately should EMS assistance be necessary. That determination is usually made by management. When possible, the patron—injured or sick—is asked what action they would like to be taken."

Emergency procedures should begin with an introduction that cites the purpose of the procedures and informs employees of what will be expected of them in a crisis. Follow this with important phone numbers such as fire, police, poison control, and security services. Then give an overview of the building and its safety features. The remainder of the procedures are divided into four sections: preemergency, emergency, post-emergency, and specialized information to deal with bomb threats, civil disobedience, stalkers, violence, and robbery.

In most places of public assembly, fire is one of the more prevalent fears. Full-blown blazes are not the only concern. During a production of *Gross Indecency* at the Theatre on the Square in San Francisco, sparks from an electric cable forced an evacuation of a capacity audience and the production company. Fortunately, a stagehand contained the fire with an extinguisher just as the fire department arrived (Carroll 1997).

Even false alarms, which can create panic among customers, must be planned for as an incident capable of causing unintentional injury and a financial burden if the show has to be canceled. If an alarm can be quickly assessed as false, often the disturbance is covered by the volume of the show. Audience members in San Francisco once thought two false alarms, resulting in sirens and lights, were part of the special effects for *Jailhouse Rock* playing at the Marines Memorial Theatre. San Francisco Opera House head usher George Weiss determined that English customers were the source of false alarms in his building because next to the elevators were red fire alarm boxes with a lift lever and "in England 'lift' means elevator" (Carroll 1997).

Preemergency

Much of the preemergency section is oriented toward prevention. Beginning with the house manager, I list each department and cover preventative measures and obligations of the employee. These instructions should be specific for the area in which the employee works.

For instance, the house manager's duties can be listed as: House manager will conduct weekly inspections and respond to any condition reported, and advise the owner of all conditions not immediately correctable.

For a stagedoor person whose job is considerably different, assign him to check nightly that the walkway to the stagedoor is clear of obstructions and trip hazards, and that exits are unlocked and are free of obstructions.

Emergency

The emergency section most often concerns the evacuation of the building. While I sometimes tell employees that they can put out a small trash receptacle fire with an extinguisher, they should not ever expect to be fighting a large blaze with available equipment. Often during life safety class when I ask untrained ushers what they would do if they came upon a serious fire, they often tell me that they know where the fire hoses are located and how to use the extinguisher. While this is admirable, they would better serve their employer by alerting the fire department. I continually remind staff that ushers seat people, and box office personnel sell tickets. Firemen fight fires.

It sometimes becomes important to reinforce to employees that they are not expected to be Superman or Wonder Woman in emergencies. They can take what measures are safely accomplished on their way out of the building, such as pulling a fire alarm or shutting doors as they exit, but crisis situations call for emergency-trained personnel. The information staff members can give about the location of a fire or injured people is far more valuable than their efforts to contain a blaze.

Postemergency

Postemergency is what takes place after the ranking head of the emergency response team—fire or police department—tells the owners or manager it is safe to reenter the premises. At this time each supervisor should assess the damage to his or her department, take action necessary to protect property, and report to the house manager.

Specialized

The specialized section of the specs should be specific to your theater and area of the country. In San Francisco, earthquakes are of great concern. In the southeast, it might be tornadoes; coastal cities have to deal with hurricanes, and flooding can be a danger for theaters in towns that are near rivers and lakes. Also in this section you will want to cover what employees should do if they receive a bomb threat, if their area is invaded with civil disturbances, if a customer or employee turns violent, and company policy in case of a box office robbery.

Appendix B has a sample of emergency and security procedures. While it can be modeled for any theater, the contents should reflect your venue, your organization, the owner's policies, and your city's laws. The local fire and police department can be consulted for additional information. Some agencies will even review your written procedures and tour your building in order to make additional suggestions.

Life safety instruction is part of emergency procedures and can be conducted a few times a year or along with fire and bomb drills. Local city colleges often teach classes in how to prepare a life safety manual. These could benefit not only you, but your staff as well. Drills can be made more interesting by presenting them as a game rather than a dull lecture. An exercise that can also be fun is to conduct a bomb drill and hide a stuffed animal as the unusual package that should not be there. Then, like an Easter egg hunt, send the staff to do their regular nightly setup and check of their parts of the building. Often an important point is illustrated when an employee comes running, stuffed bunny in hand, saying, "I found it! I found the bomb!" At the very least, they learn not to bring it to me. All employees learn that when an odd or unusual package is found, they need to report it, and under no circumstances should they touch it.

SECURITY PROCEDURES

This section also begins with a clear statement that some events are forces out of everyone's control. The employer cannot demand that employees respond in any particular way, but that the goal of the information provided is the preservation of life. An overview of the building points out areas that can serve as a natural protection during a crisis. State clearly that there is no one correct response to unforeseen events. Individuals must judge for themselves what action is appropriate. Continue with listing features of building security and instructions for entering and locking up at night. This should be accompanied with procedures for accepting deliveries, night performance versus daytime security, and measures specific to individual areas such as box office and stagedoor. Conclude the security procedures with a section on special circumstances, which details situations that could occur at your venue such as box office window robbery, invasive robbery, hostage situation, employee violence, or terrorist attack.

It is also necessary to review security information from time to time to insure what you have advised is still a valid form of crisis management. As law enforcement meets new challenges, they learn better ways to deal with violent or criminal situations. Another important element to heed is our own intuition. Gavin De Becker's book *The Gift of Fear* points to denial as a chief factor in workplace violence. Having ignored a gut feeling that something is not right, or dismissing reports from managers on security issues, employers can allow situations to go beyond the point of no return. The result can be employees who are so emotionally invested in their jobs that they see violence as their only means of addressing their problems (De Becker 1997, 141–71).

Workplace violence can have legal implications for managers as well. When a stranger entered the 101 California Street high-rise and opened fire with an assault weapon and a .45-caliber automatic pistol, resulting in one of the worst massacres in San Francisco history, the building managers as well as the owner found themselves named in a lawsuit because they did not have an emergency plan to deal with violence (Ziegler 1996).

The sample security procedures in appendix B can be adapted to your own building. As with the life safety instructions, these procedures should reflect your own venue's issues and owner's policies.

THE BUILDING

Through most of theatrical history the play has been fashioned to fit into the theater structure. "The earliest American colonial performance venues were temporary structures and converted rooms in inns or private homes fitted, at best, with a curtained raised stage and some seats. The first recorded playhouse was built by William Levingston in Williamsburg, Virginia, between 1716 and 1718" (Aronson 1993, 44). Regardless of whether you manage a ninety-nine-seat equity waiver theater or a 5,000-seat auditorium, there are, as Daniel Ionazzi (1996, 19) points out, only two minimum requirements for a theater: "a space in which the actor can perform and a space from which the audience can watch."

There are four primary stage configurations: the thrust, arena, environmental, and proscenium. The kind of space you manage will define the sorts of problems you will have and the kind of maintenance required.

"The thrust theater is designed to break through the proscenium (or 'fourth wall' as it is called), and 'thrust' the actor out into the audience" (Ionazzi 1996, 24). Depending on the shape of the stage, theater seats may be movable chairs—seats can be taken out and put back in to accommodate the production. A manager with this kind of house will want to ensure that the seats are the proper distance from the stage. Sightlines might be of more concern if sets, actors, or the stage itself blocks part of the performance.

The arena theater "has the entire stage surrounded by the house. The proscenium is no longer present and the audience has a 360° view of the stage" (Ionazzi 1996, 25). With a stage so embedded into the audience, it can sometimes be tempting to wander up on it. Security of the performers can be an issue because of proximity, and so can the security of props should a patron want a souvenir of the evening.

The environmental stage "surrounds the audience in the most contemporary concept" (Ionazzi 1996, 25). The show and audience occupy the same space, sometimes with actors and audience interacting, such as a mystery dinner theater. With the number of patrons twisting their heads, I would recommend a house manager have those accident forms ready.

Most commercial theaters have proscenium stages. It is in essence a picture frame that separates the audience from the performance. While the origin of this kind of stage is unknown, the Teatro Farnese in Parma, Italy, is the earliest recognized proscenium arch theater. It is believed that "the development of perspective drawing, and its growing use in scenic design, led artists to treat the stage structure in the same manner as they did their painting—putting it in a frame" (Pickering 1975, 124). This square has permeated our entire culture—we do not see round television sets or triangular movie screens.

A theater manager need not be an expert on backstage systems, but basic knowledge is necessary. Knowing that your theater has a proscenium stage, a guillotine curtain, and a counterweight rigging system will often answer most questions asked by a show carpenter who needs information when the theater is closed and there is no available stagehand to speak with him. The rigging system is one of the most important backstage assemblages. According to Ionazzi (1996, 27), the rigging system's "primary purpose is to fly or support scenery, or to create special effects. The hemp system is the oldest of the rigging systems." Scenery is fastened by manila ropes, which run up to the theater grid and pass though a series of pulleys. The stagehands pull the rope to raise and lower the scenic element.

More common is the counterweight system, using "wire rope instead of fiber rope for the lift lines, which are attached to a pipe batten onstage" (Ionazzi 1996, 31). Many a carpenter dreams of having the motorized rigging system with an electric winch, which "eliminate[s] the need to counterbalance the load and/or the need for strong stagehands" (Ionazzi 1996, 32).

With new technology speeding bulletlike into the twenty-first century, the building is being changed to accommodate the production. *Starlight Express* built a skating ramp out into the audience and *Miss Saigon* landed a simulated helicopter on the set. Productions of *The Phantom of the Opera* require the theater to take out their entire stage so the production can put in its own, complete with trap doors and rising set pieces. Pickering (1975, 127) points out that the structure and the drama have always affected each other, and as a designer, playwright, and director seek to "delight, amuse, shock, or instruct [their] audience, [they tend] to make ever-growing demands upon the theatre and its technical capacity."

MAINTENANCE

Moving shows in and out of a theater can be hard on the building and result in more than normal wear and tear. Typically, I do a building check after every show as soon as possible after the load-out. Some backstage damage will have to be reported to you by the department heads since it is often in areas in which the manager may not have expertise, such as the grid and hanging lines. The form I use notes the damage and specifies who needs to repair it. This form can then be copied and sent to those whose areas of responsibility need mainte-nance.

A sample form might look like this:

```
The Renaissance Theater
Inspection Report
Show that just closed: _____ Date: _____
Inspected by: _____
Front-of-House:
Main Lobby: _____
Main Auditorium: _____
Mezzanine: _____
Balcony: _____
Back Stage:
Stage Level: _____
Principal Dressing Rooms: _____
Chorus Rooms: _____
Also check: Lights, seats, walls, doors, banisters, steps, carpet, floors,
     plumbing, exits, alleys, marquee, window cases, and bathrooms.
```

Note that the form refers to superficial areas of the theater. Backstage department heads will have to let you know if there is a serious problem with the electrical board or rigging system; the treasurer would have to inform you if the box office computers are not operating; ushers can be invaluable for letting a manager know about broken equipment and tar-nished veneers. I give each department head a number of copies of this form so that employees finding a problem can fill it out and forward it to the theater manager. My form is in three parts, which allows the same form to be used for requesting a repair from the proper department (see page 61).

Patron accidents account for some of the most distressing incidents in a theater. While many of these accidents will be slip-and-fall, others will be caused by the negligence of other patrons. However, when the law-suit is filed, do not be surprised if the person who caused the accident is nowhere to be found and the theater is legally the deep pocket. There are two very separate components to keep in mind when responding to an accident. The first is to see to the needs of the person who is hurt. The second, which follows on the heels of the first, is to defend against a law-suit.

An accident report should be filled out whenever a customer is injured on theater property. Often patrons refuse to give their name, or become

---

The Renaissance Theater
Problem Form
To: Tess Collins, Theater Manager
From: _____ Date: _____
Problem:
Diagram Drawing: (Only If Necessary)
Report Made By:_____

To Be Filled Out By Manager's Office
Directed To:
Box Office ____ Backstage ____ F.O.H. ____
Janitorial ___ Subscriptions ____ Other: ____
Instructions:

To Be Filled Out By Department Head. Return To Manager's Office.
Action Taken:
Date Completed Or Date To Be Completed:
Remarks:
Signed: _____ Date: _____

---

angry when a persistent staff member is trying to fill out a report. In this case, I have employees write, "Patron refused to give name and address" on the form. The report is filled out with enough details that should this person contact us in the future, we can identify the accident. You can add a separate report to this that notes what measures were taken to help the injured person and that a check of the area showed no building deficiency that might have caused the accident.

Of course, in the event that some aspect of the building is responsible—a ripped carpet, a faulty step—that should be noted on the report as well as what action you have taken to correct it. While there is an obvious liability here, I do not recommend lying to cover up a legal negligence issue. A sample accident form (and other building-related forms) is in appendix C, but your insurance carrier may have one they prefer you to use.

OPENING AND CLOSING THE BUILDING

The house manager who functions also as a head usher may have various duties for opening and closing the theater. Some of these may be assigned to ushers who work various sections of the theater. Usually a checklist is helpful to ensure everything has been done and the theater is secure. After the usher has accomplished the task, he initials that it is complete. An example of an opening/closing list, prepared by Debra Stockton, who has worked as a head usher and assistant manager of the Curran Theater, follows:

The Renaissance Theater Opening Check List						
Day:	**Tues**	**Wed**	**Thurs**	**Fri**	**Sat**	**Sun**
Unlock Front Doors						
Remove Security Bars						
Air-Conditioning						
Store Ghost Light						
Set Up:						
Ropes/Stanions						
Ticket-Taker Areas						
Get House Count						
Check Wheelchair						
Seating Requirements						
Check Showtrans Bank						
Check Headphones						
Make Scheduling Changes						
Prepare Show/House Stuffers						

The Renaissance Theater Closing Check List						
Day:	**Tues**	**Wed**	**Thurs**	**Fri**	**Sat**	**Sun**
Balcony:						
Check Restrooms						
Deodorizers Off						
Plumbing OK						
Security Bars On Doors						
Closets Locked						
Patrons Out:						
Seating Area						
Restrooms						
Lobby Area						
Mezzanine:						
Check Restrooms						
Deodorizers Off						
Plumbing OK						
Security Bars On Doors						
Doors/Windows Locked						
Closets Locked						

Day:	Tues	Wed	Thurs	Fri	Sat	Sun
Patrons Out:						
Seating Area						
Restrooms						
Lobby Area						
Orchestra:						
Will Call/Tix Stubs						
To Box Office						
Headphones Returned						
Showtrans Bank Balanced						
Lost & Found To Mgr.'s Office						
Check Restrooms						
Deodorizers Off						
Plumbing OK						
Security Bars On Doors						
Doors/Windows Locked						
Closets Locked						
Patrons Out:						
Seating Area						
Lobby & Restrooms						
Double Check Exit Doors						
Staff Exits Building						
Set Up Ghost Light						
Turn Off Theater Lights						

The outside of the building should not be neglected. Depending on the location of your theater, first-time patrons could get lost, be unable to find parking, or be made late by forces beyond their control. Both movie and legitimate theaters along Hollywood Boulevard found their buildings sinking from the effects of a 6.7 magnitude earthquake and the construction of the city's underground Metro Rail. Additionally, the Pantages Theater was restricted "by the presence of gigantic subway cranes, trucks and ongoing digging on the block" (O'Steen 1994, 10). Posting signs or stationing personnel to aid patrons having difficulties with temporary problems such as these can head off having an agitated customer walking through the door a half hour late.

THE ADA

The Americans with Disabilities Act (ADA) has been a most challenging legislation for service industry workers. For public accommodations such as theaters, the act became effective in 1992. It required companies to take "readily achievable" measures to make the building compliant with the act (www.usdoj.gov/crt/ada/business.htm 2002). The definition of what this actually means can end up being decided in court as attorneys and advocates pursue lawsuits or out-of-court settlements.

It is not my intention to debate the merits or absurdities of what has come of the ADA, but rather address the situations in which workers find themselves. Traina observes, "This is an area that all house managers deal with in varying degrees, again depending on the age of your facility and the proactiveness of your organization." It has been my observation that front-of-house staff will usually go out of their way and beyond the call of duty to help out customers who are limited by the structure of the building. Unfortunately, older theaters that were built as early as the 1920s are not only disability-unfriendly, there often is no way to address compliancy measures in the way many physically challenged people would like. This can lead to on-site disputes with staff about the building.

It is difficult not to argue or defend the place you work when a wheelchair-bound person is screaming at you that you are not ADA compliant to their satisfaction. "The staff does offer assistance whenever necessary," says Traina, "employing the help of the porter, stagehands and ushers to help people in and out of seats, downstairs to restrooms, etc. Sometimes we will encourage people to use the restrooms in a neighboring restaurant or hotel, but folks are not always agreeable. And in a way, who can blame them?"

Unfortunately, I must recommend that you and the staff refrain from discussing the building or the ADA with a person trying to draw you into an argument or debate while you are on duty and represent the theater. Anyone with the agenda of filing a lawsuit may try to coerce or trick you into saying something that can be used against you at a later time. I explain to my staff that they do not own the building, they cannot approve construction of an elevator, an oversized bathroom, integrated seating, or anything else a person may be telling you that the building needs.

A staff member only works for the theater and can only provide assistance within their ability. If what is available is not satisfactory to a disabled person, then this person needs to contact the owner. It is not an employee's place to fight the owner's fight. A lot of "I'm sorry, that's something you'll have to take up with the theater owner," can be frustrating to both sides in a discussion. But, it is better than finding yourself out of a job because you have said something that cost your employer a hefty financial judgment. That we have declined to participate in a debate, argument, or defense of a noncompliant building does not mean we are not knowledgeable of the law or lack sympathy, but often that will be the accusation hurled at us. One West Coast theater manager relates that he

saw a box office treasurer instantly silence an outraged man in a wheelchair, who was complaining he had no way to get to his seat in the loge (he hadn't bothered to find out if the theatre had a elevator). He accused the treasurer of being stupid and uncaring. The treasurer became equally outraged and said, "How dare you accuse me of not caring. My mother has been disabled all of my life and I deal with her disability every day."

The positive side of ADA lawsuits and activists' campaigns is that as owners respond, the on-site disputes will lessen. Traina concludes, "As the theater-going population (and the American population) is getting older, we need to continue to address the challenges that will accompany those patrons."

People You Will Meet
Gary Sandy, actor

I'm an actor, always have been, always will be, never wanted to be anything else. There's "no business like show business," the greatest, most satisfying business in the world. But also the toughest. Because as I see it, you have *got* to be in it for the long haul. This is hard to explain to a youngster who has just been "discovered" walking down the street and suddenly is making more money than they had ever dreamed of. But . . . when you're hot, you're hot and when you're not, you are NOT. Longevity is the answer. To realize that you have to be READY for success, dry spells, the aging process (you're going to look different, so you may have to "reinvent" yourself into another "type"). And an actor's life always has its ups and downs. You pull yourself up to the next rung on the ladder to Success, and find hills and valleys at each level. Make no bones about it, an actor is an athlete, always ready, physically and mentally. You must keep your confidence up even after being rejected in audition after audition. A friend once argued that his being a salesman made us essentially in the same business. I replied by saying, "If they don't buy your computer, you can convince yourself it had nothing to do with you. If they don't buy my product, it becomes very difficult to convince myself . . . they didn't buy ME." Ready on the set! Just yesterday, I spent ten hours on a film, and never worked. You were expected, however, to be ready to perform when they needed you. It becomes harder to keep your energy going as the years go by. But, on a big budget film, that is what you must be ready for, take after take, while the smaller budget may call for you to be ready for the one and only take. And what of live theater? Are you ready to do the same show, the same part, 600, 1,000, 1,500 times? Eight shows a week for months? It helps me to keep in mind that at today's prices, a couple could be spending $75 apiece to see me perform, plus dinner and transportation, that could be $250–$350. They shouldn't have to care how many times I have done the show. I have to be ready for them. Sounds tough to be an actor, doesn't it? It is. Is that what you want? You have to KNOW that. To be, or not to be, that IS the question. After all is said and done, I

(continued)

am proud to be in the Entertainment BUSINESS. I've made my living as an actor for going on thirty-five years. Never had to do anything else. Some of the best work I've done was never recorded on film and will never be seen on TV. Success is what you think it is. All I know is, I'm already READY, because I'm a professional.

NOTE

1. *The Magic Curtain* by Lawrence Langner, founder of the Theatre Guild (New York: Dutton, 1951).

Chapter 6

Unions

Nearly every worker in commercial theater belongs to a union. This makes the workplace an agency shop where "the employer may hire a worker who is not a member of the union, but within thirty days the worker must pay the union an initiation fee; and the worker must pay regular union dues thereafter. . . . The worker is not required to join the union, but he is required to pay the union for the services it provides. If the worker fails to pay the money, the union may insist that the employer fire him" (Gold 1989, 13). For more technical positions such as the stagehands and wardrobe, employers will nearly always hire from the union. Most local unions are under the umbrella of the International Alliance of Theatrical Stage Employees (IATSE), including stagehands, wardrobe, box office, ushers, and ticket-takers. Musicians, teamsters, janitors, and engineers are the exceptions. Performing unions such as Actors' Equity and guilds like the Dramatist Guild are not covered in this chapter as they are primarily associated with the production rather than the theater. The manager's union, Association of Theatrical Press Agents and Managers (ATPAM), became an affiliate with IATSE in 1994.

The fact that managers belong to a union has long caused conflict and self-doubt, since we represent employers who are often at odds with unions; yet, we are unionized and share some of the same employment goals. Manager Joe Traina has always been pro-union, sometimes to his own detriment. "While there are numerous contradictions inherent in being a member of a management union, it is more necessary than ever that we have one. The old school understanding between management and labor has all but disappeared, and some producers and theater owners will agree on provisos at the bargaining table and then spend the term of the agreement trying to get around them. The integrity and honor that once existed is gone from the scene today." These sentiments are echoed by another West Coast manager who walked a picket line for a sister union, and the next day faced the effects:

> My employer made a pointed comment about me being a union activist (our company culture is one of public support for unions, but private undermining of the union agenda). My membership in a union has been crucial for my survival in my position, and I would never give it up. But I do play the game with my employer and when necessary, I will battle with other unions, but not my own.

While the great American labor movement is historically cited as having begun in the 1930s, attempts at theatrical organizing began in the late 1800s. Stagehands are credited with negotiating the first collective bargaining agreement (CBA) under the formation of the National Alliance of Theatrical Stage Employees in 1893. This organization later became IATSE (McDermott 1993, 475).

ATPAM's history was forged from the 1920s to the 1940s, in a power struggle between the New York Theatrical Press Agents and the Theatrical Managers, Agents, and Treasurers (TMAT). The two organizations competed for producer recognition and jurisdiction. In a state-mediated agreement the press agents became part of TMAT but maintained their autonomy within the group. Once the treasurers broke off to form their own affiliation in 1939, press agents and managers found their union at odds with every theatrical union and the producers. Eventually, the union was able to secure an agreement with the League of New York Theaters and extended its jurisdiction to include Canada as well as the rest of the United States. In 1946 the name was changed to ATPAM (Greenberg 1993, 5–17).

Until recently Broadway unions, as well as ATPAM, negotiated their contracts with the League of American Theaters and Producers (LATP), which represented producers and theater owners. LATP came into existence in 1930 as a trade association for commercial theaters. It defines its role as promoting "the common interests of its members; to increase awareness of, and interest in, Broadway theatre across North America; and to provide a full range of support for more profitable theatrical productions" (www.broadway.org 1998). It is looked upon by others as "a fractious assemblage of producers, presenters and landlords, each with different, often conflicting agendas" (Evans 1995). When the Walt Disney Company began producing, they declined to join LATP and negotiated their own contracts with individual unions. In recent years the Nederlander Organization has also negotiated contracts outside LATP.

For the vast majority of road theaters, the New York unions and LATP negotiations are inconsequential to their operation, except in the event of a strike, in which case traveling shows could not operate or play theaters manned by local IATSE crews. While each individual theater administration negotiates its own contracts with its own local unions, what happens in New York is probably an unspoken standard for local contracts as well. ATPAM is currently the only union whose negotiated contract with LATP covers managers and press agents who live outside New York City.

Local IATSE unions represent stagehands, wardrobe, and front-of-house employees. These organizations are under the jurisdiction of the international group, but have autonomy over their own geographic areas. While they have a president, vice-president, and treasurer, it is usually a business agent who deals with theater management. This person "may negotiate contracts, settle grievances, preserve jurisdictions, recruit new members, and handle correspondence and accounting" (Herman, Schwarz, and Kuhn 1992, 95–96).

On-site at the theater is a union or shop steward. This member of the workforce is usually elected by the workers or appointed by the union to represent its interests in the workplace. While the theater department head would be responsible for payroll, hiring, and supervision, the steward is charged with ensuring that the union's CBA and work rules are followed. Typically employees report contract infractions to the steward. Then the steward reports to the union's business agent, and "consults with employees who have or think they have a grievance, and they usually accompany an aggrieved employee in presenting a grievance to the supervisor at the initial step of the grievance procedure" (Herman, Schwarz, and Kuhn 1992, 95).

Depending on the temperament of the steward, power struggles can result with the department head, regardless of both being members of the same union. Once the department head is named, there is no getting around that he has responsibilities to management. A steward who wants to set policy may have to be pulled back in line. While there is a thin line between conditions set forth in a CBA, management should maintain their right to manage. As long as supervising does not violate the union contract or an individual's rights, then the pushiness of a steward may have to be disciplined as insubordination.

While the traveling shows work under the New York-based contract, with each production they enter local jurisdictions that might have precedents in conflict with what they are accustomed to in New York. It is wise not to assume that the IATSE and its local group have apprised each other of agreements or situations that might end up in conflict. One West Coast manager thinks the "ongoing problem is one of perceived superiority."

"That's the way we do it in New York City" is a common refrain. My answer is always "Well, you are not in New York anymore." . . . I once had a New York company manager who objected to pay rates for a local orchestra and proceeded to tear apart the local CBA as justification for not paying the musicians. After several minutes of listening to her tirade, I slammed my hand on the desk and told her to stop, that I could not change a signed CBA, and I would not listen to her complaints. She then fell silent.

But even Traina, as a New York manager, found the same kind of balking when an industrial played his theater and "the technical supervisor stated he did not require an engineer or ushers for [the] show. There was some sparring but that attraction could not ignore that those employees come with the building and are not hired at the attraction's discretion."

I found myself in a situation where the show contract specified that the theater paid all local expenses. A local union business agent decided that the production did not travel with enough stagehands. He put additional crew on the local payroll, which, of course, ended up being my expense and not the show's. After a meeting with the company manager, it was revealed that this situation had been discussed with the president of the IATSE prior to the show going on the road and had been approved as such. After informing the local business agent of this agreement, the additional people were taken off the crew and the union covered the worker's payroll.

These examples raise the question: If these details are not in the union contract, then how can a manager prepare for them? The bad news is, you can't. You find out about them when the union or a union worker voice their concerns and you learn from the experience. The outcome of an unexpected situation, like those I have described, can range from a negotiated agreement between the general manager and the union business agent to an arbitration or lawsuit. The decision then sets a precedent for similar circumstances in the future. Traina says he "always tries not to spend the show's money."

If there is an additional, unexpected cost I try to inform the show as soon as I can, and help them when possible. Sometimes premiums are due employees when there's an overtime situation pending. At a recent production of *A Doll's House* at the Belasco, the show ran to over three hours on most nights and overtime was due to stagehands, porters and ushers. The show only played seven nights a week and all staff were paid for eight. The owner and producer thought no overtime should be claimed as there was already a "bonus" show being paid, but employees and union reps thought otherwise. I tried to get the show started promptly, cut intermission down to twelve minutes but on some nights, well, the acting got in the way. Ultimately, the unions went to grievance and a compromise in overtime was paid (some got it for every show past 11:00 P.M., others for every show after 11:05 P.M.), and yours truly got to determine who got what over the course of a five-month engagement for no additional compensation.

Theater manager Robert Lazzara says that he always tries to fight additional costs because that is the job of a manager even if "I know ahead of time I am doomed to failure."

I am courteous about it, but I don't want anyone to think they can pull a fast one over me. I once had a house carpenter tell me I needed two men on the flyfloor for a show that had only one move: the house drape. One man was the flyman, the second man was there in case the flyman fell asleep. My response was, "If the flyman falls asleep, he is fired." The carpenter responded by saying he would report me to the international vice-president of the stagehands union. My response was, "Go right ahead. I had lunch with him yesterday, and I would be happy to talk to him about this." The carpenter backed down.

Perhaps Traina supplies the best summarized approach to being a union manager dealing with union employees. "Though it's difficult to be 100 percent objective at all times, I've tried to establish a management style that separates personal from professional as best as possible. I've also tried to never ask an employee to do something that I wouldn't do or haven't done in a pinch."

HOW TO READ A UNION CONTRACT

Union contracts (CBAs), also called minimum basic agreements (MBA), or working agreements, typically begin by naming the parties and a declaration of jurisdiction. Usually within these introductory paragraphs is the length of the contract and the procedure to follow by which either party can put the other on notice of termination or future negotiation. The expiration date is what most concerns the theater manager. If the Renaissance Theater is in the middle of a show when a particular contract expires, then the manager will want to ensure there is enough money to cover any increases in payroll and benefits. Provided the theater and the union are in negotiations, then additional payroll charges to the show will probably be higher when the contract is renewed. The best estimate of what this increase will be should be held on the weekly settlement.

The body of the contract contains sections that define the manpower, usually divided into the department heads and the staff. These workers may have specific designations such as ticket-taker, usher, and treasurer for front-of-house, and flyman, front light operator, and wardrobe dresser for backstage unions. The hours worked will be broken down under a show call or a minimum hourly call. A four-hour call is typical. This section also specifies when an employee can take breaks, meal periods, work that can and cannot be performed within these calls, and penalties or pay rate increases invoked when these time periods are violated.

The parts of a union contract that should be of the most interest to the theater manager are the wage scale and working conditions. This is the information that will affect budgets, payrolls, and other costs. Besides the basic minimum pay rate, the wage scale will also specify pay scales for overtime, labor outside of the defined work hours (for example, before 6 A.M. or after midnight), holidays, and benefits such as vacation, pension, annuity, and health and welfare obligations. While these rates are specific to a legitimate theater, on occasion the building may be used for television or motion picture work. Most union contracts stipulate different (and usually higher) rates for this. If an additional scale is not included in the contract, usually there will be a clause guaranteeing payment at the prevailing television and motion picture rates, which will be supplied by the union.

When working conditions are included in a union contract, they can be as general as a paragraph granting the employer the right to make rules and regulations necessary to conduct business, as long as they do not conflict with the CBA. Working conditions can also have very specific lists of the employer's obligations. The theater manager must read these carefully as they will often affect both cost and the operation of the theater. And, because these conditions will vary from city to city, the house manager will want to make the company and stage manager aware of any unusual conditions that may affect the operation of the show. She will also want to be kept informed of anything that happens during the show that increases her cost. This can be especially important when the theater is guaranteeing a show. Show personnel who are accustomed to four-wall deals where they basically call the shots can get a rude awakening when informed that because of contract violations, they must pay any excess cost incurred from their guarantee. Other situations cannot even be guessed at until they occur.

Traina once found himself in such a situation when he worked at the Richard Rodgers Theatre during the run of *Fool Moon*.

> Every night performer David Shiner would go through the second row of the orchestra with a bucket of popcorn, seeming to find his seat. Then the popcorn would spill and get a big laugh. General Manager Bob Kamlot proposed that we should leave the spilled popcorn in the row overnight to be cleaned by the cleaning staff the following morning. I objected to this for two reasons. One was the danger of attracting every rodent on West 46th Street with some of their favorite food. The other (and . . . a way more important reason) was that since this was generated by the show props, the [cleanup] was really the

propmaster's domain. We "argued" a little over the issue, then Kamlot made a deal with the house propmaster, bought a portable Dirt Devil vacuum, and the [cleanup] was done after every performance. In my experience, most rules can be compromised if there is up-front communication and trust. Some rules must be adhered to if the situation is cut and dried or if there's past precedent, but there is usually give-and-take if management and labor are honest with each other and make an attempt to work things out.

An increasingly important part of contracts is the termination language. Most managers are swiftly learning that the longer this section is, the more it is about preventing management from terminating employees. The termination section reviews the appropriate way to discipline an employee, usually by a certain amount of verbal and/or written warnings. The main purpose of these is to inform the employee of bad performance or inappropriate behavior, and to request improvement. After a certain number of warnings the employer can terminate the staff member.

This is hardly the end of the story. An employee who objects to the employer's disciplinary action can appeal to the union to file a grievance on the staff member's behalf. Typically, once this is done the employee meets with union representatives and the employer to try and resolve the matter. If resolution cannot be reached, most contracts allow for arbitration of the issue, which would bind both parties.

A difficult aspect of union–employer relations is when the union contract protects incompetent workers. It should not be assumed that the union is in full agreement with a member on every issue, though they are still required to represent the worker. In failing to reach a satisfactory resolution after meeting with the employer, a union can be expected to proceed to arbitration or lawsuit. While it is true to say that most unions will not arbitrate a flimsy or irrational issue, they risk being taken before the National Labor Relations Board (NLRB) by the union member should they refuse to proceed on the worker's behalf.

Arbitrations are generated by the union when a particular employee feels wronged and discussions between the parties have not yielded a solution. They also occur when the union believes the employer has violated the CBA, thus violating the rights of its entire membership. Traina says at one time he was known as a "scourge as far as employees who did not perform their duties were concerned."

If incompetence in the workplace is not corrected, then it affects all aspects of how I manage. There were a number of employees whom I liked personally, but they had gotten apathetic because no prior management ever expected them to give even a bare minimum of service, or they felt their union status could insure that they would keep the job indefinitely. It was a difficult approach frequently ending in a grievance hearing, but I replaced more than 50 percent of the front-of-house staff at one theater I managed a number of years ago because there were too many uncooperative staff members and not enough work getting done.

The result of arbitration is binding on both parties, but is often not yet the end of the issue. An employee who has experienced a negative decision can hire an attorney and file a civil lawsuit against an employer, file charges with the NLRB, and make a complaint to the Equal Employment Opportunity Commission (EEOC). For many years the CBA between unions and employers ruled the workplace when problems occurred. Today's workplace is more litigious and therefore it is necessary for managers to approach these situations with their eyes wide open.

Documentation is the key to protecting both you and your employer. One West Coast manager says his strategy is to

> wait and wait, knowing if you give someone enough rope, they will eventually hang themselves. In the meantime, I try to prevent myself or my staff from falling into any traps laid by the incompetent. I instruct the staff to document all failings of the incompetent, but never to overreact. The goal is to avoid arbitration and hearings, but never to be afraid of them when they occur, and to fight tooth and nail when necessary.

Regardless of which party prevails in a lawsuit, arbitration, or government agency hearing, each involves considerable attorney fees, a fact that has made both employer and union more willing to work out problems prior to engaging in expensive litigation.

BYLAWS AND CONSTITUTIONS

Bylaws are typically linked to a union's constitution. Both cover the union's organization, election of officers, finances, duties and rights of membership, and penalties for violations. While these areas are between the union and its membership, some contracts will contain language that includes the bylaws as part of the CBA. It is often an overlooked contract clause that can cause problems. While most employers have no problem with the intent of the bylaws, they seldom read them or unions may choose to make them unavailable to management.

A potential problem is that the bylaws are written and voted on by the union membership. The employer has no negotiating power over them. So, if a membership inserts a financial clause within the body of these rules, then without knowing it the employer has already preaccepted an employment condition or rule. For instance, some musician's unions insert a casual rate wage scale in the bylaws to cover work done for one-day events such as weddings, fairs, or concerts. It is possible that the theater could be bound by these rates even though they are not part of the wage scale negotiated into the CBA. A way around this kind of abuse is to read the bylaws and negotiate language into the CBA that the bylaws are accepted as of a certain date. At least this way the employer has an opportunity to broach any new additions in the negotiations of their CBA. Another alternative is to negotiate the bylaws and union constitution out of the CBA.

Work rules are sometimes written in as part of the contract, while at other times they are simply past practice that has become a precedent. When these precedents become outdated and simply do not make fiscal or practical sense, management may try to do away with them and run into a very hard wall when they find out the union is not agreeable to the change.

UNION AND MANAGEMENT RELATIONSHIPS

Theater management's relationship with unions covers the range from congenial to hostile, but by definition, it can be considered an adversarial relationship even though some business agents and managers may get along fine. Most theorists divide collective bargaining into "four systems of activity, each with its own functions for the interacting parties, its own internal logics, and its own identifiable set of instrumental acts or tactics." Distributive bargaining functions "to resolve pure conflicts of interest." Integrative bargaining seeks "to find common or complementary interests and solve problems confronting both parties." Attitudinal structuring attempts "to influence the attitudes of the participants toward each other and to affect the basic bond which relate to the two parties they represent." Intraorganizational bargaining "has the function of achieving consensus within each of the interacting groups" (Walton and McKersie 1965, 4).

Distributive bargaining is across-the-table, give-and-take negotiations to get as much as you can for your side. This type of bargaining is considered "the dominant activity in union-management relationship. Unions represent employees in the determination of wages, hours, and working conditions. Since these matters involve the allocations of resources, there is assumed to be some conflict of interest between management and unions. . . . It occurs in situations in which one party wins what the other party loses" (Walton and McKersie 1965, 11).

Theater managers typically will not negotiate a CBA, but will often be available to provide information to those who do. On occasions when managers are on the negotiating committee they will usually get permission from their union to bargain on behalf of the employer. Each of the bargaining theories probably plays a role at one time or another during the negotiation process: shared information helps each side understand the other (integrative); the relationship of the parties, either friend or foe (attitudinal); the internal politics of the theatrical organization or union (intraorganizational); and sitting at the bargaining table and working it out (distributive). The state of negotiations will inevitably affect the temperature of a theater. If contract negotiations are prolonged or do not proceed as expected, employee frustration can infiltrate work performance.

While dealing with behavior that can sometimes seem juvenile (often on both sides), few managers would disagree with the need for unions or devalue their effectiveness. Management guru Tom Peters (1997, 12) plainly states, "People do not go into labor unions just for the living hell of it. They join labor unions because management is acting like jerks." Former ATPAM president Sally Campbell Morse said in her speech to the IATSE convention in 1996, "We do not apologize for wanting to make a living in decent conditions while we do it. We cannot apologize for needing medical coverage. We will not stop protecting our right to retirement benefits after we devote lifetimes to working in this field" (Morse 1996, 7).

The nature of labor–management relations can change over time and be many different things at once. The contentiousness that shadowed the labor movement at various times over the decades, resulting in injury and death to many people, has, gratefully, seemed to have passed. Animosity that does occur often centers around a time period such as contract negotiations or an incident, perhaps a grievance. In those in-between times professional respect, even friendship, might grow between union officials and management.

When I find myself frustrated with union situations, it is beneficial to remember the historical context of why unions came to exist. Forty years after his death, I discovered my grandfather had had two fingers pulled off by coal mining equipment, and had had a foot crushed when a rock tumbled off a mine ledge. In those days there was no worker's compensation, no medical insurance, no pensions, and no multimillion dollar lawsuits for negligence. One worked with the permanent disability or one did not work.

People You Will Meet
Bill Woody, pyrotechnic special effects

Working with explosives in close proximity to the actors requires a great amount of concentration and focus. Of course, there is no room for error. Because of this, the levity of the following situation was most appreciated. A last-minute problem on stage necessitated that I run quickly to my area in the basement to retrieve another device before my cue. As I was descending the stairs, someone yelled, "Look! The 'pyro-man' is running. Now, that's what I call a reason to worry!" Maybe a T-shirt is in the want: "I am a Pyrotechnician. If you see me running, try to keep up!"

Chapter 7

Customers and Employees, or Yelling at the Usher Always Improves the Sound

Whether one works in theater or any other kind of service industry, there is one singular lie that is told by management to its patrons. The great customer service lie is: "I'm sorry, it will never happen again." It will not only happen again, it will probably happen several times. And if you hear the footsteps of some aggressive consumer affairs reporter lying in wait to catch you on concealed videotape, be prepared to explain why it happened again.

Customer problems often provoke reactions that are out of proportion to the problem, and it is tempting to answer back with "Ma'am, the Chinese military running over students with tanks is outrageous, a line at the lady's room is inconvenient." As theater manager Robert Lazzara suggests, "ignore any negativity that is directed to you by an angry patron. Your job is to see through the anger and find out why the patron is mad. Then put yourself in their shoes."

It is the staff who will encounter the patron before you, and get the brunt of anger as well. Unfortunately, a customer intent on leaving scorched earth will not necessarily calm down by the time he reaches you. The staff and the manager will face wrath from both directions, from the customer and from your employer. While your GM may be reprimanding you about all the things the staff did wrong, your only memory of the incident was that you wanted to put your hands around a patron's neck and squeeze.

After working in theater for awhile, it will become evident that most customer complaints are of the same nature: seat location is not as expected, the staff is rude, another customer irritated them, the sound stinks, the play is awful, they have come on the wrong day, the ticket is not worth the cost, they cannot see the stage, there are not enough bathrooms, and they want a refund. While the response to such complaints can be fairly standard, the way in which the customer is handled varies depending on initial contact. This can range from a quiet inquiry or suggestion for improvement to a rage of indignation that no amount of apology can assuage. It is up to staff to choose a proper response.

In dealing with patrons, it is wise to keep in mind that "[c]ustomers may not always be right, but they are seldom prepared to accept that they are wrong" (Tjosvold 1993, 138). This is not to suggest that employees must play the role of the kicked dog during such transactions. Taking control of the situation may, in fact, allow a manager to steer a situation to a more successful conclusion. Lazzara continues:

> The secret is to first remember you hold all the power. You will decide where the patron sits, what date they will attend, or if we will even allow them inside the theatre. In the extreme, management has the right to eject patrons who are causing disturbances. This power, which must never be forgotten, gives you a stable center from which to operate.

In some respects the decade of the nineties has been defined by consumerism. Rather than accepting what they get, consumers are more likely to do more than complain about a service or product they consider inadequate or of poor value. Their responses range from writing a disgruntled editorial in the local newspaper to filing legal action, to verbally or physically assaulting the staff. At a production of *Angels in America* at San Francisco's American Conservatory Theater, a "man picked up an usher and threw him against a wall after being told he was late and would have to await a break" before being allowed into the auditorium (Whiting 1995, 29).

The workplace of the nineties has responded by placing greater emphasis on customer service and employee training. The term "customer service" has become a cliché, sometimes meaning "the customer is always right," other times having a more sublime significance, such as servicing customers so well that they are not aware of it. Too often the frontline employee interprets the term as meaning another unpleasant task to engage in with a screaming, unhappy patron. It is unfortunate that such a negative connotation has attached itself to this concept, since conscientious service is the foundation of the service industry. Besides the concern for the safety of the patron, it is a principal reason for employment.

In the theatrical industry where rudeness is often expected by customers, there are excellent reasons for using customer service skills beyond being just the dictate of the employer. To smile at a customer and say "Have a nice evening" is a skill that can be taught to a parrot. To successfully handle and resolve a situation with a frustrated and upset patron is an ability that is valued by an employer and transferable to just about any job. Therefore, impart to your staff that they should not learn about and practice customer service as simply a requirement, but because knowing these skills also benefits them and makes the job easier to perform. These abilities will serve them in many situations, both professionally and privately.

WHAT THE CUSTOMER EXPECTS

Prices for theater tickets have slowly climbed over the years from as low as $3 in 1971 to as high as $90 in 2003, a 3,000 percent increase. As the expense of presenting the show, labor cost, and facility expenditures rise, so will the ticket price. As a result, customers have come to expect more for their entertainment dollar. This expectation involves more than just a captivating show. In the minds of customers, the theater's responsibility begins the minute they walk out of their home.

That a particular customer's expectations might be outrageous or ridiculous is irrelevant. What is relevant is that the staff member will have to deal with these expectations, both the normal and the outrageous. Customers arrive wanting a mistake-proof evening, where nothing will distract them from their enjoyment of the performance. In many cases, they will get it. In a few cases, they will not. Some will find that they have arrived on the wrong night, that their seats are not as they expected. Others will find the service lacking, the facilities inadequate, or the cost of the ticket, in their opinion, not worth the evening's entertainment. They will expect the show to meet their entertainment expectations, but also that their tickets are in order; that they will be able to see and hear the entire production from their seats; that they will be able to enjoy the performance unencumbered by disturbance; and that any mishaps that do occur will be handled and resolved to *their* satisfaction.

When these expectations are not met, the result can be a direct dressing-down by the customer about how rude and unprofessional you are being; a letter to your supervisor or the owner of the theater about how ignorant the staff is; a demand for a refund because of a certain employee's conduct; or a threat never to return to the theater again. Often an incident will be reported to a higher authority such as the Better Business Bureau, letters to the editor of the local newspaper, the district attorney, or the Department of Justice.

On the surface, this scenario might seem overly dramatic. But, stop and think about the last time you were in this kind of situation. Perhaps you were at a theater, a restaurant or a hotel, maybe an airport, when you found the service representative unhelpful. Did this make you believe them to be uncaring? Did you think to yourself that you would never patronize this establishment again? Did you wonder how that idiot salesperson got their job, much less keep it? Probably this and more went through your mind. You may have even taken the additional step of demanding a refund or writing a letter of complaint.

As Lazzara suggests, it is often instructive to put yourself in the customer's shoes when you believe he is being unreasonable. Chances are you have already been there and may have acted exactly as the customer is acting. What is even more important to think about is: how many times have you returned to an establishment that you believe treated you rudely or unfairly? The point of this comparison is to realize that the facts, the reality, or the truth are not what counts. It is the person's belief that determines whether or not you lose a customer.

WHAT IS EXPECTED OF EMPLOYEES

Most theaters have a basic set of guidelines about how the theater operates and what is expected within the scope of employment. Typically these guidelines focus around making the evening easy and safe for the customers, and in turn ensuring that customers adhere to certain theater policies. These policies are often quite simple: customers must sit in the right seats, do not use cameras during the show, and do not smoke or take drinks into the auditorium. Policies vary from theater to theater, and staff should understand that no one procedure is written in stone. Circumstances will always dictate decisions.

THE BASICS

As with venue policy, most theaters have basic rules and regulations about how they want employees to conduct themselves. Most will focus around the concept of acting professionally. Keep in mind that these rules and regulations are often put together to address an accumulation of problems or incidents that have happened through the years. Staff might consider that a rule stating, "Do not chew gum or smoke when working" is juvenile and obvious. But if it is in there, then I can almost guarantee that the theater has at one time had a problem with a staff member who chewed gum or took a cigarette break in front of the customers. Employees may not see the value or significance of the rule, but its genesis often lies in a problem that occurred in the past.

The unfortunate aspect of these rules and regulations is that they are often written in negatives of "don't do this, don't do that." The goal of these rules is not to try and keep employees under the hard thumb of the supervisor, but to create a professional image. Attitude reinforces the impression that is made, and staff should be aware of it at all times. The way employees look, the way they dress, and the way they wear clothing is only part of this image. Disposition and attitude are the second part. Lazzara points out:

> You must command a customer's respect. If you respond in anger or defensiveness, you lose their respect and become a punching bag. Here is where your appearance will help you. A well-groomed conservative appearing person will be listened to. A person with unruly hair and twelve nose rings will be dismissed by an angry patron, and you will get nowhere.

Very often in my own theater, a staff member will argue that their streak of purple hair and pierced body parts is an expression of their individuality. This may be true, but what I usually do then is ask them to walk to the four-star hotel located on the corner and look around. Do they see any concierges, receptionists, or doormen with purple hair and nose rings? Conservative grooming not only sets a tone of trustworthiness with the customers, but helps to ensure they take you more seriously.

Theater patrons are often older and conservative. If the theater is located in a large metropolitan city and a customer is from the suburbs, he watches the news and sees the dangers of city life. Walking into a theater and observing a staff member who looks like they live on the streets will scare them. They may feel that the trip to the theater was enough of a dangerous adventure. They will not want to feel as if being inside the theater is a continuation of all the things out on the street that makes them afraid. The first experience a customer has of the theater is the impression you make on them.

BEYOND THE BASICS

In this section, I would like to address some specific techniques that will aid in establishing customer rapport, make managers more aware of the attitudes they project, and give examples of what to do and not do in specific situations. This section involves practice—it is filled with information that is not typical of customer service training in the theater and will, at first, require a conscious effort to employ the techniques. Once mastered, many of these techniques will become automatic and you will use them without thinking. Some of this information is based on the work of Richard Bandler and John Grinder.[1]

Pace the Customer

Pacing is a kind of imitation. By imitating the positive actions of another person, you establish a rapport with them. Pacing is more formally defined by Jerry Richardson in *The Magic of Rapport* (1987, 19) as "meeting the other person where he or she is, reflecting what he or she knows or assumes to be true, or matching some part of his or her ongoing experience." In our case, we wish to pace those behaviors that lead to a satisfactory conclusion rather than the negative conduct that escalates a problem.

Consider the situation of a very upset man heading in your direction, and in a loud voice, he screams that his tickets are crap and somebody better do something about it. Naturally you do not want to pace his anger. First, quickly identify the trait worth pacing. In this case, I would suggest pacing his authority. You need to establish a stronger authority than he is projecting; otherwise, he will dictate the situation.

In a strong, deep voice say to him, "Sir, I understand there is a problem with your ticket. If you'll wait here, I'll get someone to discuss it with you." Another variation might be: "The box office manager will be able to address your concerns."

Now, suppose the person is a tearful grandmother. You would not want to use the same kind of authoritative tone with her as you used with the angry man. You also would not want to cry with her. A sympathetic tone might be the best response to her anxiety. "I understand how upsetting this is. The box office is around the corner, why don't we go there and see if the treasurer can help you out with this." By using a sympathetic tone that matches her concern, you have been able to identify yourself as someone who understands what she is going through and can point her in the right direction for help.

If you had used the sympathetic tone with the angry man, he would likely have dismissed you as someone who did not know what they were talking about and as a waste of his time. When pacing it is important to choose the correct trait to model. If you are unsure, then watch the customer's body movements and tension level and try to keep your own as calm as possible.

Also pay attention to the tempo of language. If you are speaking to someone from the southern states, and you are rattling off your answer in a mile-a-minute monotone, no amount of pacing is going to work. Typically, people from southern states speak slower. Slow down your speech pace. To imitate their accent would be condescending. What you are reaching for is similarity, not mockery. Suppose the customer were from the Northeast and has a faster speaking pattern. To speak in a slow deliberate way, hoping they will understand you better, will not help. Most likely it will only make them think something is wrong with you.

So, listen, choose, and then, pace.

Apologize without Apologizing

One of the most frequent complaints that I receive in letters from customers is, "And, after all that, they never even apologized." It is usually irrelevant that there may be nothing to apologize for. When an incident occurs, regardless of fault, a customer usually expects the retailer to come up with the solution. In those instances when we are unable to give them what they want, the allegation of rudeness will often accompany the complaint.

I recommend what I call "apologizing without apologizing." This is a technique of saying how sorry you are that a particular event happened to them. "I'm sorry you are unhappy with your seating location; perhaps the box office can move you." "I'm sorry those other customers were rude to you." "I'm sorry you missed your performance, but unfortunately tonight we are sold out." It is often a good idea to end the conversation with the same kind of apology. "I'm sorry you cannot hear; I'll forward the information to the sound department."

Using this kind of apology, you have accomplished two goals. You have met the other person's subconscious need for sympathy and responsibility. And, you have done so without admitting any fault on your part or the theater's part. If the customer huffs off after taking issue with your solution, there is less of an opportunity to accuse you of rudeness in their "sure-to-follow" letter.

Of course, there will be times when there is a genuine need for apology. If a staff member acts inappropriately or a problem occurs which is a mistake that inconveniences a customer, or even if you handle a situation incorrectly, then certainly, you should take responsibility for it, including issuing the appropriate apology.

The Way You Say It

Whether involved in a ticket transaction, seating a customer, or answering the question, "Where's the bathroom?" remember that we perform these tasks again and again throughout the evening. This repetition becomes so automatic we barely pay attention to the many steps that can be involved in getting through a performance. Keep in mind that it is the customer's first time through the procedure. If the question is answered before it is asked, because, obviously, you know what the question is going to be, that can seem rude or perceived as interrupting. Sometimes it is necessary to go through the procedure or directions with customers several times. You repeat this information over and over during a day; it is their first time hearing it.

Probably the most common question asked in theater is for directions to the bathroom. If you reply, "acrossthelobby-throughttheredcurtains-anddownthehall," you will probably hear back, "Huh?" You will have to repeat the instructions if you do not say them clearly the first time. Likewise when a customer begins the question, "What's available Sat. . ." and the box office salesperson replies, "Nothing." It could be the buyer was about to ask, "What's available Saturday, December 5th, three months from now?"

By jumping the question, you have patronized the customer and lost an opportunity. Your attitude is likely interpreted as rude and jaded, even if you were just trying to be helpful. Suppose they were going to ask about this coming Saturday's sold-out performance. If you reply, "Nothing," likely they will walk away. If you reply, "That performance is sold out, but we have excellent seats available on the following Tuesday." They may indeed decline the Tuesday seats, but, they may not.

If there is a logic in the idea that ticket sales provide the revenue that pays the employee's salaries, then be assured that it is those Tuesday and Wednesday evenings where a theater needs a ticket-seller's skill. For the Saturday evenings, we only need a body to press the correct computer buttons. For the rest of the week, the ticket-seller must use more skill. In addition to making a sale, the seller should always offer certain customers various options. Everybody wants Saturday night, fifth row, center orchestra, and this customer will complain when you give him Saturday in the balcony. You will not hear from him when he has Tuesday night in the orchestra.

Finally, be aware of voice tone. Keep in mind that deep-voiced people can often sound rude without intending to. Voices that have a nasal tone can sound sarcastic or patronizing. If you are unsure where your voice fits, tape a phone conversation (with a friend's permission) and listen to yourself. Or, arrange for a friend to record you when you are unaware of it. When speaking phrases that you say often, try varying the word choice. This will help prevent sounding as if you have said the same thing a million times today and you are bored with it. I have on more than one occasion seen customers turn to a ticket-seller and snap, "You don't have to be so snotty about it!" The stunned ticket-seller had no clue that the tone of her high-pitched, nasal voice, rapidly repeating information that she repeats numerous times a day, sounded patronizing to the customer who, of course, is hearing the information for the first time.

Do Not Argue

It was my intention to try to make this information as negative-free as possible. However, there is one negative that must be stated as "Don't" with a capital "D." It is tempting and sometimes necessary to show a customer how a mistake is theirs. You may not intend for this instruction to be argumentative, but that is likely how they will perceive it.

You will never, in the customer's mind, win an argument, even if you are right. The most you will get is their ire at how you have handled the situation, and probably a letter to the theater owner about how unprofessional the service is at this theater. Imagine how your employer is going to appreciate your efforts to be helpful now. Learn to walk away from an argument. Lazzara suggests a helpful tactic of "removing yourself from a difficult situation." By doing this it gives a way out to the customer who has backed himself into a corner.

> Give an angry customer some room. Let them mull over what you told them, give them a moment to decide what they want to do. Sometimes all they need is some privacy to collect their thoughts and calm down. You might say to the customer, "[G]ive yourself a minute to think things over. I will be right around the corner when you're ready to proceed." Then, you may continue to help them solve the problem at hand. There may be occasions where you have become the focus of all a patron's anger, and your presence is only hurting the situation. Then you must extract yourself and turn it over to someone else.

At times like this, a card with the general manager's name and address is always helpful. In the event you have not been able to give an upset customer what they want, you have at least played for time by giving them someone they can talk to on the next day.

Job Stress

Remember what "front line" refers to in the military? They are the people who get shot at. In jobs that have frequent customer contact and are usually referred to as front line positions, there is inevitably job stress. In her book *The Managed Heart*, Arlie Russell Hochschild (1983, 7) defines her concept of emotional labor as "the management of feeling to create a publicly observable facial and bodily display; emotional labor is sold for a wage and therefore has exchange value." Our interactions with customers, who are complete strangers to us, but who expect our service, are an emotional investment. When we do not meet a customer's expectations, and their reactions are negative, then an emotional toll is to be expected.

The result of an abusive outburst from a customer can bother us for days. Keeping perspective is necessary in dealing with these encounters. Consider that every night 2,500 people walk through the door of the theater. How many of them does a manager have real difficulty with? One a night; sometimes none; perhaps more on the weekends; less on the weekdays. Out of 2,500 people, it is a very small percentage of those who create stressful incidents.

Of these perhaps ten obnoxious customers per week, how much time do they have to harass us? Most shows last approximately two to three hours and the time periods when customers are most engaged are the fifteen minutes before the show, a twenty-minute intermission, and about ten minutes after the performance. Of these ten to fifteen minutes, how much is spent with the high-stress customer? Usually three to ten minutes. Out of four hours of work time, the most that could be considered stressful amounts to a total of perhaps ten minutes. When looked at from this perspective, a stressful encounter seems less overwhelming.

This is not to say that the stress of a negative experience with a customer will not continue to have an effect. It may. All employees have their own ways of dealing with stress, or should at least find them. Anger buildup can be released by "running, swimming, racket sports, and fast walking," and when that is not possible, by "[s]houting, screaming, crying, throwing things, and punching pillows." Since these pressure-releasing activities are not always available on the spot, "People can also find relief by confiding, complaining, and gossiping" (Tjosvold 1993, 148). Find what off-duty activities work for you, and in periods of high stress, schedule them.

Hochschild's (1983, 187) study of airline attendants found that the technique that worked best for those whose jobs required emotional input was acting or creating a "false self." Theatrical workers observe acting at every performance and this is an excellent metaphor to make the point. Nightly, during *The Phantom of the Opera* for example, a young ingenue is kidnapped by a ghastly monster and forced to choose between the man she loves and the fiend. Watching the faces of the audience, we see their total absorption in the play. The actors have made it real for them.

We do not necessarily know the particular techniques that performers use to enmesh themselves in their characters. Some may use method acting, others may have studied with Uta Hagan, or trained in performing arts schools. What we do know is that around eleven o'clock every night, those performers walk out of the theater as themselves, not their characters. Nor do they carry with them the emotions of their characters. The actor portraying the Phantom is not depressed that he lost the girl. He has, in effect, hung up his emotional character in the dressing room.

Hochschild (1983, 187) points out three ways in which workers tend to let themselves get involved:

In the first, the worker identifies too wholeheartedly with the job, and therefore risks burnout. In the second, the worker clearly distinguishes herself from the job and is less likely to suffer burnout; but she may blame herself for making this very distinction and denigrate herself as "just an actor, not sincere." In the third, the worker distinguishes herself from her act, does not blame herself for this, and sees the job as positively requiring the capacity to act.

When we encounter a customer's hostility, we can take that hostility into ourselves and carry it with us for days, thus building up a hatred of the customer and an avoidance of our jobs; or we can become actors who have to deal with these sorts of situations for a two-hour performance each evening. On our way out the door, we hang up our ushering jacket, shut off the box office computer or lock the manager's office, and all that goes with it. In acting with the abusive customer, we put up a barrier to the hurt of their negativity. That a stranger who does not know us would presume to stand there and shout how unprofessional, uncaring, and stupid we are is not only outrageous to our self-esteem, but an incompetence on the part of the shouter who has little or no experience of us as human beings. This "false self" that we create when we come through the door for work is a resource for us to protect our emotional selves.

It is important to recognize that the false self is a construct for the purposes of interacting with strangers. Our true selves—our feelings, hurts, and desires, in which we are sincere—are for those people that we know and have relationships with. Make sure that the distinction between sincerity and the false construct is kept clear.

Difficult and Abusive Customers

In defining a difficult customer it is important to distinguish between a frustrated patron and someone who is by nature difficult. There are people in our society whose hobby it is to complain. They may enjoy it. They may have nothing better to do. They might have grown up with the belief

---

People You Will Meet
Ginny Kolmar, press agent

A publicist in theater or any branch of show business must never expect to be thanked! If the show fails, it's her fault and if it's a smash, it's because the producer (or actors, director, designer) is so wonderful. A great exception to this rule was the late Karl Allison, who produced the first two *Greater Tuna* productions in San Francisco. On the first opening night he said "Thank you" to the two stars, director, all the technical people, dressers, front-of-house-staff and us—with a bottle of very expensive champagne for each! On the return trip he again thanked us on opening night and gave us, the actors, director, theater lessor and a few others an artists' proof of the *Greater Tuna* cast with some of their characters—by Hirschfeld! We were all so moved and pleased. . . . I cried.

that you get nothing in life that you do not fight for. They may have had past experiences that confirm to them that the squeaky wheel gets the grease.

There is no single right way to deal with difficult or frustrated customers, though there are several wrong things to do. "Most customers are not prepared to be blamed or criticized by a service provider" (Tjosvold 1993, 138). Arguing with the customer or becoming angry yourself will lead to an equally vitriolic response. It ups the ante. He will then have more reason to prove you wrong. Remember that customers think that their consumer dollars make them your pseudoemployer. Any resolution to their problems will have to be at your expense.

Listening until customers have had their say will help to deflate their energy, "as soon as the frustration has been released the problem can be addressed." Employees should "try to take the long view, and eschew counterattack because that would continue the negative interaction in which everyone loses" (Tjosvold 1993, 152). Jerry Richardson (1987, 175) echoes this view. "A mistake people often make when attacked is to try to defend themselves, their idea, or their association. . . . [D]efensiveness is a tactical error, because it can easily be taken by the other person as a counterattack and as such serves only to increase the level of anger or hostility."

Richardson (1987, 176) goes on to suggest that the best way to defuse a verbal attack is to agree with the content of the person's argument, or agree with or validate the feeling. Telling an attacker that they may be correct that they ordered tickets for tonight and not last week gives you a chance to step away from the window and print out their ticket order. (If you are unable to qualify the facts, you can always tell them you understand how upsetting this situation can be for them.) By gaining these few minutes, it can give the customer a chance to calm down, and also see that you are not accusing them of being wrong, but rather are checking to see what might have gone wrong. Even if you are unable to get the person into the show this night, from here you can make suggestions to address the problem rather than have to deal with the anger.

Lastly, I would like to address customers who are in a state of extreme distress. These are the kinds of customer that employees should not deal with but pass on to a manager as quickly as possible. People of this nature may, in fact, be dangerous, and can include screamers, intoxicated persons, drug users, and people who are verbally abusive, physically abusive, or mentally unstable. If possible, staff should try to direct the person to the outermost lobby where they will be easier to deal with by a manager or security, if necessary. A manager might have to ask such people to leave the theater or have them removed from the premises.

In the event that they are in the auditorium and refuse to leave, managers might be forced to leave them alone, especially if your presence or involvement seems to be what is upsetting them. As long as they are not disrupting the show or pose a danger to other customers or staff, a little time will give you a chance to decide what to do, or consult with security. At a more convenient time—intermission, or the end of the show— it might become necessary for law enforcement to become involved. This is an area in which the airlines are ahead of theaters—unruly passengers are likely to be arrested when a plane lands. It may be awhile before a customer who has shoved an usher finally has to take responsibility for the act.

There was once a time when the workplace was a second family. In this company teamwork was not taught, it just was. Problems were handled, not passed off, and whatever benefited the firm was also good for the employees. Perhaps this was simply an illusion which, once broken by the Depression, bankruptcy, recessional downsizing, or any other reason, caused the ex-employees of that firm to feel greatly betrayed. To some extent modern management theory has replaced the feeling of being a family firm with such teachable concepts as total quality management, empowerment, teamwork, and self-improvement.

While the gist of these concepts is for an employee to benefit by servicing the firm, the element of loyalty is usually excluded. Downsizing taught workers that there was no such thing as loyalty to employees. The increase in employee lawsuits taught firms that there should not be any loyalty to their workers. It is a harsh work environment that we now face.

Staying self-motivated is a key element for surviving in this world. Motivation can no longer be expected of an employer. How you keep yourself motivated is a personal decision. That it is necessary is my personal advice.

Twenty years ago when I first started working in theater, there were several employees left over from the previous regime. Other new employees and I could not help but think how cynical, jaded, and obtuse the older ones were. They were people stuck in their ways who fought every improvement. We agreed that they had just been there too long and we swore that we would never be like them. Now all those years later, we see employees that started out with us that could be clones of those earlier models. And the problem seems to be the same—not simply that they have just been here too long, but that they have been here and have not changed. They are doing the same job they did twenty years ago. Unfortunately, they have allowed themselves to become bitter, frustrated, and deeply ingrained with disenfranchising beliefs.

I have seen other employees who also have held the same position for all these years, but have not ended up like this. A look at their lives shows that they take classes, read books, take part-time work in other departments, and constantly revise in their own departments. In other words, they have grown, not as employees, but as individuals. There is no longer a parental company to guide you to what will make you better. Each person has to find that out for herself.

If your journey makes you better, then it also makes you a more useful employee for the company. As a capable employee you then create a more effective company. From a company of excellence grows a superior industry.

NOTE

1. Richard Bandler and John Grinder are considered the fathers of Neuro-Linguistic Programming. Others, such as Jerry Richardson, expanded on the subject, showing how aspects of it can be used in areas such as sales and customer service. An excellent beginner's book on the subject is *Frogs into Princes* (Moab, Utah: Real People Press, 1979), by Richard Bandler and John Grinder.

Part II

FINANCIAL CONCERNS

Chapter 8

Budgeting Theater Cost for an Engagement

To deal with this subject, imagine yourself as theater manager of the Renaissance Theater. When general manager (GM) Eric Edwards booked *The Time of My Life* into the Renaissance, he asked you to provide him with a budget of estimated theater costs. This budget will aid him in negotiating a contract with the show's producer. Fortunately, you have the show's tech rider,[1] which gives you much of the information you need. At times you will not have this rider and your budget will be an educated guess based on shows that previously played the Renaissance. This situation can be "very dangerous," says one West Coast theater manager. "Usually I make wild guesses and hope for the best. The best thing to do, in this case, is add a large disclaimer saying 'Budget done without benefit of tech rider. Estimates only—and all subject to change.'"

When in the position of not knowing specifics of a show you should do two things:

- Always overbudget or include a cushion-amount to cover the expenses that you don't know.
- Note on the budget that these expenses are estimates.

In all likelihood, the GM will work with a total bottom-line figure rather than the detailed work sheet, so the cushion amount may not have to be explained. If it is questioned, then your explanation is that it is necessary for budgeting purposes for a show that has no available tech rider.

The words "estimated expenses" are necessary for those occasions when the budget is written into the contract. Once a show is installed in the theater, many things can happen that affect cost and most of these are unforeseen and unpredictable. Joe Traina points out that some productions will try to perform two days' work in one day, and as a result spend more money.

> While it is everyone's hope that load-ins and load-outs will occur in an efficient and timely manner, many production supervisors will promise a producer the impossible because the producer doesn't want to hear the truth. Eight-hour days, even if there are more of them, almost always make more sense than a day that goes past eight. The workers get tired, the work has to be halted to accommodate other departments, and the money is not spent wisely as a result.

Managers can find themselves with outdated tech riders, as Orpheum Theater manager Robert Lazzara discovered.

> The tech rider has no relation to the actual show, and the costs go up. Sometimes the stagehands will try to up the yellow card,[2] sometimes the reviews are bad, and the producer wants to increase the ad budget. Usually rental fees are higher than the budget because the creative people want something different from what you got a bid on. But the biggest problem is the tech rider being out of date, or having been changed . . . [with the] producer [forgetting] to tell the local venue.

It is sometimes difficult for a company manager to resist pointing to a cost on the settlement that does not match the budget in the contract. The argument then becomes one where you are accused of violating the contract. Therefore, the word "estimated" covers those emergencies that are not foreseeable months before when you are constructing a budget.

Turning to the portion of the tech rider that sets forth the crew requirements is a good starting place. Any basic spreadsheet program will speed this process, but in the event that you are computerless, then this can be done by hand with a calculator. The tech rider specifies, for example, that the load-in be approximated at ten hours, load-out four hours, with a crew of twenty-two carpenters, eighteen electricians, eight props, and one sound. The running crew for the show is nine carpenters, six flymen, six electricians, four props, and one sound. A ten-hour load-in calculates to eight hours of straight time (S.T.) and two hours of overtime (O.T.).

To calculate this cost, the spreadsheet might look like table 8.1:

Table 8.1.   Load-In: Stagehands

Dept.	Hours	Crew	Rate	8% Vacation	Subtotal	Total
Head						
S.T.	8.00	4	$32.00	$2.56	$34.56	$1,105.92
O.T.	2.00	4	$48.00	$3.84	$51.84	$414.72
Flyman						
S.T.	8.00	1	$30.00	$2.40	$32.40	$259.20
O.T.	2.00	1	$45.00	$3.60	$48.60	$97.20

Table 8.1.   Load-In: Stagehands *(continued)*

Dept.	Hours	Crew	Rate	8% Vacation	Subtotal	Total
Extra						
S.T.	8.00	44	$26.00	$2.08	$28.08	$9,884.16
O.T.	2.00	44	$39.00	$3.12	$42.12	$3,706.56
					Subtotal	$15,467.76
					14% benefits	$2,165.49
					22% taxes	$3,402.91
					Total	$21,036.16

The way this information is read is as follows: From the tech rider we use the estimate of a ten-hour load-in. The local stagehand's union contract specifies that the first eight hours are S.T. and any hours after eight hours are O.T. Hence, eight hours S.T. and two hours O.T.

The total number of the stage crew is forty-nine. Typically these numbers include the house department heads. Subtracting your four department heads and one flyman leaves forty-four extra employees. At this point, it is a matter of plugging the numbers into the spreadsheet. Included in your spreadsheet is vacation pay of 8 percent; pension is 6 percent, and health and welfare is 8 percent, totaling benefits of 14 percent, which are paid on the rate plus the vacation. These amounts and how they are charged are set by the union contract. The theater's accountant gives you an estimate of 22 percent for taxes, which are also calculated on the rate plus the vacation. This percentage may be an item of negotiation in the show contract, so when you begin the settlement you will have to check the final contractual percentage to charge for taxes.

You will do a similar calculation for the load-out. Often load-outs take place after the final performance, so this would likely be charged at the overtime rate. I usually add several hours to this estimate because while it may take four hours to unload the show out of the theater, it may take a few more to restore the building. This could include anything from repairing the ceiling where holes have been cut to accommodate speakers and lighting instruments, to reinstalling seats removed for the show's sound console, or repainting a dressing room left damaged by a star's temper tantrum. So, we will budget our load-out at five hours (table 8.2).

The performance week has slightly different calculations because the stagehand's union contract specifies that crews be paid by performance rather than hours. For this performance, the contract specifies a rate of $210

Table 8.2.   Load-Out: Stagehands

Dept.	Hours	Crew	Rate	8% Vacation	Subtotal	Total
Head						
S.T.			$32.00	$2.56	$34.56	$0.00
O.T.	5.00	4	$48.00	$3.84	$51.84	$1,036.80
Flyman						
S.T.			$30.00	$2.40	$32.40	$0.00
O.T.	5.00	1	$45.00	$3.60	$48.60	$243.00
Extra						
S.T.			$26.00	$2.08	$28.08	$0.00
O.T.	5.00	44	$39.00	$3.12	$42.12	$9,266.40
					Subtotal	$10,546.20
					14% benefits	$1,476.47
					22% taxes	$2,320.16
					Total	$14,342.83

per show for a department head and $120 per show for crew. Most shows need some setup of the stage prior to the performance, and will have work calls during the week that can span from rehearsals to changing lights to repairing set pieces. While you do not know how much time these will take, guessing an amount can make the budget closer to actual expenses. Let us assume workers are called in one hour before the Tuesday show and any costs beyond that, such as rehearsals, work calls, and additional continuity hours, are billed to the producer.

The estimated cost for performances and one continuity hour might look like table 8.3:

Table 8.3.   Performance Week

Dept.	Shows & Hours	Crew	Rate	8% Vacation	Subtotal	Total
Head						
Shows	8.00	4	$210.00	$16.80	$226.80	$7,257.60
S.T.			$32.00	$2.56	$34.56	$0.00
O.T.	1.00	4	$48.00	$3.84	$51.84	$207.36
Flyman						
Show	8.00	6	$150.00	$12.00	$162.00	$7,776.00
S.T.			$30.00	$2.40	$32.40	$0.00
O.T.	1.00	6	$45.00	$3.60	$48.60	$291.60
Extra						
Show	8.00	18	$120.00	$9.60	$129.60	$18,662.40

Table 8.3.   Performance Week (continued)

Dept.	Shows & Hours	Crew	Rate	8% Vacation	Subtotal	Total
S.T.			$26.00	$2.08	$28.08	$0.00
O.T.	1.00	18	$39.00	$3.12	$42.12	$758.16
					subtotal	$34,953.12
					14% benefits	$4,893.44
					22% taxes	$7,689.69
					Total	$47,536.25

You will calculate similar sets of figures for each department, including every conceivable cost that the theater might incur because this show is playing the Renaissance. A sample budget is in appendix E.

While department estimates are solely a calculation of payroll, the theater may also have contractual charges. These are variable and may be based on an industry standard, theater precedent, or established fees for the venue. The GM will negotiate them into the contract. They can include rent, insurance, spotlights/sound/air conditioning rental, electricity, or an administrative fee.

The show will also incur other negotiable expenses, such as bills for phone calls, catering, or limousines. Even in the case of the show being responsible for these charges, very often they are the legal obligation of the theater since the account is in its name. Therefore, the theater would pay the bill and charge the show for the cost. To account for these amounts, I usually include a separate section for charges that I call "standards."

Once all these costs have been put into the spreadsheet, the results can be transferred to a top sheet for easy referral. I separate the top sheet into three general areas: weekly cost, one-time cost, and tech rider. The weekly costs are those expenses, mostly payroll, that are incurred every single week. The one-time cost includes such expenses as the load-in/out and preliminary box office and show bills. Tech rider expenses are those listed in the show's tech rider, which a theater does not typically pay for. For instance, a tech rider may say that the theater is responsible for crew catering, limousines to and from the theater for two stars, and the rental of a lighting system. If these are not the kind of expenses the Renaissance usually agrees to pay, then the GM will have to negate the tech rider (or parts of it) in the contract with the show and specify that the theater will not pay for certain items. Since it is impossible to predict which way a negotiation will go, this separate column lists such extra expenses and lets the GM decide what it is worth to negotiate these items. In cases where the show is a huge hit and everyone is making money, it is often easier for the GM to pay for these items. However, the risks the possibility of the next show expecting the same accommodation to be made for them. The next show may not be such a winner.

Certain categories require input from the GM. If preliminary advertising and box office are the obligation of the theater, you will need to ask what the GM wants to spend on these. If the show pays its own advertising, then a zero amount would be entered in this category.

The budget top sheet would look like this:

Renaissance Theater Estimated Show Expenses Tentative Date: June 2003	Show: *The Time of My Life*		
	Weekly Cost	*One-Time Cost*	*Tech Rider*
Payrolls			
1. Stagehands	_____	_____	_____
2. Musicians	_____	_____	_____
3. Wardrobe	_____	_____	_____
4. Box Office	_____	_____	_____
5. Engineer	_____	_____	_____
6. Stagedoor	_____	_____	_____
7. Security	_____	_____	_____
8. Ushers	_____	_____	_____
9. Load-In	_____	_____	_____
10. Theater Manager	_____	_____	_____
11. Load-Out	_____	_____	_____
Total Payrolls			
	========	========	========
Bills			
1. Advertising	_____	_____	_____
2. Insurance	_____	_____	_____
3. Housekeeping	_____	_____	_____
4. General Bills	_____	_____	_____
5. Administrative Fee	_____	_____	_____
6. Theater Rent	_____	_____	_____
7. Other	_____	_____	_____
8. Other/cushion	_____	_____	_____
Total Bills			
	========	========	========
Total Payrolls	_____	_____	_____
Total Bills	_____	_____	_____
Total Expenses	_____	_____	_____
	========	========	========

For a top sheet filled in with sample costs, see appendix E.

CUTTING THE BUDGET

On occasion the GM might ask you to cut the budget. Usually this happens when, having looked at the gross potentials (covered in the next chapter), he realizes that to cover expenses he will have to demand a ticket price higher than the market could bear; or the theater expenses, plus the show's guarantee, cannot be covered by the ticket price that he has in mind. In situations where the producers have already set the price, significant financial issues can arise if ticket receipts do not cover cost.

Any of these possibilities create a very frustrating task for a manager, who must work closely with the GM in order to cut expenses in a way that keeps the theater functioning. Ultimately, the manager may have to remind the GM or a producer that regardless of how much a budget is trimmed, when the show is actually installed in the theater, the costs end up being what they are. Unforeseen catastrophes, and few shows are without those, incur expenses. Once performances have begun, a manager may discover that the way she budgeted simply is not working and must decide that the work schedule needs to be revised upward.

When looking at what expenses to cut, the manager will often be tied by restraints not of her making. A yellow card sets forth the number of stagehands and wardrobe employees and she cannot change that. The tech rider gives a suggested number of hours for the load-in/out and weekly work calls. To lower those amounts may hamper the ability of the show to function, and in actuality, the cost will be incurred anyway because it is necessary in order for a performance to be presented.

You and the GM must look at the areas that are within your power to manipulate. Instead of opening the box office at 10 A.M. every morning, you discuss opening it two hours prior to the performance. The GM must weigh what sales he will lose during the day against the payroll cost he will save. Currently there are six security guards scheduled for every performance. After talking with the head of security, it is decided that on the Tuesday/Thursday performances, which typically do not sell out, two guards can be cut without jeopardizing theater security. In the event ticket sales increase, the guards will be replaced. The stagedoor attendant will be scheduled tightly around the work calls so he arrives a half hour before and employees will be told not to come to work earlier than that. In advertising, the GM decides to cut the television advertising at two of the major stations and stick to only one major and two independents. He also decides to increase the radio buy, but not by an amount that will burden the expenses.

"Some costs are fixed per collective bargaining agreements and are not subject to cutting," says one West Coast manager. "And budgets can be cut, if you do it early enough, before ads are placed or set up. Usually the only things subject to cutting are minor areas, like ushers and box office, which don't add up to much savings." With this new information, the manager revises the budget and again submits it to the GM.

Sometimes no amount of budgeting can cover what becomes a disaster show. The show itself may ultimately do very well and upon closing everyone may be happy, but getting the darn thing into the theater is like raising the *Titanic*. The show *Tommy* experienced such difficulties when it was first toured. Load-in costs budgeted at $30,000 ended up around $55,000. "With its state-of-the-art computer-driven projections and special effects, the show is a monster to set up. The deck took so long to load in at the Masonic [in Detroit] that frigid outside air chilled the theater, causing *Tommy's*" all important hydraulic lifts to freeze up" (Evans 1994a, 73).

THE TECHNICAL PACKAGE

This section is placed at the end of the chapter rather than the beginning because tech riders need to be studied for more than simple payroll budgeting. A variety of hidden costs can be included that are not in the contract with the show. If the contract is generated by the show then it will often contain a clause that specifies that the tech rider be considered part of the contract. Unless certain items are brought to the attention of the GM and taken out, they can greatly increase the theater's costs. Otherwise, these expenses need to be accounted for in the budget.

The technical package is sometimes called the tech sheet, tech rider, or tech information. The theater usually has an equivalent called the specs information, and in the jargon of the day, the show will call for the theater's specs and the theater will call for the show's tech rider. Both, in essence, contain all the technical information you will need to know about each other. The difference is, the theater information rarely changes while the show's information may change often. The show may also have different contractual terms with other venues, but rather than redo the tech rider, they will send everyone the same information. For instance, a presenter who is "purchasing," or guaranteeing, the show in order to get a certain star performer, might be agreeable to paying for hotels, limousine service, food, and the star's favorite furniture, while a venue on a four-wall deal has no intention of supplying these items.

The rider sets forth the show's needs for dressing rooms, offices, and wardrobe space, as well as the production's technical requirements. Conditions of the theater building are usually modeled after what is required by Actors' Equity. It is important to note that shows travel through every part of the country and meet varying conditions. While it might seem common sense to require dressing rooms be cleaned every day, the fact of having to specify this means that the show has come across theaters where it was not a priority.

Tech riders are often put together at the beginning of the tour. If the contents have not been updated recently, you will want to double-check any information that will cause a problem in your theater. This is why it is important to give a copy of the rider to each of your department heads so that they can go over it to insure compliance. If not, they can make you aware of the problem. No one wants to arrive at the theater on the day of the load-in and discover that the loading door is three inches too short for the largest set piece. Most tech riders will have an "as of" date; if it is more than six months old, all the more reason to double-check any suspect information with the show's representatives.

The information can come in any sequence, but usually starts with the crew call. First-class Broadway productions are "yellow card" shows, meaning the number of union employees has been predetermined by the IATSE. These amounts are put on a yellow card that is sent by the show to the local IATSE stagehand union, which has a collective bargaining agreement with your theater. It specifies how many crew to send for the load-in, the performance, and the load-out. Ordinarily the number of people for the in and out is the same. The breakdown is carpentry, electrics, properties, wardrobe, and sometimes hairdresser, though some venues do not maintain contracts with the hairdresser's union and the show must contract with them individually. A further breakdown can indicate how many people will work the deck (on stage), followspot (a spotlight), and flys (the rigging to raise and lower the scenery).

The next section of the tech rider details the load-in and load-out. This specifies how many car loaders—usually teamsters in larger cities—will be required to unpack the trucks, and what equipment is needed. Typically the latter means a genie lift, forklift, and their operators. This section may also have an estimated number of hours for the load-in and load-out. You will have to find out the time of the load-in to calculate out whether these hours will be straight time or overtime, and if you are going to have to provide a meal for the crew at 3 A.M., or when you will need to block off the street if this is necessary at your venue. For theaters with a street loading area, good relations with both your neighboring merchants and the police department are essential.

The next several sections will break down the backstage departments, which include carpentry, electric, sound, props, wardrobe, orchestra, and sometimes, pyrotechnics. Each section explains in detail what equipment the show travels with, what they need in the venue, and any special requirements. In addition, each section may contain a disclaimer with wording such as "failure to meet these conditions may require extra time and labor at the theater's expense." Even the most apparently simple concern, if questionable, should be noted and pointed out to the GM so that he can discuss it with the producer.

For instance, if your sound area is on the right center side of the house and measures 12' × 8' and the tech rider asks for it on the left center side of the house, you might think it won't be a problem if the show requires a 12' × 8½' area. Even if their sound person manages to squeeze into the ½ inch that you do not have, the show personnel may not be satisfied when forced to use the right side. For the rest of the run every sound complaint will be blamed on this slight discrepancy. It may sound ridiculous, but house managers have seen it happen.

Show needs in regard to dressing rooms, offices, telephones, washer/dryers, dry cleaners, security, and work calls are listed with specifications that can seem unnecessary. These are areas you can discuss with the company manager to see what is really needed for the production. While many of these specifications are dictated by the Actors' Equity rulebook, others are simply what the show would like to have. Some can be dispensed with or negotiated out of the contract. It is becoming standard for most offices to be prepared for at least two phone lines and a fax line, though on short runs a stage and company manager will possibly share the fax rather than each having their own.

A section containing show information has very standard details such as the length of the acts, intermission, and the late seating policy. It will also list any out of the ordinary facts relating to the show, like actors in the audience area, staircases to the stage which need to be guarded by ushers at intermission, set pieces that must be watched so customers do not damage them, and company equipment in the auditorium (speakers, sound consoles, etc.), which also require security when the audience is in attendance. While carrying out the associated duties can be commonplace for ushering or security staff, some tech riders specify that these employees be under the direction of particular show personnel. It is usually to the theater's benefit to work closely with the show and do whatever is required, within reason, but I would recommend to my GM that this clause be struck out. Theater personnel should report to the house manager and requests from the show should filter through him to the theater employees. The theater is ultimately responsible for the actions of its own employees, and therefore, it should be their representative who instructs the staff. A clear line of authority can also prevent show personnel from giving inappropriate instructions to lower-level staff. A stage manager who instructs an usher to forcefully take a customer's camera is forgetting that it is against the law to take another's property without permission. A theater manager who deals with these situations at every show most likely has a politer way to reach the same objective—preventing the patron from taking pictures.

Typically these riders conclude with perks for company members, which can include special foods, limousines, rental cars, gyms, and star accommodations. Depending on the venue, these items may or may not be usual for you to provide. You will want to point them out to the GM and let him tell you which can be accommodated in the budget. One West Coast house manager recounts a story told to him by a company manager for a producer who never updated his tech rider.

> During the load-in, a truck pulled up and delivered several enormous rolls of carpet. When the show carpenter asked what the carpet was for, the local presenter said, "Why, for carpeting the entire backstage, per the tech rider requirements." The carpenter was astounded and said, "Didn't anyone tell you? We bought paper slippers for the cast instead. You didn't need to buy *any* carpet!"

NOTES

1. A tech rider is a document containing general and technical information about the show.
2. A yellow card is the document sent to the local union that specifies the number of employees to send to the theater.

Chapter 9

Gross Potentials and Ticket Prices

The business part of show business comes when the producer and general manager (GM) need to decide what to charge for their product. A gross potential is an estimate of the amount of money a production can make on a show. It is one of the first steps in determining ticket prices. The gross potential usually depends on who has the most financial stake in the show. A show that is renting the theater and covering the venue's cost will have a greater interest in the ticket prices than a show that is on a guarantee. The show renting the theater will be looking to ensure that the number of seats sold will cover their obligation to the theater as well as their own expenses. A show guaranteed by the theater might not have any interest in whether ticket sales cover the theater's expenses or even their guarantee, since they are contractually assured of receiving that amount of money whether ticket sales earn it or not. An influencing factor would be the producer who, even though the production is being guaranteed, is concerned about the image of the show and therefore wants a voice in setting the ticket cost. Generally, ticket prices are set by combining the opinions of the producer and both the show and theater's GMs, and usually all parties will sign off on the final determination.

When asked to provide ticket prices and gross potentials, you will want to provide a variety of choices. The basic gross potential is simply a multiplication of the number of seats and their prices, with the result multiplied by the number of performances. This amount is a money figure that represents total earnings if you sold every seat in the theater for every performance.

Let us give the Renaissance three seating levels with different prices for each level. Get as much information as you can about whether the show will need any seats removed and subtract this from the seating capacity. Finding out on the load-in that the show needs forty seats out to accommodate a sound and light board can cut deeply into your sales, particularly since these consoles are often located on the first level within the highest-priced seating.

After you have this information, multiply the number of seats by the proposed ticket price. This resulting amount of money represents what the theater will make if all the tickets sell for one performance. Multiplying the total ticket money by the number of performances per week gives the amount of revenue the theater can earn in one week. It is prudent at this point to subtract out an estimate of credit card charges, commission, and taxes. Once this total is calculated, the final step is to multiply it by the number of weeks the show is scheduled. The last number is the gross potential for the show. It is the amount of money the theater earns if every ticket is sold for every performance.

Table 9.1 is a basic example of a gross potential.

From this gross potential, we can see that at the given prices, the show could not break even at $473,000 per week. This amount does not cover the budgeted expenses in appendix E plus the show expenses (the GM has told you these are around $550,000). Keep trying higher ticket prices until you have covered the costs.

Both gross potentials in tables 9.2 and 9.3 cover the expenses; however, even in the best of circumstances, it is unlikely that you will sell every seat in the house for every show. Therefore, there are two options: increase the price even more so that with a lower percentage of sales you can still cover cost; or go back to your budget and trim expenses.

Note that for simplicity's sake I have kept each level at a single price. Seating can be divided into separate price areas such as front and rear orchestra, mezzanine, and balcony. On one show, I had three different prices for one level. It sometimes creates anger among customers who discover that the people in the row behind them paid $20.00 less, but a price break has to be made somewhere.

This basic gross potential is intended for the occasion when the GM needed it yesterday. A truer gross potential reflects an estimate of deductions that will appear on the box office statement (covered in chapter 11). This box office statement is the actual accounting of sold tickets. It typically has a variety of deductions that are negotiated by the GM. These deductions are usually specified in the contract. Let us assume that Mr. Edwards intends to ask for a 3 percent credit card fee, a 15 percent group sales commission, twenty-five cents for all tickets sold by the

Table 9.1.

The Renaissance Theater
Gross Potential
Show: *The Time of My Life*
Tentative Dates: June 2, 2003 to June 29, 2003
Scale: Box Office Single Sales

Section	Capacity	Weekday Matinee Prices	Weekend Fri/Sat Prices	Weekday Matinee Total	Weekend Fri/Sat Total	Week Total
Orchestra	1,500	$25.00	$30.00	$37,500.00	$45,000.00	
Mezzanine	700	$20.00	$25.00	$14,000.00	$17,500.00	
Balcony	300	$15.00	$20.00	$4,500.00	$6,000.00	
Total				$56,000.00	$68,500.00	
Number of Performances				6	2	
Single Sale Gross Potential for One Week				$336,000.00	$137,000.00	$473,000.00
Based on Four Weeks						4
Total Gross for Run of Show						$1,892,000.00

Table 9.2.

Price Schedule #1
The Renaissance Theater
Gross Potential
Show: *The Time of My Life*
Tentative Dates: June 2, 2003 to June 29, 2003
Scale: Box Office Single Sales

Section	Capacity	Weekday Matinee Prices	Weekend Fri/Sat Prices	Weekday Matinee Total	Weekend Fri/Sat Total	Week Total
Orchestra	1,500	$50.00	$60.00	$75,000.00	$90,000.00	
Mezzanine	700	$35.00	$45.00	$24,500.00	$31,500.00	
Balcony	300	$25.00	$35.00	$7,500.00	$10,500.00	
Total				$107,000.00	$132,000.00	
Number of Performances				6	2	
Single Sale Gross Potential for One Week				$642,000.00	$264,000.00	$906,000.00
Based on Four Weeks						4
Total Gross for Run of Show						$3,624,000.00

Table 9.3.

Price Schedule #2
The Renaissance Theater
Gross Potential
Show: *The Time of My Life*
Tentative Dates: June 2, 2003 to June 29, 2003
Scale: Box Office Single Sales

Section	Capacity	Weekday Matinee Prices	Weekend Fri/Sat Prices	Weekday Matinee Total	Weekend Fri/Sat Total	Week Total
Orchestra	1,500	$60.00	$75.00	$90,000.00	$112,500.00	
Mezzanine	700	$50.00	$65.00	$35,000.00	$45,500.00	
Balcony	300	$40.00	$50.00	$12,000.00	$15,000.00	
Total				$137,000.00	$173,000.00	
Number of Performances				6	2	
Single Sale Gross Potential for One Week				$822,000.00	$346,000.00	$1,168,000.00
Based on Four Weeks						4
Total Gross for Run of Show						$4,672,000.00

phone ticketing agency, and fifteen cents for every ticket sold at the box office. Because ticket charges are usually written into the theater contract with the ticketing agency, Mr. Edwards is simply passing the cost on to the statement. In addition, Midtown, USA, also charges a city tax of 0.2 percent. Deducting an estimate of these costs from the gross potential gives a more accurate financial picture.

So a refined version of your gross potential would look something like what is shown in table 9.4.

The estimates on group sales, ticket charges, and credit card charges are based on your experience of what these costs have come to on previous shows similar to *The Time of My Life*. For further detailing of the figures, it is a good idea to talk to the box office and group sales managers and sound them out about whether ticket purchases are expected to be better or worse than usual. Factors such as holidays, weather, the number of other shows and special events in town, and out-of-town reviews will affect sales. If the show is not on sale yet, the group sales manager can sometimes call a few customers to determine if there is interest in the product.

Another factor influencing a gross potential is when the show is also sold to subscribers at a lower price than the box office single sales. These purchases can take place many months prior to the show's arrival, during a subscription campaign that offered not only this show but others as well. The benefit to subscribers is that they have the first choice of seats and often get a discounted price. The theater gets the benefit of an assured audience, and has access to the subscription money until it plays off in the various shows, usually several months later.

Depending on how healthy subscriptions sales are, these incoming funds can lower your total gross potential. If the subscriptions sales period is well passed, then the subscription manager can give you a fairly accurate figure of what sales are for this show.

In a pinch you can calculate a subscription gross potential the same as you did for single sales. These two numbers can be added then divided by two to get an estimated potential of a subscription show. Be aware and explain to those who need to know that this figure is not completely accurate since the percentage of subscription sales may be more or less than the 50 percent value you assigned in making your calculation (table 9.5).

With a computerized box office and subscription office, these totals are more accurate. If you know what the subscription sales are, subtract that figure from the full sale potential. The amount that remains represents what is left to sell. Keep in mind that the subscription sales figures fluctuate, so this might not be exact (table 9.6).

Table 9.4.

The Renaissance Theater
Gross Potential
Show: *The Time of My Life*
Tentative Dates: June 2, 2003 to June 29, 2003
Scale: Box Office Single Sales

Section	Capacity	Weekday Matinee Prices	Weekend Fri/Sat Prices	Weekday Matinee Total	Weekend Fri/Sat Total	Week Total
Orchestra	1,500	$60.00	$75.00	$90,000.00	$112,500.00	$1,168,000.00
Mezzanine	700	$50.00	$65.00	$35,000.00	$45,500.00	$26,000.00
Balcony	300	$40.00	$50.00	$12,000.00	$15,000.00	$3,500.00
						$1,500.00
Total				$137,000.00	$173,000.00	
Number of Performances				6	2	
Single Sale Gross Potential for One Week				$822,000.00	$346,000.00	
Less Est. 3% Credit Card Charges				$20,000.00	$6,000.00	
Less Est. of Ticket Charges 15/25 Cents				$2,500.00	$1,000.00	
Less Est. 15% Group Sales Commission				$1,000.00	$500.00	
Subtotal				$798,500.00	$338,500.00	$1,137,000.00
Less City Tax 0.2%				$1,597.00	$677.00	$2,274.00
Total				$796,903.00	$337,823.00	$1,134,726.00
Based on Four Weeks						4
Total Gross for Run of Show						$4,538,904.00

Table 9.5.

Example:	
Subscription Sales GP	$4,000,000.00
Single Sale GP	$4,538,904.00
Total	$8,538,904.00
Divide By	2
Estimated GP W/Subscriptions	$4,269,452.00

Table 9.6.

Single Sale Potential	$4,538,904.00
Actual Subscription Sales	$750,000.00
Remaining Single Sale Potential	$3,788,904.00

To further refine the last amount, the estimated deductions should be subtracted as well.

The bottom-line figure of a gross potential is what the box office would receive in ticket sales if every ticket was sold at full price. Of course, in reality that is not always the case. Actual ticket receipts are affected by discounts such as group sales, subscriptions, special promotions, or student/senior discounts. Even when factoring in an estimate of these discounts, the show still may not sell every single ticket. Therefore, it is helpful to show what money can be taken in by percentage. Usually at the bottom of the page, I will include a section that shows several percentages of the adjusted gross potential (table 9.7).

Once prices are determined and tickets are on sale, this is not always the end of the changes. Joe Traina observed a situation during a production of *A Doll's House* at the Belasco Theater when the show's GM wanted to change the $50 rear mezzanine price to $55:

> [E]ither due to the Telecharge system or an honest mistake, the entire mezzanine got scaled to $60.00. There was a lot of unhappiness on the part of the GM who felt no one would pay that price. . . . As it turned out, everyone was more than happy to pay $60 for any seat in the Belasco's mezzanine (it's a great section because it's not too high and fairly forward to the stage), and ultimately, the show's manager couldn't have asked for more.

Theater manager Robert Lazzara had a similar experience but without the advantage of a computerized ticketing system.

> During the days of preprinted hard tickets, a producer had agreed to some very low prices. When it was obvious the show would be a big hit, he decided to raise the prices. Since the tickets were already printed and on sale, the box office had to order thousands of tiny stickers with the new higher prices, and then spend many long hours sticking the new prices on each individual ticket by hand.

Table 9.7.

The Renaissance Theater
Gross Potential
Show: *The Time of My Life*
Tentative Dates: June 2, 2003 to June 29, 2003
Scale: Box Office Single Sales

Section	Capacity	Weekday Matinee Prices	Weekend Fri/Sat Prices	Weekday Matinee Total	Weekend Fri/Sat Total	Week Total
Orchestra	1,500	$60.00	$75.00	$90,000.00	$112,500.00	
Mezzanine	700	$50.00	$65.00	$35,000.00	$45,500.00	
Balcony	300	$40.00	$50.00	$12,000.00	$15,000.00	
Total				$137,000.00	$173,000.00	
Number of Performances				6	2	
Single Sale Gross Potential for One Week				$822,000.00	$346,000.00	$1,168,000.00
Less Est. 3% Credit Card Charges				$20,000.00	$6,000.00	$26,000.00
Less Est. of Ticket Charges 15/25 Cents				$2,500.00	$1,000.00	$3,500.00
Less Est. 15% Group Sales Commission				$1,000.00	$500.00	$1,500.00
Subtotal				$798,500.00	$338,500.00	$1,137,000.00
Less City Tax 0.2%				$1,597.00	$677.00	$2,274.00
Total				$796,903.00	$337,823.00	$1,134,726.00
Based on Four Weeks						4
Total Gross for Run of Show						$4,538,904.00

90% of Total Sales: $4,085,013.60
80% of Total Sales: $3,631,123.20
70% of Total Sales: $3,177,232.80
60% of Total Sales: $2,723,342.40
50% of Total Sales: $2,269,452.00
40% of Total Sales: $1,815,561.60
30% of Total Sales: $1,361,671.20

Chapter 10

Show Contracts

Show contracts and deals come in as many different varieties as breakfast cereals. They can be influenced by the clout of the producer, the quality of the production, or the amount of product available. Donald Farber (1981, 217–18) notes that prior to the 1970s, agreements between theater owners and producers "provided a modest weekly guarantee plus a payment to the theatre of 25 to 30 percent of the gross weekly box office receipts, or some combination of amounts in this neighborhood. There were also elaborate arrangements for sharing certain of the expenses of the theatre, usually at the same percentage rate as the sharing of receipts."

These kinds of terms can be in vogue for several years, then change overnight when ticket sales lag, shows outnumber the amount of theaters available, or established producers take vacations and fly-by-night operators begin touring lackluster productions on which theater owners want stronger contracts.

> The theatre owners in the late seventies decided that if they wanted to invest in the production they would do so by giving the producer cash or the equivalent thereof, but that they did not want to be, in a sense, a coproducer of every play that came into their theatre. Hence, the theatre owners increased the amount of the weekly guarantee to cover all of their weekly expenses of running the theatre and decreased the amount of the weekly gross that was shared. The concept of sharing expenses also mostly disappeared (Farber 1981, 218).

These pendulums tend to swing back and forth. And contract terms inevitably follow.

The legalese in these license agreements will remain substantially the same from contract to contract, but the contents will favor whoever

generated it. Contracts written by the show naturally have terms fa-
vorable to the company, while venue contracts contain more language
to protect the theater. Contracts are a function of the general manager's
(GM's) office, though often a house manager may be asked to review
them.

The theater manager has more firsthand knowledge of how various
clauses may be implemented in a theater or the problems they might
cause, so the GM will probably seek out your expertise on this subject.
Once the agreement is signed by the two parties, a copy is sent to the
house manager. Typically this contract is negotiated by the two GMs, but
it can be signed by producers, attorneys representing their clients, a booking agent, or a designated representative. Whoever signs should have legal authority to do so. The presentation agreement will set forth the terms
under which the show will play the venue. The portions that most concern the house manager are the settlement terms and box office fees.

Contracts are sometimes accompanied by riders or addenda that address a show's specific needs. The standard contract used for show after
show may not cover items particular to an individual show, or the parties
may not like certain aspects of the standard contract and wish to amend
these in an addendum.

Technical riders are sometimes made part of the contract. Therefore, it
is essential to study these carefully for areas that your venue cannot fulfill, and point them out to the GM so he can strike them out. Many paragraphs in a contact may have entire sections crossed out. When this is the
case, both parties initial the change. Sometimes this means that the paragraph is not in effect for this production. Other times the contents of the
paragraph has simply been rewritten and is in the rider, reproduced in
language to clarify or indemnify a particular party. Often these paragraphs will be accompanied by the phrase of explanation such as "replaces paragraph two on page ten."

Before we look at the contractual concerns of the house manager, let us
generalize a contract between the Renaissance and *The Time of My Life.*
Mr. Edwards, the theater's GM, has used his standard contract, which begins by identifying the parties and their relationship. It reads that an
agreement has been reached between the Renaissance Theater (venue)
and *The Time of My Life* Limited Partnership (producer) for use of the Midtown facility for the dates June 2, 2003 to June 29, 2003.

The next several pages cover areas and define rights and responsibilities that are of interest more to the GM. Typically these include:

- producer's use of the facility
- abandonment of equipment
- insurance coverage

- payroll tax liability
- producer's agreement to honor existing theater labor contracts
- conditions of the theater "as is"
- legal remedies in the event of default or contract violation
- sale and disposition of tickets
- designated ticketing agencies
- notice of termination or closure
- national emergency/acts of God/labor disputes and unforeseen occurrences

The house manager should read over these pages, but for the most part very little will apply to her. On those rare occasions when these areas must be invoked or enforced, people at a much higher level than she will become involved.

As you read though the contract make notes of any items that pertain to you. Most of these will be financial.

For example:

- Group sales to be commissioned at 15 percent but no groups may be sold on Saturday evenings
- Subscriptions at 18 percent
- Credit cards at 3 percent
- Box office tickets charged at fifteen cents each and tickets sold at outside agencies or by phone at twenty-five cents per item
- House and company seats limited to twenty per performance and fifty on opening night
- Complementary tickets issued only by mutual agreement of the general manager and producer

You will want to put this information into separate memos for the box office treasurer and the group sales director, if the GM has not already done so.

The final part of the contract specifies settlement terms.

To the show:

- a guarantee of $550,000.00 per week
- a royalty of 10 percent on the first $400,000.00

To the theater: all documented expenses, plus

- $35,000.00 rent per week

The remaining money is to be split 60 percent to the show, 40 percent to the theater.

A rider is attached which additionally specifies:

- Payrolls are to have a 22 percent payroll tax
- A general administration charge of $5,000
- An insurance charge of $0.20 per admission

It further specifies:

- Advertising will be the burden of the venue with not less than $175,000 spent for the run
- All ad copy and television and radio spots will be provided by the producer and must be approved by him

In handwriting on the last page of the rider is the statement, "Money split not in effect until theater expenses are completely covered." This handwritten note is initialed by Mr. Edwards and the producer.

From this information and the figures you have developed earlier in the budgets and gross potentials, you can draw up a sample settlement. In the best of all possible words, let us assume that the show sells to potential. The first week might look like table 10.1:

Table 10.1.

Weekly Gross Potential	$1,134,726.00
Show Guarantee	$550,000.00
Show Royalty	$40,000.00
Balance	$544,726.00
Theater Est. Expenses	$220,000.00
Balance	$324,726.00
60% to the Show	$194,835.60
40% to the Theater	$129,890.40

Using this optimistic example there is enough to go around for everyone and all parties are as happy as larks on a spring day in a worm field. Should ticket sales drop to indicate a negative balance at any point prior to the theater expenses, or even the show's royalty, there will be some very unhappy people in the theater administration office. At this point, you might be asked to recommend methods for trimming expenses, and with low sales, there may be places you can cut back in the front-of-house. You would not need as many ushers, janitors, or ticket-sellers; box office hours could be reduced. The GM and producer may discuss the possibility of reducing the advertising if it seems ineffective in generating substantial sales. Because Mr. Edwards contractually agreed to spend $175,000, he would have a strong interest in negotiating the reduction of advertising expenditures.

Suppose the show opens with receipts that do not reflect enough money to cover the total estimated theater expenses for the run. Then the sixty/forty split would not be calculated on a weekly basis, but at the end of the run. This way any expenses not covered in the first weeks would have first claim on any profit money in the following weeks before distribution.

In a contract with such terms as those described above, there is very little risk to the show since they are guaranteed their money. This type of contract would probably yield very little discussion of your expenses. The show would only have a stake in the receipts for their 60 percent. If receipts are nowhere near covering your expenses, then it yields them little to argue about what you have on the settlement. If, on the other hand, the company manager thinks your expenses are inflated to the point that they are deliberately cutting into the profit to be split, then the show may argue your expenses.

This is why it is wise for your actual expenses to approximate what you previously budgeted. Obviously, some areas are not foreseeable and may end up costing more than you could have been anticipated. As long as you have proper backup for an expense and are sure of your reasons for having incurred it, then it stands as a justified cost. Of course, if you and the company manager simply disagree, then the matter may have to be referred to the GMs for discussion.

The contract may or may not reflect the terms of the deal memo you received several months back, so it is important to make sure you are following the signed contract rather than notes or memos made when the show was first booked.

The contract terms discussed above reflect what is typically known as a guarantee deal. In effect the theater is guaranteeing the show. Another common type of contract is known as a four-wall deal. In this contract the opposite of the previous deal occurs and the show guarantees the theater. With the theater expenses being paid first, the company manager will examine your settlement expenses more closely, since your costs now cut into her money.

A four-wall deal might be structured something like this:

- Theater expenses plus $30,000.00 rent and 10 percent of the gross receipts
- The remaining receipts belong to the company

Variations on this would be:

- Theater expenses plus $20,000.00 rent and 5 percent of the gross receipts

- The next $450,000.00 to the show
- The remaining receipts are split eighty/twenty

Obviously, any kind of terms can be negotiated, but the main structure remains that the theater's expenses are guaranteed. Under a four-wall deal most of the preliminary work would be under the direction of the producer rather than the theater. The producer would set the ticket prices, arrange advertising, and decide when the box office opens. You or the theater's GM would be informed of these decisions, and then proceed to put them into effect.

Contracts can have a generational quality about them. For many years most shows will travel on guarantees, then a series of blockbuster shows begin to tour, and percentage splits are in vogue. Terms may stay the same for a decade and then, overnight, every show will come in under new, similar conditions. When I first worked in theater management, the four-wall deal was the most common contract at my company's theaters. Within a few years nearly every show was being guaranteed.

This forced a rethinking of how the company managed its theaters. We became more streamlined and budget-conscious. It can sometimes be a great shock to a company manager who comes in on a guarantee and must accept that the show no longer calls the shots. Some accept it better than others and several loud conversations have occurred in my theater when shows did not like the arrangement. However, remember that the producers make decisions based on what is best for their shows, so it should not come as too much of a shock when a theater also has to protect its position. The most common phenomenon I have noticed is that hit shows come in on four-wall deals and products that expect marginal sales and are of questionable quality will usually insist on a guarantee.

Chapter 11

Box Office

In 1948, producer Michael Todd brought *As the Girls Go* to New York's Winter Garden and charged $7.20 per ticket—a record high price (Botto 1984, 30). Each year theater ticket costs rise, sometimes despite poor products, and sometimes because of innovating production techniques, a discovered talent or a fresh work of art, and always because of increased expenses. These reasons make the event ticket the center of attention.

Historically, tickets came into play only for VIPs. Ancient Greek tickets had a designated seating area and a design that specified which performance the holder could attend. In ancient Rome, senators could reserve tickets made of wood and carved ivory while everyone else was required to enter as general admission, and sit in the remaining 40,000 seats—first come, first served. The first paper tickets were introduced in the late eighteenth century (Miller 1997, 10). Now, computers can create a theater ticket and sell it by phone, third-party outlets, and on the Internet. Regardless of where the ticket is generated, the box office is the place of the final accounting of ticket money.

Admissions are recorded on a box office statement that is computed by the head treasurer. The box office is the one department within the theater that has been vilified from nearly all directions. Langley (1990, 366) says of Broadway treasurers, "Because there is virtually no repeat business for Broadway shows, treasurers are less schooled in polite sales conduct than would be the case where repeat business is important." Prolific writer/producer William Goldman (1984, 345) records in his book *The Season*, "As a general rule then, box office personnel, however charming they may be—and many of them are—are thieves." These disparagements have become a burden that every honest treasurer and theater manager must deal with, whether they work on Broadway or on the road.

Joe Traina notes:

> Changing the perception of the general public is near impossible. Some people are always convinced that they are being cheated no matter what the actual facts may be. My experience with house managers and treasurers is that they are mostly hard-working people who are trying vainly to please an ever demanding public. Unfortunately, the tools that managers and treasurers are given are not always the most audience-friendly, and in many ways we offer so little (other than the actual attraction) for charging so much. Managers and treasurers are engaged to smooth over the inadequacies of the system or facility and it's often a very awkward position to be in.

This perception is not only in the minds of the general public but is also shared by incoming show personnel. Consequently, one West Coast house manager has this technique:

> [O]ne of my first orders of business with a production company that is new to my theatre . . . is to show them my honesty and integrity are beyond reproach. Point out our errors in their favor, be fair in settlement issues, whatever it takes. At the first sign of any suggestions that funny business is going on, I demand any proof they may have. If none is forthcoming, then I protest loudly.

The treasurer/house manager relationship is one of particular sensitivity. In some theaters there is little interaction between the two except at the time of checking the statement. In other venues, the treasurer may report to the house manager. In still others, employers do not allow anyone other than ticket-sellers into the box office, including managers. What have unfortunately shadowed the interaction of treasurer and manager are the uncomfortable subjects of "ice" and theft. Box office ice is a term referring to any additional money made above the ticket price by people who are not authorized to resell a ticket at a higher price. Langley (1990, 275) quotes the slang as having originated with dishonest show managers who submitted "incidental company expenses" (ICE) and pocketed the money. Kissel (1993, 60) credits politics as having coined the phrase when referring to "incidental campaign expenses."

It requires two people to engage in this activity. A reseller of tickets can range from legitimate ticketing agencies to hotel concierges and unlicensed brokers. Also included are those with access to tickets—a treasurer, theater manager, company manager, producer, or theater owner.

Tickets, usually in prime locations, are sold to the reseller for an amount exceeding the ticket price. This money is not accounted for and kept by the person who provided the tickets. The reseller then, of course, peddles the tickets for an amount that far exceeds the original, plus the kickback. This activity is considered scalping when the premium price exceeds the percentage or fee set by law, and because the broker has access to tickets not available to the general public. Nearly every employer has policies against ticket brokering, though proving the activity is difficult and rumor often persists that some employers look the other way while others even take their cut.

While the box office money is the treasurer's responsibility and the manager may have little to do with it, both people may be fired if mismanagement or theft is discovered. The financial responsibility of the treasurer borders on company religion. "I balance millions of dollars to the penny on a daily basis," says treasurer Carol Neilson. "At this time our daily box office receipts are fifty to sixty thousand dollars."

When box office shenanigans are discovered, regardless of whether the reason is ice or returning tickets to the system and pocketing the money, the result is nearly always termination. The Jujamcyn theaters fired two box office treasurers in 1996 after discovering they had diverted prime locations to brokers for *Smokey Joe's Cafe*. In 1994 the Nederlander Organization reorganized all their box offices and hired a box office overseer when a scandal at the Lunt-Fontanne on the show *Catskills on Broadway* resulted in missing cash. Also in 1994, the Shubert Organization fired five employees, including the manager of their Philadelphia Forrest Theater, but declined to publicly state the reason for the dismissals (Gerard 1994, 67; Gerard 1996, 71; Evans 1994, 67).

Neilson refers to brokers as "bottom feeders" and does not deal with them. "My policy is as far as the staff goes: deal with a broker, 'you're fired!'" Every so often various law enforcement officials will jump on bandwagons and launch investigations of ice and the notorious scalpers who buy tickets and sell them at premium prices. While *Variety* and *The New York Times* print articles following these inquiries, little comes of them. The occasional scandal results in firings, staff reassignments, resignations, the infrequent indictment, and rare conviction, but eventually the subject sleeps until the next time. *Variety* quotes an unidentified source after a 1964 investigation, which resulted in producers threatening to sue theater owners, the suicide of one broker, and other managers and brokers indicted for ticket scalping. "Ice was over . . . [u]ntil the next morning" (Gerard 1994, 193).

In 1995, after another attorney general's efforts resulted in American Express discontinuing its ticketing service to platinum card holders, which charged $175 for $70 tickets, *Variety* concluded, "Indeed, critics of the investigation, while not condoning the practice, noted that scalping has gone on as long [as] tickets have been sold to events, and investigations into scalping have gone on as long as there were politicians looking for a sure-fire consumer issue to hang a press release on" (Gerard 1995, 80). Again in 1998, yet another state attorney general investigation of Broadway theaters was launched, and on July 28, in an article entitled "Broadway's Ticket-Selling Practices Investigated," the *San Francisco Chronicle* quoted a source close to the investigation charging that "box-office workers . . . frequently cut personal side deals with outside brokers for delivering the choicest seats."

While safeguards are built into most computer systems to keep massive amounts of tickets from being returned and for tracking the history of tickets that might be released to a scalper, a dishonest treasurer may find a way around these security measures or be content with a smaller sum of money every week. The Massachusetts attorney general's office offered the following recommendations to stem ticket scalping: "Amend state laws to place a flat limit on the amount a resale broker may charge; increase criminal penalties for overcharging by a licensed broker; require brokers to provide to relevant government agencies specific data on the acquisition costs and resale prices of tickets" (Taylor 1994, 42).

The bottom line on employee misconduct and theft is that employers must hire honest people. After turning a blind eye to ice or even partaking in it, why are owners surprised that they get what they paid for? Traina notes, "It is increasingly difficult to 'steal' from the show these days, given the computerization of box offices and a general stepping up of count up procedures." A West Coast manager suggests that if a manager thinks theft is occurring he should "Call for an audit. Don't give details, don't point fingers, just firmly tell the chief financial officer you feel it is time for an audit. Put the request in writing. No matter how hard this might be, you must do it, or you will go down with the dishonest person."

THE STATEMENT

The box office statement is an accounting of ticket sales. It reflects the kinds of sales—single, subscriptions, groups, and special discounted tickets—then subtracts contractual fees and commissions. The final number represents the money credited toward the week's gross receipts. The statement is completed by a box office treasurer who then submits the document to the house manager and company manager. Once all three have signed it, the statement is considered final. The signatures do not always indicate approvals. If the statement contains errors or a charge that one of the parties disagrees with, that person may sign "under protest."

While an "under protest" signing can be used by anyone, most often it is done by the company manager. Since the house manager and treasurer are employees of the same theater, they are more likely to be in agreement about the box office statement. And in all likelihood, the treasurer has received her instructions from the manager or GM regarding deductions or percentages.

After receiving the contract for *The Time of My Life*, you made note of box office deductions and memoed them to Sally Smith, the Renaissance treasurer. Sally is responsible for box office operations, including a daily wrap. A wrap is a sales report that Neilson says includes the day's ticket sales, house, company, and group orders, and sales from contracted ticketing agencies. One of the most important financial responsibilities of her day is preparation of the box office statement.

Two types of box office statements are commonly referred to as "hardwood" statements and "computerized" statements. While the hardwood statement can in fact be done on a computer spreadsheet program, it is referred to as such because it is calculated by counting the unsold tickets. These tickets are known as hardwood.

The computerized statement is typically built by an outside ticketing agency at the request of an authorized person, usually the treasurer. Sally Smith would provide her contact at the agency with the seating capacity, deductions, pricing, and other relevant information. All the calculations, at this point, are internal since the computer is keeping track of sales. When it comes time to check the box office statement, the house manager needs to know what information the treasurer puts in manually and double-check that these figures have been entered correctly. Additionally, you would want to check the backup on the group sales, credit card charges, and any other deductions that would affect the statement that day.

Theater manager Robert Lazzara cites the difference between the two kinds of statements as being "labor intensive, bulky and hard-to-make changes" versus "fast, easy and sleek." But as Traina points out, "[T]here really is no going back. The ability to sell tickets at outlets, over the phone and now on the Internet cannot be ignored as we continue to remain as competitive in ticket selling as movie theaters and other live entertainment attractions." Both managers have had systems crash at

7:45 P.M. with no way to sell a ticket, and one suggests, "Pull open seat maps often!"

The Hardwood Statement

The night of the performance, Sally Smith pulls a preprinted form showing the theater capacity. It might look like table 11.1:

Table 11.1.

THE RENAISSANCE THEATER											

THE RENAISSANCE THEATER

Box Office Statement

Weather:_____
Perf.:_____   Week:_____

Show: *The Time of My Life*   Date:_____ Day:_____ Time:_____

SEASON SALES						SINGLE SALES					
Section	Unsold	Passes	Sold	Price	Total	Capacity	Unsold	Passes	Sold	Price	Total
Orch.											
1500											
Mezz.											
700											
Balcony											
300											
Total											
2500											

Less ___% of _____ group sales commission

Less Season Commission ___%

Less ___% of ___% of $_____

Less ___% of _____ single sales

SEASON NET TOTAL

SINGLE NET TOTAL

	# of Tickets	AMOUNT
Net Sold Season		
Net Sold Single		
Perf. Total		
Previous Total		
Total to Date		
Less ___ city tax		
TOTAL FOR THE WEEK		

We, the undersigned, have checked the above statement and found it correct to the best of our knowledge

Treasurer: _____

House Manager: _____

Company Manager: _____

Sally Smith fills in the various commissions and fees. If there were subscriptions sales on this night she would get a separate accounting of these from the subscription manager and fill in that side of the statement. These tasks can be done earlier in the day prior to the performance. The treasurer calculates across to the single sales side, which gives a new capacity. The statement would look like table 11.2:

Table 11.2.

THE RENAISSANCE THEATRE   Weather:_____
Box Office Statement   Perf.:_____   Week: _____
SHOW: *The Time of My Life*   Date: 4/3/03   Day: Tues   Time: 8pm

SEASON SALES						SINGLE SALES					
Section	Unsold	Passes	Sold	Price	Total	Capacity	Unsold	Passes	Sold	Price	Total
Orch											
1500			500	54°°	27,000	1000					
Mezz											
700			350	45°°	15,750	350					
Balcony											
300			200	36°°	7,200	100					
Total											
2500			1050		49,950	1450					

Less Season Commission 15 %   <7,492.50>

Less 3 % of 75 % of $49,950   <1,123.88>

SEASON NET TOTAL   41,333.62

Less ____% of ____ group sales commission

Less ____% of ____ single sales

SINGLE NET TOTAL

We, the undersigned, have checked the above statement and found it correct to the best of our knowledge

	# of Tickets	AMOUNT
Net Sold Season		
Net Sold Single		
Perf. Total		
Previous Total		
Total to Date		

Treasurer: _____

House Manager: _____

Company Manager: _____

Less ___ city tax

TOTAL FOR THE WEEK

After the performance begins, the treasurer counts the unsold tickets and inserts those numbers in the unsold category on the single sales side. The calculations now give you totals for single sales and the treasurer adds the numbers down to get a performance total as in table 11.3:

Table 11.3.

THE RENAISSANCE THEATRE   Weather: Rain
Box Office Statement   Perf.: ↑ 2   Week: T-6
SHOW: *The Time of My Life*   Date: 6/3/03   Day: Tue.   Time: 8pm

SEASON SALES						SINGLE SALES					
Section	Unsold	Passes	Sold	Price	Total	Capacity	Unsold	Passes	Sold	Price	Total
Orch											
1500			500	54⁰⁰	27,000⁻	1000	234	26	700	60⁰⁰	42,000⁻
						Groups		40		54⁰⁰	2,160⁻
Mezz											
700			350	45⁰⁰	15,750⁻	350	40		250	50⁰⁰	12,500⁻
						Groups		60		45⁰⁰	2,700⁻
Balcony											
300			200	36⁰⁰	7,200⁻	100	5		75	40⁰⁰	3,000⁻
Total						Groups		20		36⁰⁰	720⁻
2500			1050		49,950⁻	1450	279	26	1145		63,080⁻

SEASON	SINGLE
Less Season Commission 15 % ⟨7,492.50⟩	Less 15 % of $55 80 group sales commission ⟨837⁰⁰⟩
Less 3 % of 75 % of $49,950 ⟨1,123.88⟩	Less 3 % of $47,537.50 single sales ⟨1,426.13⟩
$41,333.62	$60,816.87
SEASON NET TOTAL	SINGLE NET TOTAL

	# of Tickets	AMOUNT
We, the undersigned, have checked the above statement and found it correct to the best of our knowledge		
Net Sold Season	1050	41,333.62
Net Sold Single	1145	60,816.87
Perf. Total	2195	102,150.99
Previous Total		-6-
Total to Date		102,150.99

Treasurer: Sally Smith	Less 2 city tax ⟨204.30⟩
House Manager: Tess Collins	TOTAL FOR THE WEEK $101,946.19
Company Manager: _____	

As performances continue through the week, Ms. Smith will carry each total forward in order to keep a final total of the week's receipts. Each evening the house manager and company manager come to the box office after the treasurer has finished the statement and checks it. This includes counting the unsold tickets, comparing them with the head usher's count, and double-checking the group sales, subscription sales, and credit card backup.

The head usher's ticket count is a good double-check to alert a manager to statement problems. Just after the curtain goes up, the head usher begins counting all the torn ticket stubs. He will need to make sure to check with all the ushers in case additional stubs are in someone's pockets. The head usher notes these amounts on a form, then brings the stubs, called deadwood, along with the form to the box office. A form might look like table 11.4 provided by Debra Stockton, who has held positions of head usher and assistant manager at the Curran Theater in San Francisco:

Table 11.4.

The Renaissance Theater Ticket Tally Sheet Show: *The Time of My Life* Date: _____ Matinee: _____ Evening: _____					
Section	Adult	Subs	Group	Comp	Total
Orchestra (1,500)					
Mezzanine (700)					
Balcony (300)					
Seating Capacity: 2,500 Final Total: _____					

After counting the ticket stubs, the head usher fills out the form like table 11.5.

Table 11.5.

The Renaissance Theater Ticket Tally Sheet Show: *The Time of My Life* Date: __6-3-03__ Matinee: _____ Evening: Tuesday					
Section	Adult	Subs	Group	Comp	Total
Orchestra (1,500)	698	476	40	20	1,234
Mezzanine (700)	250	350	34		634
Balcony (300)	70	196	19		285
Seating Capacity: 2,500 Final Total: __2153__					

What this information tells you is how many people have actually come to the theater as opposed to how many people have purchased tickets per the box office statement. These numbers can be an important indication of something wrong should the statement indicate that fewer tickets were sold, but the stub count gives evidence of more people being in the theater. By all means that is when a house manager should not sign the statement until some explanation is forthcoming. It could be as simple as customers who showed up on the wrong date and seated themselves in empty seats, and ushers not catching the mistake. The statement and stub count will never match exactly because of customers who are late or do not come. On subscription shows, subscribers are often allowed to exchange their tickets for a more convenient date. On a hardwood statement, the subscription department often cannot account for this on a per performance basis, but only validate the final subscription money. Therefore, the stub count can be off by a significant percentage with a heavily subscribed show in which subscribers have exchanged. Because there is no concrete method to determine the number of exchanges, a manager has to develop a sense of what is typical for your subscription performances. When the Curran used hard tickets, this number could be off by as many as fifty a night during the subscription period, and was even as high as seventy-five to one hundred tickets off. If that number had reached 150, then it would have been my responsibility to alert the GM to a possible box office problem.

Some theaters have the stub count function completed in a count-up room by separate personnel. In this case, when the usher tears the tickets the stubs are put into a locked box. Those boxes are then transported to a separate count-up room by staff not directly associated with the theater, and the stubs are accounted for the next day. Traina believes a count-up room "prevents some kinds of theft and certainly the types that involve selling seats not on the manifest, or trying to return tickets already sold and then trying to resell them. If the count-up room is well monitored, these types of shenanigans are very hard to perpetrate successfully."

Some managers, both house and company, may also do what is called "counting the house." This is literally counting the number of audience members. It is done mainly when a manager thinks something might be wrong with the box office statement. Occasionally company managers who come to a theater without a previous relationship with the treasurer and house manager do not know whether or not these people are trustworthy. A count of the people in the auditorium will show how closely the numbers match the sold tickets on the statement.

I once had a company manager storm into the box office, pull me aside and point to the auditorium. "There's no way the number of people in

there matches what is on that statement!" It was a shock to hear this accusation and I had no reason to believe the treasurer was dishonest. Possibly the company manager was simply playing games with me, wanting
to put me on the defensive. Or I could have been wrong. What if the treasurer was dishonest? Attendance count can be affected by people who are
late, those who do not show up, people who manage to get in with tickets for a different date, and other reasons; obviously, the numbers are not
going to match exactly. I repeated these things to myself as I maneuvered
around the auditorium in the dark counting people. With odds that are
probably one in a million, at least that evening, the count of the orchestra
matched the count on the box office statement *exactly*. This particular
company manager never questioned the box office treasurer's honesty
again.

The Computerized Statement

The computerized statement gives the same information as a hardwood
statement but there are no hardwood tickets to count. Statements from
theatrical organizations can vary depending on the ticketing agency or
software used to create them. What the house manager will need to find
out is what items are entered manually, and then double-check that the
treasurer has done this correctly.

The computerized statement might look like table 11.6.

The major difference in this kind of statement is that ticket charges
are based on actual sales. On a hardwood statement, the show would
most likely be charged for the ticket printing on the settlement. This
would be in the form of an actual bill from the ticket company for printing every ticket for every performance. A computerized box office
prints only figures for the tickets that it sells. The layout is similar, but
often the computerized statement contains more accurate information.
By virtue of computerization it is easier to keep track of different kinds
of ticket sales and subscription exchanges, and have faster access to information.

When computerized statements were first introduced, many managers and treasurers were uncomfortable with not having any numbers
to input or tickets to count, since the computer did all this. To this day,
I am somewhat uneasy depending on the computer's reliability and cor-
rectness.

The box office treasurer will depend on you to supply information
about staffing as well. If a show is planning an extensive advertising campaign for a particular span of time, it is prudent to plan for increased sales
during that period. "The house manager provides me with contract information for statement deductions, and tells me if film crews are attending

Table 11.6.

Agency Ticketing
Box Office Statement
Venue: The Renaissance Theater Subscription Performance #9
Event: *The Time of My Life* Perf. Date and Time: June 10, 2003, 8 P.M.

Section	Capacity	Unsold	Type	Comps	Sold	Price	Total
Orchestra	1,500	234	Regular	26	700	$60.00	$42,000.00
			Subs		500	$54.00	$27,000.00
			Groups		40	$54.00	$2,160.00
Mezzanine	700	40	Regular		250	$50.00	$12,500.00
			Subs		350	$45.00	$15,750.00
			Groups		60	$45.00	$2,700.00
Balcony	300	5	Regular		75	$40.00	$3,000.00
			Subs		200	$36.00	$7,200.00
			Groups		20	$36.00	$720.00
Total	2,500	279		26	2,195		$113,030.00
	==========			========			=========

Deductions	825	@	$0.15	Box Office Charge Per Ticket	$123.75
	200	@	$0.25	Outlet Charge Per Ticket	$50.00
	$5,580.00	@	15%	Group Sales	$837.00
	$60,000.00	@	3%	Box Office Credit Card Percentage	$1,800.00
	$25,000.00	@	3%	Telephone Credit Card Percentage	$750.00
	$49,950.00	@	15%	Subscription	$7,492.50
				Total Deductions	$11,053.25
				Total Net	$101,976.75
				City Tax 0.2%	$203.95
				TOTAL	$101,772.80

	Performance	Previous	Current	Attendance	Week to Date
This Week	$101,772.80	0.00	$101,772.80	2,195	2,195
Last Week	$66,000.00	0.00	$66,000.00	1,500	1,500
Difference	$35,772,80	0.00	$35,772.80	(695)	(695)

We hereby certify that the undersigned have personally checked the above statement and it is in every way correct to the best of our knowledge.

_____	_____	_____
Treasurer	House Manager	Company Manager

in case seats need to be taken off sale," says Neilson. A treasurer also completes a daily wrap that balances the ticket receipts for the day and the total sales for the production's run. This information will aid in scheduling box office and ushering staff, let the GM know the effectiveness of the advertising, and judge the popularity of the production.

Near the end of the week the head usher needs a printout of next week's sales from the treasurer. Seeing that the lower price balcony is better sold than the orchestra, he can place more staff in that section of the theater. If sales are down overall a cut in staff may be necessary, or an increase if it appears the week is going toward a sellout.

Box offices tend to have individual dynamics. Some I have been in run as efficiently as any corporate office; others have an animal-house quality as a coping mechanism for high-stress situations with the general public. Writer Helene Hanff (1989, 73) describes her summer of working in a box office, when she and her associate would play games in-between customers, or spot one another to go swimming, rowing, or to just stare at the sky, all in an effort to give them "strength to face the trauma of matinee days," which were usually

> [Two hundred] campers and 15 counselors strong, demanding the tickets they'd sent us a check for—only we'd thought they were coming Saturday so we'd saved 215 Saturday seats and sold today's seats to 215 other customers, and since the theatre only seated 300, there was no place to put the camp; or . . . we had 215 seats saved for the camp and the camp never showed up, having meant their check to cover 215 seats for next Wednesday.

As long as the work gets done, customers are attended to in a professional manner, and the books balance, it is best to tolerate idiosyncrasies within reason, and maybe from time to time, even join in the fun.

Chapter 12

Settlements

The pinnacle of the manager's work is the weekly settlement. This is a financial disbursement of the ticket money based on the contract with the show. The word "settlement" has a dual meaning. It refers not only to the discussion with the company manager, sometimes referred to as *doing the settlement*, but also to the actual packet of bills, which is called *the settlement*.

The cleaner and more concise the show contract is, the easier both settlements will be. Unfortunately, many contracts have gray areas which are a matter of interpretation, or even terms that when spelled out can be understood in opposite ways to favor each person's view. "Use them to your own advantage," says one West Coast manager. "Bend the rules in your favor and think of every reason possible why you are doing this. Argue forcibly and clearly. Stop the argument if it is going around in circles. What else would the house manager do but protect the theatre? Then end the discussion. Never give in unless you get something else in return." Joe Traina typically cites past precedent in cases like this, and "if that doesn't satisfy the company manager, I refer it to the theater owner for interpretation. What the owner says, I abide by."

While a clearly understood and mutually agreed upon contract is preferred for settlement negotiations, this is seldom the reality. The house manager must remember that the company manager is in the same position as you and will fight just as hard on behalf of the show.

Rather than hold up the settlement and delay payment to the show, certain items may be marked as having been signed off "under protest." It is then up to the show and theater's general managers (GMs) to negotiate the matter. Many disputed items are not settled until the last week of the show or even months after the production has closed. For this reason it is always prudent to hold or charge for items or payrolls that might be questionable. After the show is gone, the venue typically has no access to a show's receipts, and even if a producer agrees that the expense is a production cost, she may shrug her shoulders and say, "Go ahead, try and collect." It is always easier to give money back than it is to collect it from a business entity that no longer exists. Gray areas often depend on the relationships between the two organizations, and sometimes, a deal is simply cut on the disputed charge. In the worst possible scenario the matter may end up in court.

The type of settlement depends on the contract. For a four-wall deal where the show is paying for the theater's expenses, you will prepare all the payrolls and bills incurred because of the show, charge the production, and give them the excess money. In a deal that guarantees the show, the settlement substantiates that you have paid the show its money after deducting any mandated taxes and contractual bills. In a case like this, the show might never see your payrolls. Since the show is guaranteed, the theater's expenses are not their concern. However, even with a guarantee, you will still want to prepare an expense statement so the GM knows the cost of having booked this production.

PREPARING THE SETTLEMENT

The better organized the settlement is, the less time you will spend explaining it to the company manager. Traina's settlements have dealt with "salaries, benefits, taxes, bills, air-conditioning, box office bills, percentage for the house, etc. All listed as line items. This is usually accompanied by any specific backup necessary for the show to document the expenses." One West Coast manager says it is necessary to have a

> signed contract (or deal memo) then a clear line of authority on who does the settlement (the house manager), then clear concise backup: bills, payrolls, box office statements. Check, double check, and check everything a third time before sitting down to settle. Know your settlement and anticipate questions, have the answers ready. Be honest and forthright; make certain your integrity is above reproach, then go for the jugular and don't let go!

This same manager points out that in order to insure your position, it is important that the "theater is holding the box office receipts because this is your source of power."

There are many choices a manager can make regarding the organization of the settlement, and the information that follows is only one method. For a new manager beginning in an established theater, this procedure may already be set up and carved in stone, so you will want to follow whatever process works best for your GM.

The example below is a settlement form that itemizes each cost. Following this form are copies of the payrolls and bills, each accompanied by a top sheet that summarizes the cost and gives any information needed to understand the charge. The amount on a top sheet corresponds to the cost charged on the settlement.

A blank settlement form might look something like table 12.1:

Table 12.1.

The Renaissance Theater	
Settlement #	W/E:
Theater Expenses	Show: *The Time of My Life*
Payrolls	
1. Stagehands	
2. Musicians	
3. Wardrobe	
4. Box Office	
5. Engineer	
6. Stagedoor	
7. Security	
8. Ushers	
9. Load-in	
10. Theater Manager	
11. Preliminary Box Office	
Total Payrolls:	
============	
Bills	
1. Advertising	
2. Insurance	
3. Housekeeping	
4. General Bills	
5. Administrative Fee	
6. Theater Rent	
Total Bills:	
============	

(continued)

Table 12.1.   *(continued)*

Holdings	Prepared By: _____
1. Advertising _____	House Manager
2. Bills _____	
3. Load-out _____	
Total Holdings: _____	
Total Expenses: _____	
============	

The right side of the settlement form is often used to summarize the set-tlement money. Whether or not this calculation is needed depends on the contractual terms with the show.

Near the end of the week each department head will turn in a payroll. The theater manager checks the math and makes sure that all the charges are in accordance with the union contract. Most payroll sheets have a sep-arate area showing any union benefits, such as pension and health and welfare. After totaling a department's payroll, you will prepare a top sheet that consolidates all the cost of that department.

The top sheet for stagehands' department might look like table 12.2:

Table 12.2.

Renaissance Theater Show: *The Time of My Life* W/E: 6/8/03 *#1 Stagehands—Performances*	
Payroll	$33,138.72
22% Taxes	$7,290.52
14% Benefits	$4,639.42
Total to Recover:	$45,068.66
	============

The total figure for this week now goes on the settlement form under stagehands. You will continue making front sheets for each billable cost.

Examples of top sheets are shown in tables 12.3 and 12.4.

Some areas may require more explanation than others. For instance, load-in costs are incurred during the first week of a show, but often, this week is soft on sales. A producer may request that the theater

Table 12.3.

The Renaissance Theater Show: *The Time of My Life* W/E: 6/8/03 *#4 Box Office*	
Payroll	$5,166.00
22% Taxes	$1,136.52
9% Benefits	$464.94
Total to Recover:	$6,767.46

Table 12.4.

The Renaissance Theater Show: *The Time of My Life* W/E: 6/8/03 *#7 Security*	
Payroll	$3,456.00
22% Taxes	$760.32
Total to Recover:	$4,216.32

amortize or spread the cost of the load-in over the run of the show or the first three weeks, leaving the fourth week for the load-out cost. Each load-in payroll would be calculated with taxes and benefits and a front sheet summarizing the total. A top sheet in this case might look like table 12.5:

Table 12.5.

The Renaissance Theater Show: *The Time of My Life* W/E: 6/8/03 *#9 Load-In*	
Stagehands	$21,036.16
Wardrobe	$3,319.92
Stagedoor	$206.33
Security	$197.64
Total	$24,760.05
Over Three Weeks	3
Total to Recover Per Week:	$8,253.35

A similar request may come for the advertising, should the producer be using your local accounts. There are several ways this can be done. If, for instance, the entire advertising budget is $175,000, you could divide this amount by four (weeks) and charge $43,750 per week. As the actual bills arrived, sometimes several weeks after the show has closed, then the excess money would be released to gross receipts and it is subject to the terms of the contract.

If you have partial advertising bills incoming each week, then you can put the actual bill cost under the advertising and have a holding that approximates the cost to $43,750. Some producers would prefer only exact bills go on the settlement, with no holding until the final week when the gross receipts are typically higher and a hefty holding is not so much of a burden. Whichever choice is made, the manager will want to stay abreast of what is being spent on advertising, as this is one area that can change daily.

Usually during the final week of the show, I will call the press agent to ask about any last-minute expenditures and double-check my holding against the current budget. Should the money I have held not cover the expenses, it may be difficult, if not impossible, to recover it from the producer later on, especially if the show has closed. A theater manager does not want to be in the position of explaining this situation to the GM.

After all the costs are entered on the settlement form, the manager needs only to wait for the final performance of the week in order to finish up. The last box office statement of the week will show the gross receipts and these are now subject to the contract terms. For contracts that are fairly straightforward, such as a four-wall deal, you can put the payment figures on the right side of the settlement top sheet.

For example, a four-wall deal where the show is paying the theater's expenses might look like table 12.6.

This verifies that on a week with ticket sales amounting to $850,850.00 and theater expenses of $250,547.17, the balance of the receipts is $600,302.83. According to the contract this amount is to be given to the show. The state tax of 3 percent is charged to out-of-state companies, so that must be subtracted and sent to the state tax authorities. The resulting balance is the actual amount of the check to be given to the company manager, $582,293.75.

If the contract terms were that after theater expenses the show received the next $550,000.00, and any further amount be split sixty/forty, then the right side of the settlement might look like table 12.7.

This settlement does not reflect the money that you give to the show. Contract terms determine the way you will set up the settlement. If you

Table 12.6.

The Renaissance Theater Settlement #1		W/E: 6/8/03	
Theater Expenses		Show: *The Time of My Life*	
Payrolls			
1. Stagehands	$45,068.66	Gross Receipts:	$850,850.00
2. Musicians	$39,788.08	Theater Expenses:	$250,547.17
3. Wardrobe	$23,303.83	Balance:	$600,302.83
4. Box Office	$6,767.46		
5. Engineer	$2,780.00	State Tax 3%	$18,009.08
6. Stagedoor	$660.24		
7. Security	$4,216.32	Balance to Company:	$582,293.75
8. Ushers	$9,265.37		=========
9. Load-in	$24,760.05		
10. Theater Manager	$3,243.00		
11. Preliminary Box Office	$11,444.16		
Total Payrolls:	$171,297.17		
	===========		
Bills			
1. Advertising	$43,750.00	Make Check Payable to:	
2. Insurance	$2,500.00	The Time of My Life L.P.	
3. Housekeeping	$3,000.00	Deliver to house manager	
4. General Bills	$5,000.00	by 8:00 P.M. Tuesday	
5. Administrative Fee	$5,000.00		
6. Theater Rent	$20,000.00		
Total Bills:	$79,250.00		
	===========		
Holdings		Prepared By: _____	
1. Advertising	_____	House Manager	
2. Bills	_____		
3. Load-out	_____		
Total Holdings:	_____		
	===========		
Total Expenses:	$250,547.17		
	===========		

Table 12.7.

The Renaissance Theater Settlement #1		W/E: 6/8/03	
Theater Expenses		Show: *The Time of My Life*	
Payrolls			
1. Stagehands	$45,068.66	Gross Receipts:	$850,850.00
2. Musicians	$39,788.08	Theater Expenses:	$250,547.17
3. Wardrobe	$23,303.83	Show Guarantee	$550,000.00
4. Box Office	$6,767.46	Balance:	$50,302.83
5. Engineer	$2,780.00		
6. Stagedoor	$660.24		
7. Security	$4,216.32	60% to Show	$30,181.70
8. Ushers	$9,265.37		
9. Load-in	$24,760.05		
10. Theater Manager	$3,243.00	40% to Theater	$20,121.13
11. Preliminary Box Office	$11,444.16		=========
Total Payrolls:	$171,297.17		
	==========		
Bills			
1. Advertising	$43,750.00	Make Check Payable to:	
2. Insurance	$2,500.00	The Time of My Life L.P.	
3. Housekeeping	$3,000.00	Deliver to house manager	
4. General Bills	$5,000.00	by 8:00 P.M. Tuesday	
5. Administrative Fee	$5,000.00		
6. Theater Rent	$20,000.00		
Total Bills:	$79,250.00		
	==========		
Holdings		Prepared By: _____	
1. Advertising	_____		House Manager
2. Bills	_____		
3. Load-out	_____		
Total Holdings:	_____		
	==========		
Total Expenses:	$250,547.17		
	==========		

live in a state which taxes money paid to out-of-state companies, then a separate page reflects this deduction, as well as any other bills payable by them. Suppose the theater is guaranteeing the show $550,000 per week plus 5 percent of the gross receipts, and 70 percent of the gross receipts over $800,000. The remainder of the money belongs to the theater.

The show guarantee sheet might look like table 12.8:

Table 12.8.

```
Renaissance Theater
Show: The Time Of My Life
W/E: 6/8/03
Show Money Week #1

Company Guarantee                              $550,000.00
5% of Gross Receipts:       $42,542.50
Gross Receipts:             $850,850.00            $42,542.50
70% over $800,000.00        $35,595.00
Amount:                     $50,850.00             $35,595.00
                                              _____
Company Money:                                    $628,137.50
                                              =============
State Tax 3%                                       $18,844.13
Show Bills                                          $6,000.00
Holding for Show Bills                                      0
                                              _____
Total to Company:                                 $603,293.37
                                              =============
                                              =============
Make Check Payable to: The Time of My Life Limited Partnership
For the Theater: _____
```

The settlement form showing the theater's expenses might look like table 12.9.

This expense sheet shows a loss to the theater on the first week. In this case, carry the loss forward to the next week until the theater's expenses are entirely covered. If you are going into a show with receipts that fall short on a weekly basis, then you might choose to do a cumulative settlement.

For instance, the contract terms of a sixty/forty split on the receipts after the company guarantee and theater expenses are paid require a running total of expenses rather than settling the sixty/forty on a

Table 12.9.

The Renaissance Theater Settlement #1		W/E: 6/8/03	
Theater Expenses		Show: *The Time of My Life*	
Payrolls			
1. Stagehands	$45,068.66	Gross Receipts:	$850,850.00
2. Musicians	$39,788.08	Show Money:	$628,137.50
3. Wardrobe	$23,303.83	Balance	$222,712.50
4. Box Office	$6,767.46		
5. Engineer	$2,780.00	Theater Expenses:	$250,547.17
6. Stagedoor	$660.24		
7. Security	$4,216.32	Loss to Theater	($27,834.67)
8. Ushers	$9,265.37		=========
9. Load-in	$24,760.05		
10. Theater Manager	$3,243.00		
11. Preliminary Box Office	$11,444.16		
Total Payrolls:	$171,297.17		
	===========		
Bills			
1. Advertising	$43,750.00		
2. Insurance	$2,500.00		
3. Housekeeping	$3,000.00		
4. General Bills	$5,000.00		
5. Administrative Fee	$5,000.00		
6. Theater Rent	$20,000.00		
Total Bills:	$79,250.00		
	===========		
Holdings		Prepared By: _____	
1. Advertising	_____	House Manager	
2. Bills	_____		
3. Load-out	_____		
Total Holdings:	_____		
	===========		
Total Expenses:	$250,547.17		
	===========		

weekly basis. This ensures that theater's expenses are covered prior to a split. A cumulative expense report is a variation on the settlement. Table 12.10 is a sample cumulative expense form.

The cumulative settlement is calculated by taking the amount guaranteed to the show from that sheet, and subtracting it and the theater

Table 12.10.

The Renaissance Theater Settlement #1 W/E: 6/8/03					
Theater Expenses Show: *The Time of My Life*					
Week Ending:	*6/1/01*	*6/8/01*	*6/15/01*	*6/22/01*	*Total to Date*
Payroll					
1. Stagehands					
2. Musicians					
3. Wardrobe					
4. Box Office					
5. Engineer					
6. Stagedoor					
7. Security					
8. Ushers					
9. Load-in					
10. Manager					
11. Preliminary Box Office					
Bills					
1. Advertising					
2. Insurance					
3. Housekeeping					
4. General Bills					
5. Executive Fee					
6. Theater Rent					
Holdings					
1. Advertising					
2. Bills					
3. Load-out					

(continued)

Table 12.10.   *(continued)*

Week Ending:	6/1/01	6/8/01	6/15/01	6/22/01	Total to Date
Total Payrolls					
Total Bills					
Total Holdings					
Total Expenses					
Gross Receipts					
Company Guarantee					
Theater Expenses					
Balance					
Balance to Split					
40% to Theater					
60% to Show					

expenses from the gross receipts. By the final week of the show you will show a profit or a loss. The profit is to be split sixty/forty.

As table 12.11 shows, settlements are as varied as contract terms. The key to an excellent settlement is to be organized and know what you are talking about. This means you must understand every item on your settlement. Of course, there may be times when a GM instructs you to charge certain bills, and of course, barring something illegal, you will probably do so. To protect yourself it is wise to make sure those instructions are in writing. Traina says he has never been in this position and that his "primary loyalty and accountability has to be to the house. Otherwise, my position becomes compromised and in this small industry, it's not a label that I would have wished to have." If the issue borders on unethical or slimy, a West Coast manager says to "make certain the GM knows you know this is wrong, and the possible consequences of doing this. Then you must follow instructions, but be certain the opposing party knows you have been ordered to do this by a higher up, and you have no choice but to do it. Still give it your best shot, even if you personally don't agree with the action."

The only remaining item to deal with is the release of holdings. Usually on the last week of a run you will have held money back for bills that have not arrived by the time the show closes. Typically, these are advertising expenses, show bills, and sometimes load-out costs. When the bills arrive, you will deduct them from this holding. If there is a remaining amount,

Table 12.11.

The Renaissance Theater Settlement #4	W/E: 6/29/03				
Theater Expenses	Show: *The Time of My Life*				
Week Ending:	*6/8/03*	*6/15/03*	*6/22/03*	*6/29/03*	*Total to Date*
Payroll					
1. Stagehands	45,068.66	45,068.66	45,068.66	45,068.66	180,274.64
2. Musicians	39,788.08	36,430.00	36,430.00	36,430.00	149,078.08
3. Wardrobe	23,303.83	23,303.83	23,303.83	23,303.83	93,215.32
4. Box Office	6,767.46	6,767.46	6,767.46	6,767.46	27,069.84
5. Engineer	2,780.00	2,780.00	2,780.00	2,780.00	11,120.00
6. Stagedoor	660.24	660.24	660.24	660.24	2,640.96
7. Security	4,216.32	4,216.32	4,216.32	4,216.32	16,865.28
8. Ushers	9,265.37	9,265.37	9,265.37	9,265.37	37,061.48
9. Load-in	18,253.35	18,253.35	18,253.35		54,760.05
10. Manager	3,243.00	3,243.00	3,243.00	3,243.00	12,972.00
11. Preliminary Box Office	2,861.04	2,861.04	2,861.04	2,861.04	11,444.16
Bills					
1. Advertising	44,625.00	22,950.00	62,300.00	10,500.00	140,375.00
2. Insurance	2,500.00	2,500.00	2,500.00	2,500.00	10,000.00
3. Housekeeping	3,000.00	3,000.00	3,000.00	3,000.00	12,000.00

(continued)

Table 12.11. *(continued)*

Week Ending:	6/8/03	6/15/03	6/22/03	6/29/03	Total to Date
4. General Bills	3,600.00	2,500.00	1,500.00	3,500.00	11,100.00
5. Administrative Fee	5,000.00	5,000.00	5,000.00	5,000.00	20,000.00
6. Theater Rent Holdings	20,000.00	20,000.00	20,000.00	20,000.00	80,000.00
1. Advertising				25,000.00	25,000.00
2. Bills				3,000.00	3,000.00
3. Load-out				20,000.00	20,000.00
Total Payrolls	156,207.35	152,849.27	152,849.27	134,595.92	596,501.81
Total Bills	78,725.00	55,950.00	94,300.00	44,500.00	273,475.00
Total Holdings				48,000.00	48,000.00
Total Expenses	234,932.35	208,799.27	247,149.27	227,095.92	917,976.81
Gross Receipts	850,850.00	650,000.00	920,000.00	990,000.00	3,410,850.00
Company Guarantee	550,000.00	550,000.00	550,000.00	550,000.00	2,200,000.00
Theater Expenses	234,932.35	208,799.27	247,149.27	227,095.92	917,976.81
Balance	65,917.65	(108,799.27)	122,850.73	212,904.08	292,873.19
Balance to Split					
40% to Theater					$117,149.28
60% to Show					$175,723.91

and there should be if you have held enough, this money becomes subject to the terms of the contract. In the example we have been studying, that would be split sixty/forty. And remember the show's 60 percent is also subject to the 3 percent state tax.

A holding release might look like table 12.12:

Table 12.12.

Renaissance Theater Show: *The Time of My Life* Date: August 31, 2003 RE: Release of Holding . Holding For: Advertising and Bills	
Total Holding:	$28,000.00
Advertising	($15,362.20)
Show Bills	($2,065.36)
Total:	$10,572.44
	===========
40% to Theater:	$4,228.98
	===========
	===========
60% to Show:	$6,343.46
3% State Tax	($190.30)
Total to Show:	$6,153.16
	===========
	===========
Accounting Department: Please Wire to: The Time of My Life Limited Partnership	
For the Theater: _____	

The financial work of a manager can be the most important aspect of the job. While there is a philosophical belief that theater is about art and entertainment, it is also about money. When GMs and producers need financial information, the person who knows the workings of the theater the best is the manager. Becoming an expert at budgeting, keeping track of expenses, and forecasting profit/loss can make a manager indispensable. This knowledge can serve as a stepping-stone to higher positions such as GM or producer. More importantly, mastering this area helps create the self-confidence needed to work for any theater, any time.

Part III

CAREER DEVELOPMENT

Chapter 13

The Drama Offstage

The movie *All About Eve* is an entertaining and well-written theater melo-drama about an ambitious and vicious ingenue backstabbing her way to stardom. Along the way those who helped her are used and discarded. In an ironic twist, the movie ends with an even younger woman plotting her way into the new star's circle. The lives of actors make interesting fiction. There are seldom plays or movies written about a love triangle of ushers who end up in a screaming match with one woman striking the other, a fight I witnessed when I decided to cross the theater on the mezzanine level rather than my usual walk through the main lobby. It is doubtful anyone would pay to see a film about the conflicts of bickering ushers, customers threatening to go to the local consumer affairs reporter if you do not refund their money, or producers shouting at press agents that they will never work again. And yet, these small dramas play out in every department of the theater. Sometimes people let simple situations spin out of control. Too many hours of work, combined with a couple of mis-understandings, can make a usually normal person look at everyone around them as the enemy. Director Edward Dmytryk (1984, 63) says of these outbreaks on movie sets: "Each one is certain all the others are gang-ing up to do him in. Only one thing can be done about it; recognize it for what it is, a temporary aberration of perception. The act of recognition serves to defuse its more dangerous effects."

Dramas aside, there are also very real work issues among employees, de-partment heads, managers, show personnel, and customers. The carousel ride that cumulates in an 8 P.M. performance begins early in the morning when the janitors enter to clean the building. With each department's ar-rival a variety of skirmishes can occur. It is also the time when work gets

done despite the drama. The house manager's decisions during these skirmishes can be unpopular, and accepting the responsibility of the outcome
is yours alone. Manager Robert Lazzara says, "Steel yourself, for going will
be rough. Have the facts ready to defend your position, and make them
known loud and clear. If your decision is right, make other people see that.
If your decision is wrong, you may have to admit you made a mistake, but
no one should ever question your right to have made the decision in the
first place."

Whether working backstage or front-of-house, the focus required at
performance time is total, and this intensity can often spill over into the
personal. Bob MacDonald describes a situation when he worked for
the New Mexico Repertory: "This woman wanted my job and tried to
undermine the staff, but was fired by the board because of her under-the-
table tactics. It hurt badly at first—it made me question myself. Confidence was shot for a brief time. I wanted to hide out." Another West Coast
manager who has experienced being made the scapegoat for other's bad
decisions says, "I once made the foolish decision of covering a grave error
made by someone below me and my boss thought I had made the mistake. It was too late to correct the mistaken impression. I suffered rather
severe consequences. I will not make that mistake again."

Such incidents are not specific to theater. A plethora of books have been
written about these kinds of situations in the corporate world. Whether
we call it backstabbing, lunatic bosses, office politics, customer warfare,
theater rage, whatever, most managers will at some point in their careers
have to deal with certain aspects of aberrant behavior. It is hard to say
why it happens. Oddly, William Goldman (1984, 176) cites sadism.

> The majority of people not involved with any particular production gener-
> ally wish the majority of those who are involved just enough pain to prove
> unbearable. Psychiatrists disagree about the reasons behind the high sadism
> level, but there is a general head-nodding over the following famous dictum:
> "It's not enough for me to succeed. My best friend also has to fail."

It is not surprising to learn from managers that most often they are expected to bring order to chaos and fix it. They are expected to mediate the
cat fights in the box office; placate ranting customers; not respond when
attacks become personal, but obey their supervisor's order, "You must be
above the fray," and yet look the other way if the supervisor's own tirades
violate the law; and then, be blamed for low employee morale. The
dilemma becomes a struggle of one's ethics and what is necessary to survive, both emotionally and career-wise. Facing an environment where
ethics are situational can be "a living hell," says one West Coast manager
who has witnessed unethical activities.

It can cause you to question your own goodness and morality, even your own sanity. From situations I have seen happening to other people, I know there is no defense against this kind of activity should you be discovered. And no one above you will defend you; in fact, you will be thrown to the wolves so fast your head will spin. Your only options out are resignation or suicide. Another job can be found, another life not so easily done.

Oddly, within the dramas that can emotionally freeze a company, the people somehow continue to operate. Even the most hateful organizations seem to carry on with a minimum of output from staff and management. As long as the performance takes place, tickets are sold, and the place locked up at night and opened on time the next day, the company can report high grosses to *Variety* and give the impression of being as solid as a rock.

> Like a ship at sea, it will float by itself and sail by itself helter skelter whether there is anyone at the helm or not. One salient trait of corporate executives is their skill in marketing the fantasy that they have the ship on course—some course. Sometimes the course is the wrong course and sometimes the officer in charge is completely lost—but the goal is to keep the ship afloat under circumstances that cause a casual observer to conclude that someone is, indeed, at the helm and that the ship is, indeed, going somewhere. If those in charge of the corporation can create such an illusion, they will become greatly sought after by other corporations, admired by all, and deemed highly successful (Spence 1995, 271–72).

New managers often make the mistake of assuming that "organizations are rational places. We think the people in authority are smarter and understand the big picture better than we do. We figure their decisions, no matter how demented they sound, must be based on superior knowledge" (King 1987, 16). By the time managers wake up to the realities of the workplace, they can become disgusted and quit or end up corrupted themselves in an attempt to fit in. Those who stay and attempt to remain above the fray often find there is still a price to be paid. "[I]f you daily face the unethical behavior of others, your own self-esteem will be eroded. If you see people whose methods you despise being rewarded, you may have to pay for your tolerance of such villainy with the lining of your stomach" (King 1987, 243).

There are alternatives to ulcers. For example, some managers will fight back. Their approach is not necessarily like coming out as Mike Tyson or passively looking the other way. Some might choose to play the game and wait for better days, while others will keep out of the way, learning the spoken and unspoken rules, and cover their backside in a crisis. Revenge might appeal to the very bold, but only for those who deserve it, of course. Regardless of what strategy is used, all should be boxed in knowledge and wrapped in understanding.

Educating oneself as to how the company covertly operates is a necessity, regardless of whether one works for a corporation or a theater. In his book *Moral Mazes*, Robert Jackall (1988, 109–10) reports that corporate managers survive bureaucratic life by observing a series of rules:

> (1) You never go around your boss. (2) You tell your boss what he wants to hear, even when your boss claims that he wants dissenting views. (3) If your boss wants something dropped, you drop it. (4) You are sensitive to your boss's wishes so that you anticipate what he wants; you don't force him, in other words, to act as boss. (5) Your job is not to report something that your boss does not want reported, but rather to cover it up. You do what your job requires, and you keep your mouth shut.

I would submit that surviving in some entertainment companies is not so different from corporate America. However, more people than your actual employer will think you work for them—the customers, the stars, the producers, and oddly enough, sometimes even the employees.

THE ORGANIZATION

With such a variety of individuals claiming authority over you, let us refer to all of them as "the organization." While a manager can remind a producer they are not your supervisor or recommend to a customer that if they do not like your decision they can write to the general manager (GM), still you are going to have to deal with the fallout of these disputes. However unjust this sounds, especially considering a manager's immense responsibilities, we are still limited in our strength against these people because they are more elevated in the hierarchy.

Peter Scott-Morgan's *The Unwritten Rules of the Game* and Gerard Egan's *Working the Shadow Side* provide comprehensive studies of how organizations work beneath the surface. Scott-Morgan (1994, 22) cites the unwritten rules as originating at the top of the hierarchy. "They typically start with top management. On the one hand the unwritten rules come from the way top managers behave—their actions and their pronouncements—and on the other hand with what you can think of as the written rules that they create or maintain." Egan's definition (1994, 4) of the shadow side leaves out the everyday policies that govern an organization's actions. This suggests images of dangerous waters crawling with sharp-toothed creatures. "[T]he shadow side consists of all the important activities and arrangements that do not get identified, discussed, and managed in decision-making forums that can make a difference. The shadow side deals with the covert, the undiscussed, the undiscussable, and the un-mentionable."

That these covert activities exist is not the worst thing in the world. It is an environment that managers need to be aware of and need to know how to negotiate. This world is not to be feared, but understood. "The unwritten rules are the *missing link in our understanding*" (Scott-Morgan 1994, 27). MacDonald tries to stay clear of the kind of situations and environments where ethics are situational: "if I can't, I try not to pass judgment." A West Coast manager notes that if a lower level employee is playing politics, it is often easier to ignore it.

> If it affects your own responsibilities then any illegal activities must be brought to the attention of your superiors, or you will be as guilty as the other person. If the situation involves your superiors doing unethical, im-moral or illegal things, this is very difficult. If you want to keep your job you may be forced to do things against your will. If they are illegal activities, you may want to consult a lawyer and protect your own interests. Or you may want to quit.

Losing a job in an industry you love can be an extreme measure, but it is even more upsetting to leave a job because you can't stomach the politics. "'Forewarned is forearmed' is a critical guiding principle. In the end, however, there are no magic formulas for managing the shadow side— just courage and hard work" (Egan 1994, 71).

One might conclude that the grief is not worth the paycheck. After all, most of us simply want jobs we can work at, go home, be with our loved ones, and return to work again the next day. Even those of us who are so addicted to our careers that we nearly live at the theater would still pre-fer to do our work without having to deal with a lot of political nonsense. Let me suggest that the breadth of a theater organization is not so differ-ent from that of a family or a relationship or even a friendship. The work-place is simply another environment in which *stuff happens*. Learning how to deal with the difficult aspects of organizations makes you valuable to an employer, and even more so to yourself. "Mastering the unwritten rules of the game is the way to become a modern day troubleshooter. You can react to or predict barriers to performance, rapidly track down the real causes, and correct them. And like any troubleshooter, you build on ex-perience and recognize patterns" (Scott-Morgan 1994, 39).

Not every person in an organization is lying in wait for a manager to make a mistake. You will find mentors in this world, friends, and even ac-quaintances whose intentions are to make the workplace better. Even more important is that your skills will constantly improve. "Effective managers and supervisors understand the vagaries of people and know when to intervene and confront, when to encourage and reward, when to coach and counsel, and when to leave things alone. While this is only common sense—let's rename it extraordinary sense" (Egan 1994, 138).

A mistake many of us make is being loyal beyond a reasonable point. We cling to the belief that our good work will make the company take care of us; our efforts to please a customer will be appreciated; our honesty with a show will be returned in good faith. We believe that our organization will recognize us in the same way we see ourselves, and when it does not, we are as hurt as if a family member had betrayed us. However, what we might work out with a relative is misplaced allegiance in the workplace. Our loyalty is put to better use if it is directed at ourselves. "Loyalty means you should be doing the best job you can, not that you become emotionally dependent on an organization" (King 1987, 269).

Strategies for dealing with organizations can be multifaceted, complex, or as simple as recognizing that truth and reality are not always the same. If you work for a fairly straightforward organization, then discussion of a touchy issue with perhaps a memo to the file as backup will cover you. A company staffed with bullies, manipulators, and relatives of the owner may require more thoughtful tactics. Egan recommends that managers ask themselves a series of "prevention-oriented" questions before making a decision or embarking on a project:

> What are the hidden stumbling blocks? How will X (some difficult person) react? What silent arrangements will throw this project off course? How disruptive will this project be to current social arrangements? What power plays will be initiated by key individuals? key units? How compatible is this course of action with the covert culture? What inertia will we run into (Egan 1994, 70–71)?

Of course there are always times when an organization lurches toward disaster and no amount of goodwill, talent, or hard work can help it. This situation can often be recognized by the way individuals try to force the organization to bend to their will. MacDonald remembers legendary producer Joe Papp: "You never knew what to expect. He was a genius but so cruel to people." An East Coast manager finds the subject of out-of-control organizations too difficult to speak about: "Some stories are too intense to be repeated while the participants are still alive. And the only reason some of these people are still alive is because murder is illegal." The bitterness of those working under extreme pressure often results in grievances, lawsuits, lists of rules, downsizing, firings, and even sabotage. These deep feelings are as authentic with management as they are with employees, and neither group can be held solely responsible.

Often when a covert war breaks out, it is due to stereotyping rather than realizing that each side has reasons for its behavior. *Management hates us. The employees are lazy. All management cares about is demonstrating its power. Those workers get so much and do so little.* The generalization becomes entrenched with emotions and the tug-of-war begins. "People's true values do not change under duress. Even under exigencies of war, where some pretty nasty approaches have been tried, no one has ever been able to change what was really important to people through force. Instead, resistance goes underground" (Scott-Morgan 1994, 50).

It may take powerful but poorly-run organizations years or even decades to fall, yet short of a new regime from top to bottom they often continue to function in a kind of slow rot. Scott-Morgan (1994, 50) points out that organizations like those are in the "death throws of *corporate suicide*. Most people within the body of the organization will still mourn its passing—not because of what it became but because of their lost jobs and because of what it once was. But, since it degraded to a tyranny, it's better off dead." What is important to understand is that these situations occur not because management is bad or the workers are bitter, but because management is bad *and* the workers are bitter. There is enough fault to go around equally.

THE PEOPLE

Imagine how you might react when meeting a star you have admired all your life, and the first words out of her mouth are a diatribe on the ugly dressing rooms. This happened to me after the theater manager and I had spent the previous month working on every aspect of the backstage dressing rooms. A lifetime of admiration was wiped away with one comment that could not really be responded to because of who the star was. The manager and I had to stand there and listen to her disparage our hard work.

One customer brought her family of nine to a performance for which she had prime orchestra seats, and discovered the tickets were for the night before. We were not sold out, so I arranged for her party to be seated in the best available seats, the rear center of the side orchestra. She was elated. A few minutes later she charged toward me yelling that I had given her the worse seats in the house, and ordered me to seat her family in the center orchestra. When it became obvious that this was not an option for that evening, she grabbed me by both arms, shaking me and screaming, "You're not going to do this to me and get away with it!"

Another patron who had chosen an inconvenient time to go to the restroom discovered he could not go back into the auditorium until the seating hold was over. After loudly taking my name and returning several times to shout about how outrageous my stupid policy was, he lowered his voice, glared, and said, "You blew it, and I'm going to get you for this."

A producer with his first national road show had posters for his production put up all over town two weeks prior to the show's official on-sale date. Radio ads gave the ticket phone number of the theater in an East Coast city; then he changed the show schedule, changed opening night, changed the ticket prices which required refunding customers, and demanded computer programming changes which caused the box office and subscription departments to delay their normal work. Even with these and other slips, the GM worked with the producer and many times *saved his butt* while taking his blundering (or lack of experience) in stride. The show was not selling well and his company manager okayed comping a certain amount of tickets on the first week. When the show's sales picked up, the producer accused us of costing him at least $20,000 by comping those tickets. When it was pointed out to him that his own company manager had approved the comping, he responded, "She's not authorized to do that." Opening night, the press agent had a tirade about how awful her locations were, shook a seating chart in my face and yelled, "These seats say to me 'fuck you.'"

A West Coast manager recounts the time an actor ordered a private phone, then refused to pay for the installation. "I went to his dressing room with a bolt cutter and snipped the line." This same manager had the misfortune of working a show where the "three stars called in sick twenty minutes before curtain. The company manager told me there were no understudies. I made the company manager go to their hotel to drag them to the theater. At the hotel he found they had left for Los Angeles and a vacation!"

With some people actions are subconscious manifestations of their personalities—they are just like that and probably have no idea that they have inconvenienced anyone. Others are more premeditative—power trips, control freaks, bullies, narcissists. Still others are constantly trying to protect their position or may simply have a hidden agenda. During the pre-Broadway production of *42nd Street*, producer David Merrick is reported to have positioned his creative team "at each other's throats. He would phone them individually, generally at two in the morning, to complain, in his deep, solemn voice, of their colleagues' poor work. . . . The next morning all those who had received phone calls regarded each other with extreme wariness. They were unable to speak to each other. It left Merrick the only one able to speak to everybody, the only one with unmitigated power (Kissel 1993, 13–14).

While most situations might not be so high-powered, they can be equally traumatizing. An actor who demands premium seats from you behind the back of the company manager puts you in a difficult position. A customer screaming so loud the performance is disrupted causes several problems, not one. Crew members who sulk and barely work when they do not get their way can be demoralizing to other staff. A GM who berates you in front of the staff or a colleague who whispers innuendoes behind your back and smiles to your face can undermine your confidence and your ability to manage.

Once we realize we have been played for fools the question still gnaws at our minds, why in the world did this person do such a thing? There was no need for it. In all likelihood, you never did anything to them and had they approached you more sincerely, most of us would have done anything to help out. What has been attacked is more than our self-esteem. A hostile encounter can shake us to the core because it requires a response or acceptance of despicable behavior.

> *Honor* is a word not often used, but it can be argued that we traffic in "honor" every day of our lives. We present a face and a self to the world and, for the most part, we expect to be accepted and treated as a fully fledged member of that world. But it doesn't always happen. When we're treated with a lack of respect, we tend to become angry and aggressive, especially if we cannot foresee a time when that attitude will change (Barreca 1995, 120).

It could be that these kinds of people are crazy, or insecure, immature, maybe even a little pathetic. I do not pretend to have expertise in psychology, but do keep my eyes open for methods to protect myself from such people. Jay Carter's wonderful little book *Nasty People* (1989, 10) describes an invalidation cycle used by abusive personalities. In the case of theater managers, this can include bosses, customers, stars, colleagues, or employees. "The major reason invalidation occurs so often is that it works (in the short run). . . . The big part of the cure for invalidation is achieved when we simply spot it. Remaining undetected and unchallenged is what gives invalidation its power."

Whether or not to oppose someone depends on who the person is. Often it is unwise to directly challenge a boss, especially one who is temperamental or unstable. "The smart employee of the crazy boss, therefore, *does not say no*, does not disobey per se. He becomes devious. The first tactic is simply to stay out of the line of fire" (Bing 1992, 53). This advice can be equally apt when dealing with a producer, production personnel, or star who is out of control. When the ranting begins it can be better to wait out the tantrum in another part of the theater rather than make yourself available as the kicking-boy. Of course, at times when you are unable to escape, you may have to decide on a response to this kind of attack. A producer might be directed to the GM, a customer can be given a refund and told to leave the building, an employee can be given a written warning for insubordination, an actor referred to his own management company. But, this will not be the end of the matter if the individual does not like your response. Carter (1989, 68) warns: "Never, never say 'you're wrong' to an invalidator; this is a cardinal rule. If you contradict, point out, demonstrate, or in any way show an invalidator to be wrong, sooner or later he will get you."

MacDonald once had a customer ask him if he "was the asshole who ran this theater." This kind of bullying is rarely challenged and you will likely not be backed up by your employer should you complain about it. Instead, bad behavior often seems to be rewarded. "Management by terror is a time-honored technique, because it works. The most mediocre man or woman can suddenly seem dynamic, forceful, fearful—passing anxiety and hatred down the managerial pipe until it infects all who work under him" (Bing 1992, 100). A colleague who invalidates you often becomes all the more valuable in the eyes of management. The truth can be of little consequence as long as the accuser is loud enough and appears to be kicking butt. The good news is that in time, incompetent people usually trip themselves up.

Another dangerous type is the person who has been with the company for so long that they have spare time to stir up trouble.

> Too often, top management knows that a manager has serious shortcomings and leaves him in the job anyway. There are many reasons bad bosses escape the ax. They are expert in some function and therefore considered technically indispensable. They know where the bodies are buried and top management is afraid to incur their wrath by firing or even demoting them (King 1987, 217).

Customers come under this description as well. Just because they are customers, their word is often taken before yours or a staff member's who has had to deal with them. How you have handled the situation then becomes suspect and subject to criticism as having been inappropriate.

Once you are able to see abusive people in perspective, they start to seem like spoiled children. Their actions spring from a need to dominate and get their way no matter what they have to do. "[T]he invalidator does whatever is necessary to control you. He is control-crazy, and any time he perceives himself to be not in control, he will be scared" (Carter 1989, 16). Dealing with him then becomes your priority.

Bing describes a long-term, fivefold path to dealing with temperamental bosses. It is just as apt for dealing with others in the organization. He suggests breaking the cord of emotional dependence on the boss's authority, remaining competent in your job, staying sane within the crazy environment, using his craziness against him, and being prepared for his downfall (Bing 1992, 97). While this may keep you focused on the future, you must also devise tactics to deal with this behavior day to day. One manager used to take a few minutes in the restroom after the boss had humiliated them and visualize the woman standing in the unemployment line. "I collected all the 'I hate my boss' jokes I could and would repeat them to myself with the GM's name in the punch line. It got me through the day."

Certain strong-willed people are willing to engage an abusive personality in a knock-down-drag-out fight. I have always admired them, and their courage is a trait to emulate even if you choose different methods. The battles I have witnessed were usually screamers who tended to shut up when screamed back at. Then consistently they apologized after their outbursts, as if that could make up for what they had done. Do not be surprised if they try to revise the scenario to make themselves the victims. "It's ironic that the best way to make an invalidator lose his grip is to invalidate him. A person who is trying to hurt another will use the methods that would hurt *him*. If you want to hurt an invalidator, all you need to do is watch what he does or says to others. If you use his own methods against him, he will cave in sooner than anyone" (Carter 1989, 69).

The question also arises, why put up with all of this? It is the first question you will need to answer. It could be that you like the job and have much to learn in it. After all, this is your career and to walk away from it while certain people are bad-mouthing you may be detrimental, so it is better to stay and overcome the situation first. Perhaps you cannot afford to be unemployed, or maybe you simply want revenge. Whatever the reason, it is important to your physical and emotional health to know why you are doing what you are doing.

There are pros and cons to staying and you must weigh them carefully. Management consultant Patricia King (1987, 90–91) points out: "If your boss doesn't know much, he can't teach you much. If your boss is a featherbrain, your own growth in your field will be severely curtailed." But also, "if you have to take up the slack for the boss and work at a higher level, the boss's ignorance can create more challenge for you. In such cases, your growth can be enormous—a fine arrangement provided you don't resent your boss collecting the bigger paycheck while you do two jobs."

When the time comes that you are unable to stand the situation any longer, your choices should be considered along with your future goals. If conditions are intolerable and you are not in the position to quit, you will want to start your search for another job. While doing this, develop a support system of friends and family. If you do not have that, take a class to improve your skills. If you cannot do that, buy a book that will give you some encouragement. During one of the worst episodes of my theatrical career, when another employee was lying about me and sabotaging everything I did because he wanted my job, I ran across Betty Lehan Harragan's book *Games Mother Never Taught You*. Reading a chapter a day helped me cope and gave me the breathing space to stay calm and wait out the culprit. By the time I finished reading the book, he had overstepped, done himself in, and had been fired.

In the meantime, dealing with hostility as best you can and disassociating yourself from the situation is one technique. Remember that no matter how loud a boss or fellow employee is yelling at you, you are still going home to your own bed. They cannot come in to get you. And very soon, you will have a new job where this person will not be part of your life. Often the culprit's tantrums can then seem quite humorous. "While you are looking for a better job, understand that you are staying *temporarily* because being there serves your needs. If you remind yourself that you are there by choice, you'll stop feeling like a dupe" (King 1987, 144). Keeping focused on your own goals is necessary for more than simply the job, it is good advice for an entire career. "Remember, no matter who signs the paycheck, we always work for ourselves. No matter who hires or fires, we always please ourselves. Always we live up to our own standards. In the end, that is how we always win" (Spence 1995, 283).

If you feel required to do more than quit your job, it can be a weighty decision. Grievances and lawsuits sometimes have a way of not working out the way one expects. In the eyes of the law, what you feel as wrong might be interpreted differently by an arbitrator or jury. Attorney fees can mount, but far more important to consider is the effect of your decision if a future employer finds out. While clearly against the law, many employers will not hire someone they feel might sue them too. "[L]awsuits are emotionally draining and time-consuming. It may be worth your while if the payoff is substantial. I don't mean that we should allow the law to be broken and do nothing about it. Realistically, though, I must warn you that legal action may not be worth it" (King 1987, 180–81). If you decide to go down this path, think in realistic terms about the effect on you; and disregard the media hype of multimillion-dollar settlements. They are not every day occurrences and appeals cannot only take years, but often reduce the judgment until all that is left covers no more than attorney's fees.

Leaving loudly with a trail of reporters taking down your every word can also backfire in one's face.

If resignation cannot be avoided, there are selfish reasons for doing it quietly. Most resignees would like to work again. Only Nader's Raiders love a blabbermouth. Speaking out is not likely to enhance one's marketability. A negative aura haunts the visibly angry resignee, while the individual who leaves a position ostensibly to return to business, family, teaching, or research reenters the job market without any such cloud (Bennis 1994, 147).

THE DECISIONS YOU MAKE

The common function of every manager, department head, supervisor, or employee is that all of them have to make decisions. Some will be mere Band-Aids until the problem can be passed along to someone else. Others will involve the input of colleagues and some will be yours alone. And it could be you will be by yourself with your judgment up for scrutiny. Frequently, there will be no right decision, only the one you make. "A judgment call occurs when a decision maker must make a tough choice between two or more options based upon ambiguous information and conflicting goals" (Mowen 1993, 9).

Nothing is worse than making the wrong decision, but it should be expected that with the amount of decisions required in the average day of a manager, some of them will be incorrect. Perhaps the little ones will slide by. The others may have a price to pay. Someone has to be the scapegoat. "[W]hen blame is allocated, it is [to] those who are or become politically vulnerable or expendable, who become 'patsies,' who get 'set up' or 'hung out to dry' and become blamable" (Jackall 1988, 85). This leads most people to look for ways to protect themselves. Even so, MacDonald is not sure that is possible. "Those hard decisions involve taking risks as long as you know you are making the right decision, or what you think is the right decision." At times all you can do is trust in yourself.

When a decision falls in the category of a judgment call, getting as much information from as many different people as possible is a first step. Some will not want to commit themselves while others will take the off-the-record approach. "High-stakes decisions involve trade-offs between important goals, and frequently no absolutely best choice exists. You can call in the most outstanding experts available and they will disagree on what to do" (Mowen 1993, 15). When a manager finally decides on a course of action, it can be frustrating to sense the tentativeness of staff who are not sure you will be their manager tomorrow.

Since judgment calls can rarely be avoided, decision makers tend to look for ways to protect their position.

> When a manager gets into a difficult situation that demands a hard decision, even when he knows that others are fully aware of his decision, he must actively involve them in his problems if he is to hope for their support later. Committees thus reduce the plausibility of "deniability" although, of course, when things go wrong, instant amnesia always seems to become a widespread malady (Jackall 1988, 80).

Other ways that managers protect their position when a decision is questioned is to consult with other managers, especially those who have faced similar circumstances. If you choose the same action that someone else used, it is defensible to say that "so-and-so did it that way and it worked fine, so it seemed the reasonable thing to do." Ultimately, it is always good to put your actions and reasons in writing. It clarifies what you did and why. Should anyone dispute the facts of a situation, a memo or note to the file documents your understanding of the situation at that moment in time. Jackall (1988, 89) points out:

> CYA [cover-your-ass] memos proliferate during a crisis, as managers who sense jeopardy try to "get their views on the record" or stake out defensible ground against opposition or construct plausible alibis. In fact, it is said that one can gauge the seriousness of an issue or the importance of a decision and its potential dangers by the amount of paper it generates.

Managers must also deal with decisions made at higher supervisory levels and, at times, be the implementer. Since the manager is the on-site representative, the decision then becomes associated with you and is as good as yours. If the policy is a disaster, someone gets the blame once everything blows up, and it might not be those who formulated the policy to begin with. Spence (1995, 280) points out that higher management will "quickly lodge responsibility at the door of some defenseless underling who will find himself out on the street without a recommendation."

MORALS, ETHICS, AND A GOOD NIGHT'S SLEEP

Whether making judgment calls or dealing with the fallout from the decisions of others, if we are going to sleep peacefully or wake up every ten minutes in a fit of rage depends on how acceptable our actions are to ourselves. Reconciling a job and one's private life seems easier when we separate our personal beliefs from what I will call workplace beliefs.

> In the welter of practical affairs in the corporate world, morality does not emerge from some set of internally held convictions or principles, but rather from ongoing albeit changing relationships with some person, some coterie, some social network, some clique that matters to a person. Since these relationships are always multiple, contingent, and in flux, managerial moralities are always situational, always relative (Jackall 1988, 101).

The conflict of workplace activities and our own values is often weighed on an uneven scale when doing what we personally believe is right can lead to being disciplined or fired. The choices made to deal with these possibilities are changing the organization, accepting the reality and living with it, or battling the circumstances. Changing the direction of a company or the mind of an individual requires the agreement of both or all parties involved. In a showdown or covert situation, trust is not a likely element. A customer who refuses to get out of his seat and return to the box office possibly feels certain you are planning to move him to a less desirable location. An employee who continually tells customers that the sound is always this bad and lots of people complain might be secretly overjoyed by this small exercise of power that will take a few hours out of a manager's day to deal with customers' complaints. A company manager who's had a bad experience with the house manager at the previous theater might arrive at yours with a cynical attitude. Jackall (1988, 204) notes that many managers "take their world as they find it and try to make that world work according to its own institutional logic."

> They pursue their own careers and good fortune as best they can within the rules of their world. As it happens, given their pivotal institutional role in our epoch, they help create and re-create, as one unintended consequence of their personal striving, a society where morality becomes indistinguishable from the quest for one's own survival and advantage.

These thoughts are not put forth as a judgment of workplace beliefs, but rather are meant to be a discussion of their reality.

Sometimes a refusal to recognize facts of the workplace hinders an employee's adjustment to a job. As one of my GMs was fond of saying, "this company is not a democracy." Often employees will assert their views on how the theater should be run, and when their ideas are not implemented they embark on a campaign of bitterness, making everyone who does not agree with them miserable. Challenging management's right to manage can be like running into a brick wall. While it can lead to grievances and lawsuits, the more dangerous results are sabotage and revenge. Even small retaliations can take up more time in a week than you would like to allot. "Revenge is most often regarded as an affair of the heart, but the workplace has become a primary site for the need to get even because of the growing emotional investment we have in identifying ourselves by and through our work" (Barreca 1995, 110).

Organizational structures involve power constructs that have probably been in place long before you were hired. Often power itself is not necessarily a problem; rather, it is how people use it. Abuse of power is mostly blamed on management, but other organizational players can be equally at fault. Stars throw temper tantrums, customers write letters of complaint about you, employees threaten grievances and lawsuits if they dislike the way you manage. These are just as much an expression of power misuse as anything that management might do.

Once we understand how power is misused by those in power and why, their power no longer intimidates us. We see it, shrug our shoulders and press on. We do not lend it reverence. We are not afraid of it. We do not worship it. For who would worship a squawking child, a screaming, aching, lonely man, a frightened judge, a stupid person with power (Spence 1995, 42)?

Though proclaiming he is not proud of the trait, talk show host Montel Williams (1996, 109) admits "[I]f you burn me, I'll burn you back, and I'll make sure it takes you twice as long to heal." Revenge is often seen as a method of the powerless. Not many people acknowledge having thoughts of revenge, much less actually following through on an action. Revenge is considered negative, ugly, bad karma, something to avoid, and yet, "Fantasies of revenge at the office easily equal fantasies about affairs at the office: Neither is a good idea, but they remain difficult to avoid when you're cooped up in close quarters with a wide range of personality types, energy levels, and standards of performance. In a world seasoned by ambition and flavored with complex interpersonal relationships, revenge is a dish difficult to refuse" (Barreca 1995, 106–107).

It could also be said that there may be levels of revenge that are acceptable, especially if one has unjustly suffered at the hands of another. "A simple sense of dignity and self-esteem are what most workplace revengers are trying to regain" (Barreca 1995, 119). There are some people who learn only when the point has been made to them in the form of payback. One West Coast manager says:

Yes, I got my revenge. Long and slow revenge. Afterwards I felt empty, a bit foolish, and that just maybe the person the revenge was directed against was a better person than me [sic] because they had allowed me to get my revenge and did nothing back to me. . . . Generally, I feel revenge is best if it can never be traced back, but also, give someone enough rope, and if they are truly bad, they will hang themselves. And then, I laugh.

So assume the organization resists small changes as well as major ones; revenge may or may not have brought some measure of personal satisfaction, and the work situation remains the same. There is still one other path, one more change that can be made. You can change yourself. Recognize that you can walk away from the situation. Put up a barrier against the stream of negativity directed at you and know deep within yourself that you need not judge yourself by another's standards.

So, I offer you, as a final alternative, what I believe is the best choice. Change yourself. Choose the kind of person you want to be and by doing that, perhaps you will accomplish the ultimate revenge of success. As Spence (1995, 283) points out, "One also wins by not expecting a pat on the back from the handless bureaucracy, but by patting oneself on the back for having satisfied one's self."

Chapter 14

Management and Imagination

As a child I had a nightmare of wandering alone in my house. The back-door squeaks open to a view of the forest. Outside a dark and ominous mountain begins to shake. The wind roars. Then the mountaintop spurts volcanic-like blood and everyone in the world, except me, is burning in its acidic vapors. I am safe as long as I stay in my house where I can do nothing to save the world. The guilt of my inaction fills me because I am afraid of stepping outside and dying. There were also nightmares about vampires, werewolves, and assorted ghosts, usually of dead little girls haunting the woods behind my house. There was no obvious psychological reason for my nightmares. My brothers did not have them. I lived in a fairly normal and happy household. The dreams seemed to be solely a product of my personality.

My parents said I had an overactive imagination and limited my viewing of horror movies and the monster magazines that my cousins devoured every weekend. Even with this parental guidance, my nightmares never stopped. They continue to this day and I have recently turned forty-five. What has changed is my fear of them. When I have a nightmare now, I awake excited, trying to remember every detail of it, sometimes saving the memories in a tape recorder kept by my bed. Some of my nightmares have worked their way into my fiction writing. In the transition from child to adult, I found a constructive use for an overactive imagination and conveniently, one that pays—fiction writing. My nightmares have become imagination I can use.

Making use of imagination can be a foreign idea in the business arena, although it has been fully explored in the theoretical world. Everyone from employment gurus to psychologists has taken their stab at incorporating what many see as the "magical" into very structured environments. Each expert usually creates key words to describe his version of working creatively—reengineering, total quality management, empowerment, the fifth discipline, to name a few.

One well-known writer is Gareth Morgan (1986), who uses metaphor to draw the concept of "imaginization" in his book *Images of Organization*. Morgan visualizes the organization as a machine, an organism, a brain, a culture, a political system, a psychic prison, an instrument of domination, and as a medium that undergoes flux and transformation. Within each of these images he demonstrates that companies are many different things, not just a monolith whose structure is unmovable. In terms of imagination, the metaphors differ in how the organization operates. For instance, the brain organization is information-oriented. Its managers make decisions through very formal methods, such as procedures and rules, and try to avoid uncertainty. As a psychic prison, an organization can become a victim of itself whether through groupthink or unconscious neurosis. This is to demonstrate that the workplace functions under the influence of more than one metaphor.

In *Managing with Power*, Jeffrey Pfeffer (1992) looks at the workplace as if it were a chessboard. One person's loss is another's win. Building power bases and cultivating influence is necessary for survival within an ever-changing work environment. Above all, he suggests that unless you use power, you will likely stagnate not only in your organization, but also in your career. In his world, power is not a dirty word. Peter M. Senge's (1990) *The Fifth Discipline* introduces the learning organization. This workplace exists in the imagination of its workers who bring it to reality; it has the feel of "the church is not the building." A shared vision and teamwork are at its foundation while keeping focused on personal mastery. Organizational learning relates to imagination through individuals exerting the effort to overcome ineffective and limiting mental states and replacing them with a new worldview that enhances generative learning.

The Empowered Manager by Peter Block (1991) puts forth the idea of breaking the paternal dependency of a patriarchal organization and empowering employees to become their own bosses within the workplace. This entrepreneurial spirit is meant to promote enlightened self-interest, which, in the long run, also serves the organization: a kind of "what is good for you is good for the workplace" mentality. Tom Peters has explored a variety of business theories, most of which revolve around shaking up the humdrum workplace. His book *The Tom Peters Seminar: Crazy Times Call for Crazy Organizations* suggests that employees should think like independent contractors so that every job is turned into a business. Peters suggests that change and revolution will be or already are the norm in most organizational life. In his view, if this world is crazy, it does not make sense to act sensibly. Therefore, it is better to embrace a particular world on its own terms rather than be swallowed up by it. Organizations are in a state of transition from the Industrial Revolution to the Information Revolution and "imagination is the main source of value in the new economy" (Peters 1994, 12).

All of these authors have addressed the workplace and a person's mark upon it, whether it is bucking the system or encouraging teamwork. The common denominator in many of the theories is the making and influencing of one's own niche within the system. Other writers have looked directly at the individual and examined what makes them creative. Linking creativity with genius is the subject of Gene Landrum's two books on men and women, *Profiles of Genius* and *Profiles of Female Genius*. His earlier study of thirteen men includes media mogul Ted Turner, Federal Express founder Fred Smith, Sony's Akio Morita, Microsoft's Bill Gates, and the Price Club's Solomon Price. Landrum notes that the element of risk is a key factor in the careers of successful entrepreneurs who, in his opinion, have changed the world. He describes three management types: risk-takers, care-takers, and under-takers. The risk-takers are the creators and innovators; the care-takers are the experts, bureaucrats motivated by security; the under-takers have a brain-dead operating style with negative and past-oriented perspectives (Landrum 1993, 28).

The women in his later book include philosopher Ayn Rand, pop diva Madonna, activist and actress Jane Fonda, politicians Margaret Thatcher and Golda Meir, and feminist writer Gloria Steinem. Landrum cites that their lack of formal education, limited opportunities, and gender bias shaped their approach to their goals differently than with the men, who often had strong mentors. "They gained their knowledge through a heuristic, trial-and-error approach to problem resolution earned at the grassroots level of innovation. These women learned by doing. Their knowledge was their power and they tended to know more about their given profession than anyone, including those who had superior educations in the field" (Landrum 1994, 84). However, he finds their core impulses and motivators very similar to male risk-taking in that these women have

> the unique ability to tap their internal resources, their dreams and fantasies, while resisting all external distractions. They never allowed their quantitative minds to get in the way of their qualitative images. Our unconscious can be an evolving, ever improving source of imaginative power. Unfortunately for most people it becomes a fixed resource which is reinforced in its existing state (Landrum 1994, 401).

The average workplace may not have as many opportunities to allow a person to be as entrepreneurial as Landrum's geniuses, so instead many people seek smaller successes. In their individual worlds activities are not so earth shaking, but can be equally creative. At the Curran Theater some highly paid project managers were about to build stairs to level out a disabled seating area. This left the possibility of causing every able-bodied person to trip in the dark on the unseen ascent. A theater carpenter looked at the window behind the area and asked, "Why can't that be made into a door?" After some investigation the door was approved and installed, allowing wheelchair access to the disabled section and eliminating the need for steps around it. Morgan (1986, 343) says that the use of "[i]mages and metaphors are not only interpretive constructs or ways of seeing; they also provide frameworks for action. Their use creates insights that often allow us to act in ways that we may not have thought possible before."

Brewster Ghiselin (1985, 10) says in the introduction of *The Creative Process*: "It is evident that in both art and science the inventor is to some degree incited and guided by a sense of value in the end sought, something very much like an intimation of usefulness." Managers judge the end value in almost every decision they make. Back before the Curran Theater had air-conditioning, the audience sweltered on those rare hot days when a capacity-filled auditorium heated the space even more. The backstage crew came up with the idea that stringing a water hose punched with holes across the fan's intake window cooled the air as the water dripped down. This rather simple but effective measure kept many theater patrons from demanding refunds, as they had during previous performances.

Confronting a situation that demands the active use of imagination is like setting up a cauldron where all the ingredients mix to become a different product, just as carrots, celery, meat, and potatoes are separate foods, but when cooked together become stew. Ghiselin continues:

> A great deal of the work necessary to equip and activate the mind for the spontaneous part of invention must be done consciously and with an effort of will. Mastering accumulated knowledge, gathering new facts, observing, exploring, experimenting, developing technique and skill, sensibility, and discrimination, are all more or less conscious and voluntary activities. The sheer labor of preparing technically for creative work, consciously acquiring the requisite knowledge of a medium and skill in its use, is extensive and arduous enough to repel many from achievement (Ghiselin 1985, 18).

This process can also be imbued with a dose of what some call magic— a thought that occurs to us and we are unsure where it came from, a dream that gives the right answer, a passage of poetry that inspires an unrelated thought. Some psychologists have referred to this as the collective unconscious. Others have called it inspiration or imagination. It seems to be the broth that cooks the vegetables and allows it to become stew. While cooking may be a simplistic metaphor for an alchemical process of bringing the unknown into the known, what is consistent between the two images and not within the context of magical thinking is that it happens. A person is in the position of being lost, not knowing what to do. Their work is in danger of amounting to nothing and then, the answer comes. If some part of this process is a gift, then that part is the unconscious working of imagination that has taken our labor and found the answer we could not yet articulate. This step seems to require removing logic from the process. We, or our minds, become a receptacle, much like a cooking pot.

One example of how a person prepares for creativity is related by mathematician Henri Poincaré, who acknowledges intention in his efforts. "To create consists precisely in not making useless combinations and in making those which are useful and which are only a small minority. Invention is discernment, choice. . . . Among chosen combinations the most fertile will often be those formed of elements drawn from domains which are far apart" (Poincaré 1985, 24–25).

What connects distant concepts and allows them to transform seems to be making the conditions or ourselves ready for the information. In that sense we are like an empty vessel filled with the necessary cooking ingredients and which must now wait for them to mix. While working on Fuchsian functions and being fairly certain that they did not exist, Poincaré would go through a daily routine:

> I seated myself at my work table, stayed an hour or two, tried a great number of combinations and reached no results. One evening, contrary to my custom, I drank black coffee and could not sleep. Ideas rose in crowds; I felt them collide until pairs interlocked, so to speak, making a stable combination. By the next morning I had established the existence of a class of Fuchsian functions (Poincaré 1985, 25).

Another time he used distraction as a means to encourage creativity:

> I turned my attention to the study of some arithmetical questions apparently without much success and without a suspicion of any connection with my preceding researches. Disgusted with my failure, I went to spend a few days at the seaside, and thought of something else. One morning, walking on the bluff, the idea came to me, with just the same characteristics of brevity, suddenness and immediate certainty, that the arithmetic transformations of indeterminate ternary quadratic forms were identical with those of non-Euclidean geometry (Poincaré 1985, 26).

What makes a person follow the footsteps of others or blaze their own path might have to do with environmental factors as much as personality. Warren Bennis (1994, 2) makes a distinction between what he calls the once-born and the twice-born. We are all born once, but, "[t]wice-borns generally suffer as they grow up; they feel different, even isolated. Unsatisfied with life as it is, they write new lives for themselves." Self-invention plays a part in managerial imagination. When viewing how a person has acted creatively, it often shows that their accomplishment has as much to do with themselves as the end result. Poincaré's life was about math, the theater carpenter knew there would be lawsuits from people tripping on the stairs. Bennis says he recognized his own uniqueness when, as a child, he impressed his teacher and friends with a presentation on shoe polish during a school function when other kids' hobbies were likely to outshine any of his own interests. From that small success he began to develop "a growing sense of the power of imagination, which may be the only real power children have" (Bennis 1994, 2–6). The danger Bennis cites is that too much success can lead to arrogance.

> Anyone in authority . . . is to some extent the hostage of how others perceive him or her. The perceptions of other people can be a prison. . . . People impute motives to their leaders, love or hate them, seek them out or avoid them, and idolize or demonize them independently of what the leaders do or are. Ironically, at the very time I had the most power, I felt the greatest sense of powerlessness (Bennis 1994, 33).

A combination of self-invention and following footsteps allows knowledge to build upon knowledge. At one time in our history we used to walk as a means of travel, then someone had the idea of getting up on a horse. Then, another person decided to put a saddle on the horse, then someone hitched a wagon to the horse, realizing it could pull a load, then a steam engine was invented and the train became our mode of travel, then a car, then an airplane, and now, in science fiction movies we see warp drive and imagine the day when the words "Beam me up, Scottie" are more than TV trivia.

How we marry the two, genius/imagination and the workplace, is sometimes a risk in itself. An owner who makes risk-taking a part of the job description and gives his employees a safety net to grow, may produce either loyalty or sloth, depending on the ambition of the individual. The employee who labors under tyrants and succeeds despite adversity may patent a discovery, or lose to a legal system when the employers claim the invention as their own. Sadly, how many creators do not survive corporate structure or have the strength to forge their own iron is not known. It is easy to imagine small lives of despair that end with only an untended tombstone and thoughts of what might have been. This waking nightmare keeps me aimed at worthy goals no matter what I have against me. In *Profiles of Female Genius*, Landrum (1994, 394–95) expresses the belief that:

> [C]reative geniuses are bred not born and that the Mozarts of the world are an aberration not the rule for any great creative endeavor. The creative and

entrepreneurial women . . . [in his study] received their visionary behavior characteristics not from some genetic luck of the draw but from their own experiences in coping with a dynamic changing world. These critical traits are: self-confidence, comfort with ambiguity and risk-taking, a renegade behavior, 'Type A' work ethic, intuitive vision, heuristic learning skills, and an obsessive will. Experiential influences account for these traits. Most are firstborns, the father is a strong role model and is usually self-employed, there is a permissive family environment, often a crisis in early childhood, and all were intelligent with IQs ranging between 120 and 140.

Just as the combination of a variety of food ingredients needs the application of heat in order to transform in to stew, individual and organizational creativity are not mutually exclusive. On an individual basis, factors that influence creativity and imagination are a combination of the right physical conditions and a motivated individual. Organizational creativity and imagination are shaped by a secure environment where the individual can flourish and be transformed while carrying out daily work. The two go hand in hand.

Whether owner or employee, genius or a carpenter with a good idea, the workplace is like a church that is nothing without its people. It is not the workplace that changes, but the people. Those who choose to do so or those who have natural gifts learn to use their imagination within their jobs. They overcome their fear of nightmares. They make necessity an opportunity for solving problems in the same way that geniuses do. They claim their own managerial imagination, which is a combination of following footsteps and awakening their own inner knowledge. We can call this inner knowledge many things: intuition, collective unconscious, a knowing certainty that might border on arrogance. It is perhaps a little bit of all of these. It is, most of all, a gift whose combinations can be stew or poison. Only when aimed at worthy goals do we give it a pleasing name: managerial imagination.

Chapter 15

Managerial Imagination

Creativity and imagination are often considered the province of those on stage. The people who work in other areas are looked upon as glorified accountants, clerical workers, or craftsmen. From the outside, the glamour of performing overshadows other jobs. And yet, when a thousand people are milling around the lobby at showtime and further delay will cost overtime, everyone is looking at the manager to figure out something—anything! At various times each department will face challenges requiring an imaginative solution. The process of discovering these resolutions can be as creative as any characterization on stage. I call this ability managerial imagination.

As discussed in the last chapter, many experts have taken a stab at defining the theory of working creatively, calling it by different names: empowerment, total quality management, twenty-first-century thinking, imaginization, reengineering, managing with power, swimming with sharks, and searching for excellence. All of these concepts contain useful information, and yet exact definitions can be vaporous when applied to real-life situations. Even as I struggled to understand management theory, the explanations often seemed either too laced with unrealistic circumstances or the implementation was too dependent on the goodwill of other people. It seemed sensible to read the how-to and management theory books, take what was useful, and discard the rest. This resulted in a patchwork of serviceable strategies that work some of the time, but not in every circumstance.

I knew examples of managerial imagination when I saw them, but did not truly know what it was, how to explain it to someone else, or how one could learn it. Managerial imagination often seemed as nebulous as a fairy godmother waving a magic wand. The times I had experienced it were as instantaneous as an "ah-ha," a realization that something incredible had been accomplished in the intensity of the moment, or even an "of course, how could I have been so stupid." Manager Bob MacDonald is also unsure of what it is or if it is learnable. "It becomes part of you—maybe that's learning. I don't like the word but it is like breeding—good breeding. Imagination is taking that chance with common sense." A West Coast manager defines managerial imagination as

> the ability to dream wide awake in order to find a solution to a problem which may not be readily apparent. I believe some people are born with this ability, but it can be learned by people who are willing to give it a chance. It can be learned by imagining what you'd do in difficult situations and then practicing on the job. As managers get more experience using skills in this area, they will become better at it. This ability is underrated and overlooked and should be part of the training of any manager, along with the more mundane aspects of learning to manage a theatre.

Some of what I can relate about managerial imagination are examples of how people demonstrated it and references to useful literature, but neither I, nor any other management expert, can define it precisely or chain it to a definitive management theory. And perhaps that is rightly so, for its strength is in its flexibility. Managerial imagination is as elusive as a holy grail, ever-changing to become what it needs to be.

The use of on-the-job imagination can be found in every kind of profession. FBI profiler John Douglas recounts how he gets into the minds of serial killers (Douglas and Olshaker 1995, 151).

> What I try to do with a case is to take in all the evidence I have to work with—the case reports, the crime-scene photos and descriptions, the victim statements or autopsy protocols—and then put myself mentally and emotionally in the head of the offender. I try to think as he does. Exactly how this happens, I'm not sure. . . . If there is a psychic component to this, I won't run away from it, though I regard it more in the realm of creative thinking.

Notice that imagination is only one slice of what this man is using. He does not neglect his homework, the facts of the case. Just as studying evidence is a preliminary step to profiling, gathering information is central to the theater manager's decision-making process.

Knowing what you are talking about and grasping the particulars of what kind of decision is required is just as necessary as thinking creatively. It would be foolish to simply rely on the instrument of imagination. In situations outside your expertise, slowing down the process and forcing those who do understand to walk you through the issue in baby steps will aid you when you have to explain the problem to your supervisor. "Nothing is so complicated that it can't be broken down into a series of simple, easy-to-understand and easy-to-accomplish steps" (Witt 1983, 90). When Bob MacDonald faces unfamiliar situations or problems he recommends the following: "Always back off at first—saying I am not really sure or don't know, but will come back with the answer when I've had a chance to review. I research past experience, if available. I will bite the bullet and solve a problem with what I feel is the best resolution if necessary." Manager Robert Lazzara recommends first determining how much time can be spent to examine the issue. "If there is time, gather opinions from knowledgeable staff, then weigh pros and cons. Never forget the 'gut' feelings—those are almost always the right ones. If there is no time, zero in on the gut feelings, quickly review consequences of any decision, and then don't delay. Hope for the best, but be prepared for the worst."

In business, viewpoints represent a variety of agendas. Guarding against the ill will of others is as necessary as recognizing naiveté or stupidity. "With competition so keen, there is little room for mistakes—and no room at all for misinformation" (Witt 1983, 79). Witt (1983, 79) describes how the president of a tool manufacturing company defends himself against misinformation. He watches out for "'facts' from people who have a personal stake in the matter; observations of people who have little training or experience in that particular field; hastily prepared data that may have typographical and numerical errors; superficial reports that don't go thoroughly into the subject; preconceived notions that were never right in the first place."

Vigilance can be especially important when dealing with people who are not as versed in a job as you, or those in need of a scapegoat. The circling of wagons can be as prevalent with those above you as with staff personnel, as one theater manager found out when ADA issues began to rise at their theater. Built in the 1920s, the building was not ADA compliant for many years, prompting letters from disabled people and activist organizations.

When one of the letters came to the attention of certain higher-ups, a flurry of phone calls and memos ensued—the focus being why [there was] no procedure for disabled patrons. In reality, the front-of-house staff and I had been aiding disabled patrons with the theater's lack of access long before the ADA became law. When this was explained, I was sent correspondence from a representative of the owner, who had concluded that perhaps theater management should be more concerned with and have a more helpful attitude toward disabled patrons. It was classic shift the blame for the inadequacies of the building onto the staff. It not only insulted the staff, who were on the receiving end of a disabled person's hostility, but showed management's lack of knowledge as they tried to move the focus of the problem out of their court. Being sure of what instructions had been given to staff for dealing with customers in these instances prevented me and theater personnel from being blamed for conditions which were beyond our control, and had not been addressed—namely ADA compliance.

Becoming bogged down in policy, procedure, or by a this-is-the-way-we-do-it attitude limits the options in solving problems. When I worked as an assistant manager at the Golden Gate Theater, the house carpenter posted a large sign over his office door for every traveling crew to see: "We don't give a shit how they do it in New York." Clinging to what worked last time provides a kind of security that is not reliable. A response may work twenty times, but if we trust completely in the implementation, we lose sight of the overall effect and end up with another procedure.

> What works for us intellectually speaking, in one time and circumstance may not work for anyone else or at another time. In today's world, certainly in tomorrow's, every situation calls for completely novel solutions. Unlike uniform, assembly-line thinking, precisely measured formulas and cookie-cutter outcomes, creative adaptive minds seek one-of-a-kind answers and believe, "If I can't solve this problem one way, I'll try another" (Sinetar 1991, 12–13).

Lazzara says some key factors for stimulating creative solutions are "a willingness to try something, anything that might work; the time and the energy to see it through, but most importantly, an open mind."

If we can think outside the lines, then we can place ourselves ahead of problems rather than constantly chasing behind them with a mop and bucket. This "21st-century thinking," as Sinetar calls it, is centered yet flexible, and reasoning must occur outside the obvious. It requires actions that lend themselves to the situation rather than trying to squeeze circumstances into a predesigned equation with a known answer.

> [T]he creative adaptive mind *learns* to use itself in whatever way works best and develops its own wholesome expansion. . . . [I]t seems sufficient to say that it is not so important what models we design as it is that we experiment with the progression, play at "figuring out." It's precisely this tinkering, this noodling about with one idea or goal, that stretches thinking skill, helps us become objective observers of our minds, teaches us to hear our unique thought-language. Remember: "Figuring out" is a skill (Sinetar 1991, 77).

Our *figuring* begins in knowledge that is cushioned by experience or information we have learned from other sources. "Creative ideas, then, typically emerge from a skillful blending of old and new information." What we know forms a basis from which to build toward a solution. "Deploying old knowledge in the service of new ideas . . . can bring forth expedient solutions, set the stage for further developments, and prevents us from becoming hopelessly mired in frivolous pursuits." It is important to note that old ideas and information can, at times, impede progress. One example from the transportation industry states when the first train cars were built, the only previous model was the stagecoach where the driver rode on the outside of the cabin. This proved to be obviously unfeasible for an engineer to ride on top of the train (Ward, Finke, and Smith 1995; 30–31).

One West Coast manager believes in trying to find the way out of problems.

> A man and woman were disturbed by latecomers and began causing a scene both in the house and the lobby. They were arguing furiously with the head usher. Someone came to get me and I got refund money from the box office—I wanted them out of the theatre. I interrupted their screaming with these words: "You must be the people who are disrupting the performance. The stage manager just called me about you." This shut them up long enough to draw them outside so I could refund them. Once outside, they could vent without disrupting the show. They both began screaming at me at once. They even blamed me for their bad day at the office and their terrible meal before the show. I shouted "Stop! I will not let you gang up on me. I will discuss this in an adult manner with just one of you." I pointed at the man, as he seemed the calmer of the two, and told the woman to go away. When she did, I drew the man aside, apologized, and asked him what he wanted. Good seats to another performance was the reply. I reopened the box office and sold the man two good seats on his choice of dates. The tickets cost more, but I paid the difference for him out of my pocket. By the time he left, he was eating out of my hand.

Circumstances may dictate what is possible, and some facts must be dealt with for what they are—unfair but still realistic. Jose Vega, who retired as a general manager for Broadway shows, told me about the time he managed a musical group in the 1940s which had an African American pianist. During those days train travel was common and when the group went to dinner they were informed that a black man could not enter the dining car. There are many decisions Mr. Vega could have made. He might have refused to allow his troupe to eat in the dining car. Or, he could let the white members eat in the dining car and have food brought back to the pianist. Mr. Vega chose neither of these easy answers. Being showmen of a bygone era, the troupe accompanied their colleague back to their compartment and fashioned part of a sheet into a turban around the pianist's head. They returned to the dining car, and when asked about the race of the pianist, explained that he was from India. Recognizing that he was not in the position to fight the battles that would soon be fought in 1960s, Mr. Vega encountered no further questions as his troupe traveled and ate well in the South during the 1940s.

To express some of what I have discussed in terms of a metaphor may be helpful. Therefore, a three-tiered pyramid would have its base built of logic: the work we have done, the facts we know, the past experiences that we have had, and the realities of what we encounter.

The next level might be identified as attempts at problem solving. "[T]he natural tendency in problem solving is to pick the first solution that comes to mind and run with it. The disadvantage of this approach is that you may run either off a cliff or into a worse problem than you started with" (Adams 1986, ix). This pyramid level is naturally smaller, because we try out different tactics to see what works and what fails. We try what has worked in the past, discard ineffective strategies, and limit the use of those that increase the problem. Often a great deal of fear accompanies this part of the process. If what we are doing does not work, we may still be on the line for the implementation of a solution. This limits the amount of risk we are willing to take if we are afraid of getting into trouble.

At this point the danger is in limiting our thinking to the nuts-and-bolts of what has broken down. We think of machines as metal contraptions, relationships as job descriptions, buildings as piles of brick. We respond to their breakdown by reading the operations manual because that is what is safe to do. "What blocks a creative solution to a problem is often an overly narrow and single-minded concentration from a single frame of reference. The person who can combine frames of reference and draw connections between ostensibly unrelated points of view is likely to be the one who makes the creative breakthrough" (Shekerjian 1991, 41).

Actor Hal Holbrook recounts how the stage turntables made so much noise as they revolved prior to the Philadelphia opening of *I Never Sang for My Father* that the cast could not hear each other. A stage manager had an unusual suggestion, which the prop man successfully implemented. The most surprised person involved was the drug store pharmacist when the prop man asked him for five gallons of vaginal jelly ("Thanks" 1993, 59).

Some key factors are evident: noticing and curiosity. Both lead to the question, "What would happen if. . . ?" Denise Shekerjian (1991, 153–54) cites these two qualities as common in recipients of the MacArthur Foundation Fellowship, sometimes referred to as the genius award. She points out that these two traits "share the same bloodlines because one is usually shadowing the other. Curiosity leads, noticing follows. Or perhaps it's the other way around, noticing coming first, spotting some wrinkle and insisting on a closer look; curiosity wondering how the wrinkle affects half a dozen other things. In time, a connection is made and a revelation discovered."

The *what if* part of the equation is where our imagination kicks in and our metaphorical pyramid begins to peak. Dreaming about a snake swallowing its own tail led chemist Friedrich August Kekule to the realization that the benzene molecule had a circular shape. Imagining himself riding a moonbeam led Einstein to the theory of relativity. Clearly these are also cases of complex problem solving, not just flights of fancy: but how easily they might have been discarded by a lesser mind!

> [T]wo conflicting positions have dominated theories of problem solving. One position has it that problems are solved incrementally, by applying bits of knowledge piece by piece until all of the components together produce a solution. The other position focuses on the phenomenon of insight, which is a sudden and unexpected realization of a solution to a problem (Ward, Finke, and Smith 1995, 90).

This dynamic becomes a jigsaw puzzle, pieces being tried and discarded until a picture begins to emerge. The work goes faster once that image is formed. "Creativity requires the manipulation and recombination of experience. An imagination that cannot manipulate experience is limiting to the conceptualizer" (Adams 1986, 50). It is an individual who must do this work as he sits atop the pyramid, forming the peak from his own way of thinking, his own way of doing, and his imagination. These individuals come to answers by simply being who they are: creative people.

> The creative person thinks in nonsterotypical, unconventional ways, insightfully spotting his best answers and options, breaking out of intellectual and emotional ruts. . . . [T]he special openness or receptivity of 21st-century thinking results in extremely sensitive antennae; the individual is psychically open, will use anything as a tool to better understand problems or the world at large. To develop this receptivity one must relinquish old thought-modes (Sinetar 1991, 107).

In his book *Conceptual Blockbusting*, James L. Adams (1986, 10) points out that "for most of us, creativity is more of a dull glow than a divine spark. And the more fanning it receives, the brighter it will burn." Often it is our circumstances that dictate whether creativity can flourish. It is hard to be creative when you are hungry, when you are worried about paying the rent, when a customer or employer is screaming at you, when you are afraid your activities will get you fired. The safe action is to do nothing.

> The distressing truth is that few people expect themselves to be truly resourceful—either at work or in their personal lives. Americans have been among the most innovative people in the world, but recently we seem to have lost our edge. Only those rare independent, self-trusting souls whose minds shy away from mass-produced answers or robotic responses still contribute to our national heritage of resourcefulness (Sinetar 1991, 76).

Being a creative person is often dependent on having the courage to take action. *Doing it* is different for everybody. Some people break projects down into parts and work to completion. Others spin the whole theater into a whirl of activity like dervishes worshipping a personal god. Creativity occurs because of the kind of people we are as much as the necessity of the moment. One of our ancestors discovered that striking two pieces of slate together caused sparks which made fire. People who cannot hear learn to make letters with their fingers. A New York manager related to me his frustration at there being no heat in his theater and offering a complaining couple the pint of bourbon he kept in a closet. The idea worked.

The Managerial Imagination Pyramid might look like figure 15.1:

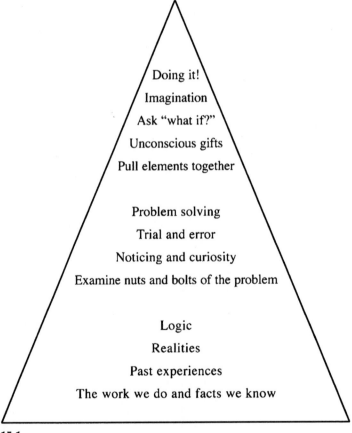

Doing it!

Imagination

Ask "what if?"

Unconscious gifts

Pull elements together

Problem solving

Trial and error

Noticing and curiosity

Examine nuts and bolts of the problem

Logic

Realities

Past experiences

The work we do and facts we know

Figure 15.1.

Shekerjian (1991, 141–42) says of the MacArthur recipients:

What carries creative people through from the conception to the completion of a project is drive and concentration born from a sense of purpose. Purpose is what dictates the entire range of the enterprise. Through intention, goals are shaped and ideas generated to fulfill them. Through relentlessness the cultivation of skills and the perfection of technique. Through motive come the decisions as to which projects to pursue and in what order. Through resolve, resources are marshaled and the necessary strength mustered to overcome obstacles rather than to be overcome by them. Through tenacity, friends and collaborators are selected. And through will comes the wisdom to know when to part paths with influences one has outgrown.

All creative people need not be geniuses. I doubt that many of the MacArthur fellows consider themselves so; they simply are doing what they do. This is the next important consideration for theater managers, for much of what you do can be undone. One West Coast manager recalls the time when he tried to get the staffs of three different theaters to work together. "I underestimated their long held and deeply felt hostility—it never worked. They were bent on destroying any good will. They only wanted to hate each other. I suppose that is why they never moved beyond their positions. They were firmly in their ruts."

The consideration then becomes, Why do it? Bob MacDonald answers this question in his recollection of working at New Mexico Repertory:

I tried to make substantial changes in programming. It won over a whole new audience. Some of those people were just plain afraid of that building that housed the New Mexico Repertory. Once I got them in there, and they saw that it was about them—and for them—the change was thrilling. It actually brought tears to my eyes. The arts are truly terrific—they are about "us"—what we were and what we can be.

The political nature of the workplace can squelch all the good we have done. Sometimes it is necessary to know when to draw the line and withhold our talent, knowledge, and creativity. At other times we play along to get along, judge when to keep our mouth shut, when to quit, when to sue, when to adjust to the things we cannot change. We act as we do because in some sense there is a deep obsession that does not allow us to walk away. While it is doubtful a theater manager will ever be awarded a MacArthur fellowship, we have tenacity in common with the recipients.

The MacArthur Fellows are not quitters. Even in the face of insult. Or when confronted with defeat. Or when up against humiliation, despondency, hostility, boredom, or indifference. They find a way to make adjustments, to keep at it, to stay buoyant, to believe in themselves. There is a sense of the carpenter about them, of making things work and of turning mistakes to good account. There is a smoothness of attitude and a sense of endurance, and of continuity. Smiling at each fresh indignity, they find in themselves the seeds for survival and for leadership (Shekerjian 1991, 196).

Being realistic about what your job is and then recognizing under what conditions you must work is essential. Within those perimeters, you will find ways to be creative and make your job work for you. One West Coast manager points out, "My own well-being is important to keeping an open, creative mind. If I am run down or beaten down emotionally, then the ideas don't flow." I have outlined only some of the elements of managerial imagination. There are others not yet discovered. What works for one generation of managers is outdated for another.

The new generation must forge a path and find their strategies. Managerial imagination is a constant for everybody all the time. There were certain problems I ran into that I had no idea what to do about. Nothing, as it turned out, was often effective. With other situations the steps of the pyramid may prove helpful:

- Gather the facts logically, compare against past experiences and acknowledge the realities of the workplace.
- Problem solve by thinking outside the frame of reference.
- Wake up curiosity and ask "what if?"

Then, come to the best decision that you can.

Earlier in this chapter, I made the suggestion to read books about management theory, learn what works for you, and discard the rest. My advice is the same for this chapter and this book. Read it, learn from it, decide what works for you, and discard the rest.

Chapter 16

Creating and Thinking

The greatest thinkers of the twentieth century could be counted on one hand: Einstein, Freud, Tesla, perhaps Yeats. In human history, we might add Aristotle, da Vinci, Mozart, and perhaps others depending on one's definition of *genius*. Another perspective is that some thinkers simply have better PR than lesser-known or unknown counterparts. There is hardly any among us who does not wish for equivalent brainpower. Popular techniques for increasing intelligence have ranged from vitamin supplements to meditation routines. In considering management, imagination, and managerial imagination, it is instructive to look at some of the mental processes that comprise creative thinking.

As a scholar of Neuro-Linguistic Programming (NLP), Robert Dilts has written several books on the nature of genius. He believes that great thinkers can be studied and their mental strategies modeled and made available to anyone. These patterns are as useful in problem solving for a manager as they are for a scientist or artist. Dilts (1994, xx) cites NLP techniques as providing

> a way to look past the behavioral content of what people do to the more invisible forces behind those behaviors; to the structures of thought that allowed these geniuses to accomplish what they accomplished. NLP provides a structure and a language to be able to put into a set of chunks or steps the relevant mental processes used by a Leonardo or an Einstein so that those mental processes can be taught to others.

The prospect of being as smart as an Einstein seems an unlikely result of any learned technique. It is important to understand that talent, intelligence, and cognizance vary in every individual. What can be taught and implemented to any level of competence is the manner through which a genius creates. NLP does this by modeling "the process of taking a complex event or series of events and breaking it into small enough chunks that it can be repeated in a manageable way" (Dilts 1994, xxv).

In this chapter we will look at two NLP models, TOTE and SCORE First, consider Dilts's example of a very ancient creation formula:

> "And God said, Let there be. . ."—Conceptualization
> "And God made. . ."—Implementation
> "And God saw that it was good. . ."—Evaluation
> Each cycle leads to a successively more refined and personal expression of ideas. With each cycle the idea takes on more and more of a life of its own—the idea itself is able to "bring forth," "multiply," and sustain other ideas. The ultimate expression reflects the process of the creator so much that it is able to "replenish" all the other creations as well as multiply itself. (Dilts 1994, xvii).

This strategy of conceptualizing, implementing, and evaluating is common among creators. Dilts expands on the subject by rendering a Test-Operate-Test-Exit (TOTE) model. In this model, behavior is goal-oriented. As the individual tries out or "tests" various methods to reach a goal, he uses his senses to judge whether that objective is being achieved; if not, he tries something else until the goal is accomplished. In other words we keep trying until we judge the outcome as good (Dilts 1994, 41–42).

The way a theater manager might use this model is on a busy opening night. Assume the theater has reopened after having been redecorated and with a new bar installed in the main lobby. The immediate problem is that customers going to the bar are blocking those who want to be seated. The goal of the manager is to get the audience seated prior to the show starting. After observing the flow of the crowd, it becomes obvious that the old lobby setup does not work with the new construction.

The manager realigns the stanchions and ropes, easing the nondrinking customers around the bar. This gets the people in question seated quickly and easily. Goal reached. Test-Operate-Test-Exit. Now another factor comes into play. The new lobby setup does not allow for easy entry to the bar. The concessions manager has complained to the general manager (GM) that sales are being lost because of this lack of access.

The manager tries other setups. One backs up the customers into the street, causing more of a people-jam and even placing life at risk when the crowd rounds out in a lane of traffic. Continue testing. Another configuration allows for easy bar access but strands many drinking customers on the opposite side of the theater from where they are seated. Fighting the crowd to get on the right side makes them late for the performance. The manager continues testing.

Finally, the manager thinks outside of the-way-its-always-been-done. The ropes and stanchions are used for crowd control. They have always been used, so when testing out various ways to set up the front-of-house, the manager has used them again. But why? After studying the main lobby, the manager sees no reason for them. If the entire lobby is left open, there is more room for customers going to the bar and also for those who simply want to go to their seats. Tickets do not need to be taken until a person reaches a staircase or decides to enter a door to the main floor.

By getting rid of the ropes and stanchions all together, placing a ticket-taker at each of the two staircases and two others at the door on each side of the bar, the manager has accomplished both goals. There is access to the bar and clearer paths to the auditorium. A third goal is unwittingly accomplished in that the lobby is generally less crowded than when the ropes and stanchions were used to hem in customers into exact areas. Test-Exit.

The continuation of testing is a key element in creating and problem solving even when the impulse has originated from sudden intuition. Arthur Koestler (1989) in his book *The Act of Creation* calls the Eureka act "the sudden shaking together of two previously unconnected matrices." He looks past the initial discovery at the aftermath, from which he concludes, "If all goes well that single, explosive contact will lead to a lasting fusion of two matrices—a new synthesis will emerge, a further advance in mental evolution will have been achieved. On the other hand, the inspiration may have been a mirage; or premature; or not sufficiently impressive to be believed in" (Koestler 1989, 212).

Disciplined thought is therefore necessary to continued testing. A pitfall to the creative process is refusing to acknowledge that one has taken the wrong path or made an error in judgment. Sometimes years of work can be wasted on what seemed like a good idea. "A false inspiration is not an ordinary error committed in the course of a routine operation, such as making a mistake in counting. It is a kind of inspired blunder which presents itself in the guise of an original synthesis, and carries the same subjective conviction as Archimedes's cry did" (Koestler 1989, 212).

In the subject area of creating, we have previously examined both the inspired idea and the use of incremental work that adds linkages to our knowledge. Combined with a dose of imagination the mixture often leads to unexpected conclusions and solutions. Koestler finds the linkages to be a process of adding and subtracting, which bring about an amalgamation of knowledge. He also notes historical examples.

The new synthesis in the mind of the thinker may emerge suddenly, triggered by a single "link"; or gradually, by an accumulation of linkages. On the map of history the "links" are the discoveries of individuals; and here again the process of integration may be sudden, or the result of a series of discoveries by several people. The unification of arithmetic and geometry—analytical geometry—was a one-man show, accomplished by the formidable Descartes. The unification of electricity and magnetism, on the other hand, took a hundred years—from 1820, when Hans Christian Oersted [*sic*] discovered by chance that an electric current flowing through a wire deflected a compass needle which happened to lie on the table, to 1921, when O. W. Richardson explained ferromagnetism in terms of electron-spin; and it needed a whole series of original discoveries by Ampère, Faraday, Maxwell, and others to act as links and bring the crowning synthesis about (Koestler 1989, 230).

If we focus this knowledge on the area of management, Dilts and Bonissone's recommendation of looking at problem areas that also have solution areas is instructive. By expanding into an area rather than limiting the problem to an exact issue, a manager can ameliorate varying mental capacities, differing expectations or other detrimental influences that exist between people.

[I]n the past several decades there has been a big difference between American and Japanese creativity strategies in the development of technology. American technology companies tend to be oriented toward big breakthroughs and visions of new and innovative technologies. The creative style of Japanese technology companies, on the other hand, has been to incrementally refine something to make it better and better. Both are creative, but in different ways (Dilts and Bonissone 1993, 89).

It is essential for a manager to break out of the kind of thinking that continues the problem, whether it be one of the individual or the culture. "The whole goal in creative problem solving is to find a way of thinking that is not the same thinking that is creating the problem. Then, hopefully, this other way of thinking will lead to a solution space, that is at least as broad or broader than the problem space, in which the appropriate alternatives and resources can be found" (Dilts and Bonissone 1993, 188).

Dilts and Bonissone (1993, 97) point to three processes to enhance and manage creative problem solving:

1. Adding: What can one add to what already exists and operates effectively in order to improve it?
2. Transferring: Are there creativity strategy patterns in one context that can be applied to another?
3. Coordination: How can one coordinate one's own style of creativity with the style of another in order for them to be complementary (rather than conflicting)?

The model Dilts and Bonissone use to apply creativity to problem solving is called S.C.O.R.E., which stands for symptoms, causes, outcomes, resources, and effects. They recognize change and transition as the situations most in need of creative problem solving.

> Creativity may be applied to:
> 1. Perceiving change and resistances to change.
> 2. Managing change. Creative problem-solving ability involves defining the "problem space" and identifying potential areas of "solution space" by establishing the relationship between the various S.C.O.R.E. elements (Dilts and Bonissone 1993, 194).

These elements determine the boundaries of the problem area and help name the direction of the solution area. Symptoms are the "most noticeable and conscious aspects of a present problem or problem state." Causes are the "underlying elements responsible for creating and maintaining the symptoms." Outcomes are the "particular goals or desired states that would take the place of the symptoms." Resources are the "underlying elements responsible for removing the causes of the symptoms and for manifesting and maintaining the desired outcomes." Effects are the "longer term results of achieving a particular outcome" (Dilts and Bonissone 1993, 195).

A typical theater problem put through the S.C.O.R.E. model might unfold like this: At show time of a sold-out performance a customer has come to you with tickets for the night before.

- Symptoms: Unhappy customer who is going to miss tonight's performance.
- Cause: Customer did not look at their ticket; the box office ticket-seller did not repeat the show time and date.
- Outcome: Customer wants to see the show or get a refund; producer wants to be paid for the ticket.
- Resources: House manager offers to get customer into another performance, another show, or as a last resort, offers a refund. This may mean taking a loss in order to pay the producer for the ticket.
- Effect: The theater keeps a customer.

Whether problems are as momentous as seeking an outcome that will change the world or as simple as a ticketing mistake, it should not be forgotten that the creator or manager has more to consider than his or her area of influence. In a manager's world, organization policy sometimes limits the options. A creator's world can be restrained by what the public and benefactors are willing to believe. Koestler (1989, 253) sees the history of scientific discovery as one of recurrent cycles.

The various phases in the historic cycle correspond to the characteristic stages of individual discovery: the periods of creative anarchy to the period of incubation; the emergence of the new synthesis to the bisociative act. It may emerge suddenly, sparked off by a single individual discovery; or gradually, as in the history of electro-magnetism, where a series of individual discoveries acted as "links." Each revolutionary historic advance has a constructive and a destructive aspect: the thaw of orthodox doctrines and the resulting fertile chaos correspond to the regressive phase of the individual reculer-pour-mieux-sauter phenomenon. Lastly, the process of verification and elaboration of individual discoveries is reflected on the map of history as the consolidation of the new frontier—followed by the development of a new orthodoxy, a hardening of the collective matrix—until it gets blocked and the cycle starts again.

Outside the scientific community, artists can find similar cycles that obstruct their progress. They develop strategies to live in the world and still create. Dilts (1994, 278–83) notes ten common patterns of creative genius in his study of the mental processes of Aristotle, Walt Disney, Mozart, and Sir Arthur Conan Doyle's fictional character, Sherlock Holmes. These abilities are used as much to create as they are to deal with the world. Walt Disney creates the entertainment empire of his imagination. Mozart creates symphonies. Aristotle evolves a way to think. Sherlock Holmes unraveled mysteries and unveiled murderers.

1. Have a well-developed ability to visualize.
2. Have developed numerous links between the senses.
3. Use multiple perspectives.
4. Highly developed ability for switching between perceptual positions.
5. Ability to move back and forth between different chunk sizes and levels of thinking.
6. Maintain a feedback loop between the abstract and the concrete.
7. Balance of cognitive functions: Dreamer, Realist & Critic.
8. Ask basic questions.
9. Use metaphors and analogies.
10. Have a mission beyond individual identity.

The theater manager overloaded with mundane duties, employee complaints, and higher management expectations might question the worthiness of developing such thought processes. I would remind them that the mental processes of a genius can be most useful at the times of greatest stress. If, in the craziness of the moment, a manager can only implement a portion of a strategy, this is better than repeating old mistakes and be-ing responsible for the same negative outcome. Our lives are about more than a job even if the theater is our life. Most of those working in theater intend to leave it a better place. That better place begins in our imagina-tions. "Imagination is what brings knowledge to life. Imagination and creativity are the driving force behind change, adaptation and evolution" (Dilts and Bonissone 1993, 6).

Dilts (1996, 86) once asked a top business leader how he created the future in the face of uncertainty. The response was, "I continually make successive approximations until I reach a point of 'no return.'" Dilts con-cludes, "This notion of making 'successive approximations' as a way to manifest a vision seems to be the essence of the strategic thinking skills necessary to achieve goals."

This might be another way of saying, do the best you can with the re-sources you have and continue to do it until you reach the goal you seek. Knowing when you have reached that goal can differ for each person. Some will see concrete evidence of their work. Others will hear of the ex-cellent job they have done from bosses and coworkers. Still others will sit down at their desk and feel satisfied with the personal answer, "Yes, this is good. This will do just fine."

Both models are written about in other NLP literature with Mr. Dilts as author and co-author. That I've chosen Mr. Dilts book should not slight the work of other authors who have contributed to this knowledge. If the reader wants further in-formation about NLP, the author recommends any book written by Richard Ban-dler, Judith DeLozier, Todd A. Epstein, and John Grinder.

Chapter 17

Industry Interviews

Wisdom could be called that thing that happens to us as a result of our life journey. Partly an outcome of our hard work, wisdom is often equidistant to experiences born of pain. I have interviewed four wise individuals in this chapter. They have lives in the theater and each struggles in it even as they make their mark upon it. In their words is found not only the key to who they are, but why they have made the decision to make theater part of their life journey. Peter Botto addresses important issues of ethics in this industry. Mitchell Brower explains the day-to-day operations of a major New York theater. Gordon Forbes forecasts the future the manager's union as it goes into the twenty-first century. Edward C. Powell discusses the historical significance of unionism of theatrical workers.

PETER BOTTO

Peter Botto, general manager of Oakland, California's Paramount Theatre from 1972 to 1999, supervised the restoration of the 1931 Art Deco theater which has hosted such artists as Margot Fonteyn, Chet Atkins, Dolly Parton, George Carlin, Jerry Seinfeld, Lily Tomlin, Anita Baker, Harry Belafonte, Natalie Cole, Keith Jarrett, Al Jarreau, Billy Joel, Lyle Lovett, Bonnie Raitt, Bruce Springsteen, and Stevie Wonder. It is also a venue for musicals and plays such as *Ain't Misbehavin'*, *Annie*, *Cats*, *Chicago*, *Evita*, *Hair*, *The Wiz*, Hal Holbrook as *Mark Twain*, and popular attractions like Harry Blackstone, Victor Borge, Ella Fitzgerald, Sarah Vaughn, Ray Charles, Tony Bennett, and Maya Angelou.

TC: How did you start in this industry?

PB: I wanted to be an actor. Tony[1] and I worked in little theater in the San Francisco Bay Area. I wanted to be a dancer. When I got out of high school I went to State College for a semester; I hated school and quit after the semester. I hitchhiked to New York for something to do, planning on coming back in the fall to go back to school. When I was in New York I ran into my high school drama teacher who was the general manager of *The Fantasticks*. He got me a job as house manager and I never went back to school. I ended up working there about a year for $45.00 a week, which was decent money. After a couple of months I realized there was no merchandise or concessions, or anything being sold. There was this hatcheck room with a Dutch door and I went around the corner and bought some sodas and candy bars. I made another $60.00 a week selling that. Why I didn't stay in merchandising food and beverages is beyond me because that's where all the money is in this business. Even if the show is scraping by there is money in the auxiliary things. I stayed there about a year and then went to Europe. When I came back I continued working on shows, helping people build sets and so forth. I worked mostly in box office as treasurer for shows that would usually close the day before they were supposed to open, or the day after they opened. I continued doing that for several years, went back to Europe, returned and worked the first major job I had which was with Theater Guild. The American Theater Society was the ticketing and subscription arm of the Theater Guild. I don't think either organization exists anymore. We had subscriptions for sixteen to eighteen cities around the country—Boston, Washington, Cleveland, Cincinnati, San Francisco, Los Angeles, St. Louis. Basically, we did all the solicitation from New York for subscribers and then we processed all the ticket orders for all the shows. We'd pull the subscription tickets, mail them out to subscribers then ship the balance of the tickets to the box offices in those towns. Thinking about this is funny because we'd use little 3 × 5 cards with the names of all the subscribers. We'd have file drawers with all these names on it. We used hard tickets. It's different now with computers! I did a lot of box office work and that was my main occupation. After a year or so, I decided I wanted to get out of New York and do something different. I was going to go to Los Angeles and work for James Doolittle. He competed with the Theater Guild. He called me and wanted to hire me. When the Theater Guild heard that, they were not happy so they made me an offer I couldn't refuse to work for them in Los Angeles. That was a real disappointing experience. I shouldn't have done it because it was a lateral move, though it was an interesting job.

I was there about eight months when I got an offer to come to San Francisco and be ticket sales manager for the San Francisco Opera. I came up and did that. I was with the Opera for about six years. I met Jack Bethards there. He was a management consultant for the Opera and he saw some potential for me to expand my position there. He moved me up the ladder in that organization. I stayed there for a couple more years. Jack ended up with the Oakland Symphony in 1971 and I did some consulting for him with the Symphony. They bought the Paramount and were going to renovate it to use for their home.

TC: So how did you end up at that theater?

PB: I wasn't interested in the Paramount, so Jack said, "Come over and look at the building and if you say 'no,' I won't bother you about it." I came over and saw this wonderful old 1931 movie palace that was a mess, but such a beautiful space. So I told Jack, "I'll start the project but I'm leaving in six months." I was married at the time with a two-year-old son. We were going to move up to Auburn where we'd just bought some property. There were a couple of old houses on it. We were going to move into one of these houses and I was going to be a painting contractor with my brother-in-law. Well, in six months I was in the process of a divorce, working seven days a week, fifteen hours a day. Once the building opened, obviously the personal part of my life had changed, so I wasn't interested in moving. With the restoration done there was still the process of preparing for the continuing operation—setting up guidelines for running the building, policies and procedures, job descriptions for staff—all that had to be done from scratch. It was interesting because I'd never done any of this before, including the construction and restoration element, nor had I been a manager of a facility like this.

TC: Most of us got thrown into these jobs without any training program. We were just told to go in and manage.

PB: Right. I've found that to be a problem over the years in this industry. People who are managers of buildings don't know anything about stagecraft, anything about janitorial, box office—don't know anything about the various operations, and there were a lot of things I didn't know either. I'd built some sets and done some odd work, but I'd never had any formal management training. To this day I feel I could be a better manager if I had, but I learned a lot during the restoration process— I had to. The work had to be done. Fortunately, the one talent I've always felt that I have is the ability to hire the right people to do the job, or the right consultants. I've no other qualification or talents myself, but if I hire the right people the job will get done right! I definitely learned a lot that way and it's important when you're operating a building to know a good deal about all the elements of it, to know what to look for, and the qualities of the people you hire. When you're walking around backstage just glance around and see that things are safe, that they look right. When you're looking around the theater where the public is check that things are clean and safe and people are comfortable. Much of that was learned during the process of the restoration. That's important when you have [the] responsibility to take care of a building and the people who are using it and working in it!

TC: I'm always amazed that people who work in this industry, even though they might switch jobs, they nearly always stay in it in some capacity, as opposed to switching from banking to insurance to computers. Their whole lives are their jobs.

PB: Right.

TC: It is interesting that you started out in box office and switched to management. The relationship between box office and managers is sometimes shadowed with the perception that there is something dishonest going on—like ice, kickbacks, or dealing with brokers.

PB: It is a valid belief. It does happen. You've probably read in *Variety* recently about the stuff going on in New York. It must be political—every [time] there's an election for state attorney general there's another investigation.[2] When I was in New York thirty years ago—1962, almost forty years ago—that was going on. It went on before and it's been going on ever since! It's always reported like it's some new discovery. There's no way to control it and I'm sure it happens from the level of producers, promoters, box office people, managers—as long as the opportunity is there some people are going to take advantage. The opportunities may change. Maybe the treasurer has less opportunity, but the opportunity will be there for someone else. It's problematic. I don't know what you do about it except set up strong controls and make sure that the staff knows how you feel about it. If you find out about it you warn the person that it's not an acceptable practice, or if it's repeated, fire them.

TC: Some managers want to protect their reputations when they work around people who take part in this activity. How would you advise a manager whose staff brokers tickets on the side while the owner looks the other way?

PB: Yeah, that's totally inappropriate. First of all, if there's any money to be made I'm going to make it. For example, the Shorenstein Organization has house seats. The owner's pals call up or I call up and can get house seats, but I pay an extra $25.00 a ticket.

TC: It goes to a charity.

PB: It goes to charity, right. Well, we started getting some hot shows here a few years ago and everybody's calling me for tickets, so I decided to do the same thing. I charge an extra $10.00 per ticket and we put that money into our endowment fund. It's a legitimate thing to do.

TC: Yes, I think people think of it a little differently if it's going to a charity rather than into someone's pocket.

PB: On the other hand, I've never discussed doing this with promoters. There are a few promoters that bug me for tickets regularly so I make them pay for them and the $10.00. So promoters know about it even though I've never discussed it with them. Maybe some promoter wouldn't think that was an appropriate thing to do. You're holding out seats and selling them for a higher price. But from my point of view you have people in the industry and people you're associated with who want to be taken care of. As the manager of the theater, I'd like to take care of them, but at the same time it's a pain in the ass for me to do. So, they pay a little extra, put it in the endowment and I don't mind so much! The promoter's tickets get sold and I make a few bucks for the endowment!

TC: It's a different case when the money goes into someone's pocket.

PB: The bottom line is who's being hurt when the treasurer or whomever is selling tickets to agents or others and making money on it. The producer's not being hurt 'cause the tickets are being sold. The promoter's not being hurt. The management of the theater is not being hurt. The box office manager (or whoever) is making some money. So no one is being hurt, except the customer! The producer sets a price on tickets and says, "This is what I want to charge and I don't want to 'gouge' patrons for anything more." So it's just not right. There are individuals who are greedy or weak or for whatever reason they need the money. There are other individuals who if they know it's not the right thing to do and management doesn't want them to do it, then they don't do it. It certainly is something that does happen and people who come out with touring shows—company managers who are so concerned about it—they're also concerned about the theater manager and the treasurer trying to stick them for costs. And that happens, too. Maybe the deal you made wasn't the right kind of deal and you want to make up for it some way. All of this depends on your perspective but the fact is that the promoters and producers of these shows and their representatives know stuff goes on like that. They also know that there are stupid box office people who don't know how to do a statement—so they have to deal with that. They have to look for all this stuff.

TC: And sometimes they do it themselves.

PB: Yeah, Sure.

TC: A manager trying not to get that reputation—because ultimately it does hurt you in the long run—how would you advise a manager to respond to someone who offers them money for premium tickets?

PB: If somebody did that to me—it'd depend on how well I knew them, I guess. If it was somebody I knew I'd just say, "That's not the way we want to do business. We take care of you the same way we take care of every other agent" (or concierge or whoever it happened to be).

TC: Do you think there is a long-term corrupting influence when managers have to look the other way, or if they act against their personal moral code?

PB: An employee shouldn't look the other way. For instance, if a manager wants the employee to participate in something illegal then the employee should say directly to that person or supervisor that they don't want to participate. If they see it continuing to go on around them, whether it's corrupting or not depends on the individual. If I saw that coming on in an organization that I was working in, I wouldn't want to work there because there would be other things wrong with that organization. Any time there's dishonesty you can see there are going to be other things too. I remember my mother used to say, "Anything you do and everything you say always comes back." Somebody more recently, I forget who, said, "The truth never changes." If you're doing stuff that is dishonest—it's like telling a lie. If you tell a lie to somebody, are you going to remember that you told that lie, are you going to remember what the story was? What if later you tell the same story and you tell it different? Suddenly you're in a situation that's uncomfortable. And that's what's going to happen when you're in an organization where that kind of thing is going on. There's going to be other issues going on as a result of that dishonesty that's going to make it difficult and uncomfortable to work in that environment, and to have a smooth operation.

TC: Like what's happening at the White House[3] now.

PB: Exactly! And here's his people—you hear the reports from the media, and I'm sure to a great extent it's got to be right even though you can't believe anything the media says—his people want to support him, but it must be really hard to do so. Look at Barbara Boxer[4]—her daughter or son married Hillary's[5] nephew or whatever, and Boxer's coming out and saying, this is really screwing up my campaign. So that's a good example of how this kind of thing spreads out throughout an organization—in this case the government. It hurts everybody. So the answer is if an employee sees that happening, if he's asked to participate he should say, "No, I won't have any part of it." If it's affecting his work, he should work some place else 'cause [it's] not going to be fun to work in an operation like that. The other thing you can do is to go to supervisors. It depends on who your boss is; if it's the owner, then you can't go any further, unless you want to bring in the police. I was in a situation with the Opera where the box office people were stealing and I researched it, found out what was going on, had everything all laid out so I could prove everything. I went to the "powers that be" and told them what was going on and it was stopped. Now, mind you, it wasn't stopped by the people I reported to 'cause they were either in on it or they were too lazy to do anything about it, but that was about the time that Jack Bethards advanced my position with the Opera so I was able to fire these thieves.

TC: So you really stopped it.

PB: I changed it myself, yeah. But I did go to higher-ups to try to deal with it. The experience was pretty negative. It wasn't like they were all participating in it but they weren't interested in following up either. I remember I showed them all the documentation and they said, "Well, we need to do an audit." They called the box office treasurer, who was one of the thieves, and told him they wanted to do an audit, and he said that they were real busy and he wanted to do it in a few weeks! I was sitting there, and they're on the phone with this guy, and I'm going: you don't do it that way. You storm in there and say we're going to do an audit. Well, of course, I don't think they ever did the audit. It was a very short time after that that the thieves were gone. So you can do that too—go to higher-ups, but it may be with unsatisfactory results. Partly I think people don't want to know. People higher up might not necessarily care.

TC: How prevalent do you think nepotism is in this industry and what are some good strategies around it?

PB: Well, nepotism isn't bad if you hire good people. [Laughs.] I'll give you a couple of examples. When I was at the Opera, I hired my mother. She couldn't type, and she wrote all of the documentation by hand! She was a terrific worker. We didn't tell anybody she was my mother. She had a different name. Nobody knew she was my mother for years. She was just Mrs. Clark, but she was a good worker, she came in when I needed her and she was on time. I could call her and say I'm going to need you tomorrow. Or she'd be there for a couple of hours and we'd get caught up and that was fine with her. What a terrific situation that was for me to have somebody like that. You don't find people like that. I trusted her. So, there's that kind of nepotism. The Paramount security chief, Don Wysinger, over the years has hired a couple of nephews as extra security. There was one nephew [who] didn't work out, and we agreed that he wouldn't work here. Gene Morrison, my house manager—over the years he's had his own kids working here as porters and ticket-takers, and his foster kids have worked here. One of them is now my custodial chief. So it's not a problem if they're good people and they're qualified. What can be a problem is when there's conflicts when you're unhappy with one member of the family! When they don't work out and you have to lay somebody off, or fire them, it can be difficult if you have other employees from the same family. That's really the problem—whether it's family or with friends.

TC: Let's take it from the other way around such as an owner or producer's child. Someone who hasn't worked their way up, but is suddenly in charge, and you have no connections and are trying to break in.

PB: I assume you're referring to producers.

TC: Something like that.

PB: In a case where the owner is doing it, it can be demoralizing to the employees. If you have somebody coming on board who's taking charge and they don't know anything, they don't know what's going on and they never will, it's a problem. Your good people are going to leave. The organization's going to flounder eventually. What do you do about that when it's the owner? The owner is the owner.

TC: The average employee who's trying to survive a bad situation can't necessarily leave when they're being scapegoated for bad situations. Typically, the scapegoated person or people are fairly innocent. It's not going to be the top-level people who get the blame. What do you think are some good ways to avoid being the scapegoat and if it's too late—how is the best way to deal with the situation?

PB: It's tough to answer that without specifics. I'm not even sure how to generalize it. I guess it depends on the kind of person you are and how secure you are. That's happened to me. I've always felt that I've done a good job at my work. At least I know I work hard at it. So I don't have any fears I'm going to get criticized for being lazy or not following through—that sort of thing. That's a start. So if anyone wants to accuse me or lay the blame for something—I don't have a real problem with that.

TC: As a person negotiates all these kinds of situations in the workplace, maintaining personal integrity becomes a job in itself. What do you think is the best way or ways to do this?

PB: A lot of it can be judged on whether you'll be able to sleep at night. Don't do anything that you wouldn't want your mother, father, sister, brother, wife, or child to find out about!

MITCH BROWER

Mitch Brower's career spans over forty years. After graduating from Yale University and receiving his MBA from the University of Chicago, he worked as a company manager on Broadway and/or the road over a span of years for such shows as *All the Way Home* (Pulitzer Prize winner), *A Passage to India, They're Playing Our Song, Glengarry Glen Ross, Arsenic and Old Lace, Joe Turner's Come & Gone,* and *Noises Off* during different phases of his career. He has worked as a film producer for *McCabe and Mrs. Miller,* directed by Robert Altman, starring Warren Beatty and Julie Christie; *The Getaway* directed by Sam Peckinpah, starring Steve McQueen and Ali McGraw; and *Larry,* a CBS-TV drama that received the First Humanitas Award. He has worked as a theater manager, general manager, press agent, consultant, and has also stuffed envelopes. Mr. Brower supervised the opening of the Mark Taper Forum and the Ahmanson Theatre at the L. A. Music Center and was its first general manager. Currently, he is once again the general manager of the New York State Theater at the Lincoln Center for the Performing Arts, a venue he also opened in 1964.

TC: Can you tell me about how you came to work in theater?

MB: I decided to work in the theater while I was getting my graduate degree in Business Administration at the University of Chicago. Part way through that program, I realized that I didn't want to work with the people around me who had come out of industry and business, and I asked myself, what shall I do with my life? I thought about it awhile and decided, well, I'll work in the theater. But in those days, which is now a very long time ago, there was no easy entry point into that world and there was no regional theater, so I went back to New York where I lived and found a job as a volunteer stuffing envelopes in a not-for-profit theatrical office—at a place called ANTA which I don't think exists anymore. I earned enough money to do this by working at Macy's as a salesman at night, and through that entry point, when jobs became available, I then spent a summer as an assistant in the box office at the Jacob's Pillow Dance Festival. Later I spent six months touring for Sol Hurok as an advance man, which in those days paid $120.00 a week. I did everything. I traveled three weeks ahead of the show, which I'd never seen. It was a group of dance suites from Agnes De-Mille musicals. I literally took care of arranging the housing on the spot, and the technical needs and sent all sorts of information back to the company manager. I did that for six months and covered 107 cities.

The reason I dwell on this is because that's how I got my experience: doing it, out there, and that's a large part of what everyone has to think about—where you accumulate the experience to be of enough value so that you can get a meaningful job. Then I got to manage an all-star summer stock company in Rhode Island for a couple of years with people like Mae West and Marlon Brando, another form of education. And then three summers in Philadelphia as house manager at the Playhouse in the Park, a tent theater in the round. In between that, I went to Milwaukee and opened the Fred Miller Theater. It was the conversion of a movie house into a theater in the round. Gradually, through all that, I found my way to Broadway. After working a lot of shows, most of which opened and closed quickly, I realized that what I wanted to do was work with serious theater, which was dying on Broadway.

TC: That was about what year?

MB: The late fifties. What I chose to do, which I think is the wisest course, was to find the best people you can work with, the people you can learn the most from, even if you have to work as an intern, not being paid, but to get your foot in the door with good people so that you can learn the quickest and the best way to do things. This involves an enormous sacrifice but, if you're not willing to make those sacrifices early in your career, you shouldn't be choosing this career.

TC: What factors influenced you?

MB: Careers go in a zigzag, not a straight line. The main thing is that you have to know that you need it. If you're looking for glamour, if you're

looking for the high life, you're in the wrong place. After many years I realized I stayed with it, whether it was in film, television, or theater, because I needed it as a fulfillment. I was involved in what became known
as the cultural revolution, then the counterrevolution—whatever. But
with the way various governments, federal and state, are cutting back
now on funding for the arts, people have got to be much more willing to
work as interns or at low paying jobs even with their fancy degrees. Just
because you've got this academic background doesn't mean you know
anything about what really happens in the theater on any level. So the important thing is to examine yourself and see whether this is really what
you want to do and how badly you need it, and whether you're willing to
make economic and emotional sacrifices to stay with it. Happily for me,
I was willing to do that. There were times when I was unemployed because a show closed or because what I was trying to do wasn't doable, yet,
but I stayed with it because I needed it.

Back to the main question: I was working on Broadway and the things
I wanted to do—serious theater—were not doable so I got involved in the
idea of doing art films based in New York. I had the good fortune to be
invited to be the general manager and open the New York State Theater
at [the] Lincoln Center, thirty-four years ago. By doing that I had economic stability [year-round] while trying to get film ideas going.
I worked at the State Theater six months before it opened, and another
six months, then Lincoln Center moved me over to the Beaumont Theatre, which I opened and ran maybe another six months. By that time I
had an opportunity to go to California to open a theater which never
did—it eventually became the Shubert in L.A. in Century City with a different architect. But luckily I had known Gordon Davidson (earlier—he
had been assistant stage manager and I the house manager at the American Shakespeare Festival in Connecticut). He was in L.A. with the Center Theater Group, ready to move from UCLA to the Mark Taper Forum,
which was about to open, and invited me to be the general manager of
both the company and theater.

My experience at Lincoln Center and on Broadway made this right up
my alley. I spent two years at the Center Theater Group. Again, working
in the not-for-profit world—which, when you move back and forth like
that, can be distracting because you have to make many adjustments. In
professional theater, you have to get something done today or tomorrow
or you may not be in business next week. In regional not-for-profit theater you can take years to get something done because timeliness is not
what it's about. It's about process, bureaucracy, and boards of directors.
But those two worlds are very different and many beginning managers
choose the latter because that is where most opportunities lie in music,
opera, ballet, whatever. They must understand that it is a hard road. It's

not going to be easy. They should try to go to work for a good, professional organization where the most skillful people are, to learn how to do things right—just absorb and assimilate everything you can. If beginning managers are really good and they do a good job, they'll be noticed by the people they work for and promoted, and from there they can move right on.

That's the way I did it and the way I've seen it done. I've done it with people who work with me now. All of us do it. So you mustn't come into the professional theater world with a lot of hubris and presumptuousness because you have a degree. The degree doesn't teach you anything about the way things really are. It gives you some tools to work with, the way my MBA did back then. But other than that, it is just another tool. So put away your ego and your vanity, and focus on going to work with organizations that you can help with your energy and your focus and willingness to lend a hand, and do whatever you are called upon to do. Even if you one day want to be a producer, you begin as a press agent or a manager, working as an apprentice to those people. You learn what producing is about, and so I did this gradually.

After I made my big detour into films, then television—[I spent] fourteen years in L.A.—[then] I wanted to get back to the theater and New York. I called old friends from my earlier life on Broadway like Manny Azenberg and Joe Harris, and Manny said, "Mitchell, come home." And that's how I met you, Tess. That's when I did the tour of *They're Playing Our Song*. It was about to go into rehearsal in L.A. By that time there were computer payrolls, everything had changed. I used to do manual payrolls. One thing I did early on was take a company of *St. Louis Woman*, a Harold Arlen flop, to Europe with an assistant who did the international payrolls all day long, francs and guilders to Belgium francs, etc. It was another great adventure.

The thing is you have to accrue experiences of all kinds relating to your job. That's how you learn how to do it. So what you learn in school is useful, but it basically gives you little grounding. You've got to get out there and do it. Also, you should try to go on tour with shows. Touring with shows is really managing, you're really out there, fully responsible. You're not sitting in New York doing payrolls, answering phones, and making Xeroxes. You're literally in charge of the show or working as an assistant to someone who is responsible, and that way you learn how to deal with people, how to travel people, house people, how to work with box offices and press agents and theater managers.

Anyway, when I got back into the theater, I toured with several shows. It was my dues-paying to get back into New York. *Hollywood/Ukraine. Glengarry Glen Ross. Arsenic and Old Lace.* And then, I began to manage shows in New York again. There was a whole new generation of people

I didn't know, but I knew enough good people who'd grown up into the business that I could work with them. I was always professional and took my job seriously, and wasn't presumptuous because I produced films. Sometimes you've got to bury your ego. You can't let it bother you in any way. You're in the service of artists, producers, directors, etc.

I'll tell you a quick anecdote. When I was at the Shakespeare Festival in Connecticut as house manager, Katharine Hepburn was there doing *Twelfth Night* and the air-conditioning broke down. It was just before the weekend, and we had to do the Saturday matinee with all the exit doors open. She liked it cold, and it was hot and the lights were bright, and she called me backstage between shows. I went down to her dressing room. The whole company was there, and she gave me a public dressing-down. I told her everything was in the works, it would be fixed on Monday—we had flown a plane down to Pennsylvania to get the part. And she just ripped me up and down and I could have killed her. I was so humiliated. The director was standing right there, and of course I disciplined myself and I didn't react. But the whole company heard it. We got the problem fixed on Monday and I stayed away from her for a couple of weeks. Finally I wandered by and heard, "Young man, come in here." She wanted me to know, "The squeaky wheel always gets the oil." That's where I learned that expression, and thereafter applied it in my career.

Anyway, what became of me is that after touring Broadway shows again . . . I got to reopen the Shubert Theater in New Haven in 1983–1984, which had been closed for seven or eight years. I used to play there years before when I traveled with shows, pre-Broadway. Now it was not-for-profit and had a board of directors that knew nothing. All they wanted to do was sit in the third row again every Friday night to watch *My Fair Lady* open. It was an interesting experience, but I got away after a year because it was so provincial and I had too much experience in the big leagues to put up with that. I went to Europe for a few weeks and then to L.A. where my kids lived. I got a phone call from Joe Harris saying, "Mitch, you've been resting too long. Come back to New York." He was opening an off-Broadway theater, so I returned and ran the theater and managed the show for a while, and that's how I got back to Broadway.

I did that for a number of years, went on the road from time to time, and then, ten years ago, I got a call from an old friend, Roy Somlyo. He asked, "How would you like to come back to Lincoln Center?" They needed a new general manager at the Avery Fisher, the symphony hall. So I went out and met with the executive vice president for two hours and he asked, "Why do you want this job?" And I said, "I'm at the point in my life when I'm older now, and I want to be in New York." I missed it too much. I missed everybody. He wanted me to meet the president of [the] Lincoln Center for the Performing Arts. I saw him for another two hours and then I heard nothing for three months. One day I received a letter in which they said they'd found somebody else.

I was working Broadway the whole time, *Joe Turner's Come and Gone*—I believe that was my last show. Anyway, after a few weeks I got a call out of the blue from the chairman of the New York State Theater who wanted to see me. He'd heard about me from the Lincoln Center people. I was hired to come back to the State Theater where I worked behind the scenes and just observed for three to five months with my predecessor to get me up to speed. He, by the way, had also been my successor decades ago, and had been there twenty years, an ex-police lieutenant who wasn't a theater man but had learned enough along the way.

TC: So you came full circle—starting at Lincoln Center and ending up at Lincoln Center.

MB: Exactly. So here I was. Anyway, he didn't bring me up to date very much. He left a bunch of files, but with my considerable experience, I sat down at the desk and within a week I was running the place. I learned all about the horrors of working in a city-owned building, the difficulty and bureaucratic endlessness of it all. I had to get into the business of lobbying the city for capital. Being the resident home of the New York City Ballet and City Opera, city officials were busy with their own deficits and not concerned with the building. I found a whole new world: lobby the city, lobby the mayor's office, lobby the city council, lobby the state. I spent a lot of my time doing that. One thing I realized early on was that the building was aging rapidly and badly needed help, and everybody else was too busy with their own problems. "The city will take care of it," they said, meaning I would go lobby the city. But it didn't mean the city would give me the money.

We didn't have a lobbyist. I got there too soon in terms of knowing what was needed, and then five years after I told them about it, they hired a lobbyist. I moved back from some of this. I'm not so much on the front lines any more, but have enough else to do. I have to run a very large enterprise, which includes rehearsal halls and administrative offices for separate ballet and opera companies. I'm responsible for keeping the whole building functioning, and the show crew of twenty-eight men reports to me. We have twenty-four-hour maintenance people, security guards, engineers—all seven days a week. A full-time painter spends the whole week repainting and touching up. We go five stories underground where we have only a small fraction of the storage space we need. The building was not designed for opera, just for ballet, and the opera moved in and the place is like—there's no space for anything anymore, hasn't been for years. Anyway, with all the experience I'd had, I was able to be of some use there, but also found it was very difficult because the priorities of the two artistic companies were their needs and they didn't consider the building.

So even if I got a new set of rigging for the stage because my predecessor hadn't maintained it, and even though I got them 750 modern stage lamps—whatever I've done, it's because I'm a professional and take great pride in my work, and want to make the place work. I'm not going to say, "To hell with it." So you have to be proactive and you have to be your own person, and not be dispirited or demoralized by indifference, or by people who have other priorities, people who have very large egos. You must not let your ego get in the way of what has to be done. You have to do the best you can do. Don't be vindictive, don't become hostile because it is really a service business. And people who get into this business have to understand that. You're serving both the artist and the public—whatever.

TC: Becoming demoralized is one of the biggest problems managers face. It's very easy to become that way.

MB: Sure. But you see, one of the great pluses I was able to bring to this job was that I've worked on both sides—both production and theater management. The active one is the company manager. The theater manager waits passively for the show to come, and then provides the crew with electrical outlets—whatever they need. It doesn't quite work that way at the State Theater. We have a resident crew for at least forty-two weeks a year. I also have two house managers who do the day-to-day payrolls and administration, and they're there every evening—fixing problems and all that. They're both valuable, good people. I also have an assistant who is the glue and does a million chores. It's hard to describe a typical day.

TC: How would you advise someone who ultimately gets in that state where we're demoralized, and feel bitterness all around you, and you have to go on anyway. How do you deal with that?

MB: I suppose you can leave and find another job! What I learned to do many years later, when I was touring *They're Playing Our Song*, was to ballroom dance. That was my way of doing something to get me mentally and physically away and clear my head. When I toured with *Arsenic and Old Lace*, in every city I'd arrange to have classes. Marion Ross and the stage manager danced; Larry Storch and his wife came. We were in each city a long enough time so we could do that. And it was great, so when I got back to the New York State Theater, I focused on it because essentially I had evenings and weekends free. You just find a way to get your head some place else. Don't be so absorbed in it. It takes a great deal of focus to get the work done and put up with everything. Find something else—whether its yoga, meditation, or aerobics. Just find something to take your head away from it on a frequent basis.

TC: You've hit on a number of elements that I think comprise managerial imagination—needing to do it, getting your head somewhere else, and also just doing it.

MB: Glamour is not part of it.

TC: Absolutely.

MB: That's what people who are considering entering this industry have to know early on. Whenever I interview a young person, I just let them have it straight. If they wilt, then they shouldn't be in the business. I come upon someone on occasion who is willing to do what is necessary and have gotten some people jobs by recommending them. I really back those I feel can deliver and they move up in the company's ranks. If a person thinks an MBA or MFA means earning a good living right away, that's a mistake. Remember, with two fancy degrees from two fancy universities, I still stuffed envelopes. My contemporaries with the same degrees I had were getting jobs as captains of industry. I did what I did because I needed it. I didn't want it for the glamour, I knew that. Somehow my intuition told me where I belonged.

TC: That reminds me of a time when you brought a show to the Curran, here in San Francisco, and had assigned some task to your new assistant who told you he wasn't here to do your crap-work. I think you put him straight pretty quickly.

MB: [Laughs.] He used to work in Manny Azenberg's office. He was presumptuous. Boy, I . . . that was pretty funny. You know who was my assistant opening the State Theater? Peter Neufeld. It was the first theater job he ever had.

TC: And he went on to become a general manager.

MB: You have to really need it and go through a lot, and hopefully save your money so you can afford to do it between jobs, or find a way of working part time while you're doing it. All of this is part of the need.

TC: What about dealing with temperamental people?

MB: As far as that goes, I find you have to subsume your ego once again. There was a star I worked for, I can't remember the show—someone on Broadway, I forget her name, and everybody feared her. I went to the stage manager and asked, "What do I have to know about this woman? And tell me how I can make her happy, how do I defuse her, de-fang her? I asked the stage manager, I asked everyone I could, so when I was introduced to her, I just said, "How can I help you? What can I do for you?" Stars just dissolve.

You know, that's the way you do it. I've worked with big stars. Steve McQueen, Warren Beatty in those movies I made. That's the only way to deal with temperamental directors or anybody. You've got to just let them know that you're there for them. That's the important thing. You have to show them how you can be of value to them. When you go into a job its not to say, hey, I'm great, I have a degree. You've got to say to them, I'm here to work for you, I'm here to help you anyway I can to make your job easier. That's what people appreciate. If you think the other way around, they'll say, who the hell needs him or her—and be unpleasant, if that's their style.

TC: Describe your day-to-day functioning with the theater staff.

MB: I've never in my entire career, no matter how much I've learned or how big a job I've had, thought I knew everything. I always listen to everybody. The door to my office is literally open and I will talk to anybody who has anything to tell me or bitch about. Otherwise, I don't know what's going on around the theater. Every day I learn something new. But there are always a lot of other people who have very good ideas. People on any level. I pick up good ideas whenever I can. I thank them, and make it clear that it was their idea, that I didn't come up with it, and they appreciate that. That's the way people learn to work with me. They know I'm not going to be some kind of holy god although there are a lot of people like that who work in the arts. I'm very open to ideas. If I stop being like that I wouldn't be of any use. I try to relate to everyone who works for me in a personal way. I don't mean that I'm especially concerned about their personal or family lives, but they all have an interest. That's another way to reach people, by the way. You listen to what really interests them and you talk to them about it. That flatters them. It makes them feel that they matter. I have a prop maintenance guy who I discovered loves to go to restaurants and cook, and I give him my *Bon Appétit* and *Good Eating* magazines, and you know, we now have a whole other relationship. It always takes a while to do that. I'm not one of these guys who jumps in. I wait for things to evolve in a natural way. But everybody knows that I'm there for them. I'm not saying it to flatter myself, but it's a way to operate, a modus operandi. When the crew needs equipment or materials or something, I make every effort to get it because that way they know that I'm there for them.

TC: That's a strong grounding for your success.

MB: Joseph Campbell said, "Follow your bliss." I realize that's what I've done. I can look back on my crazy career that went in a zigzag—success doesn't go straight up, but in a wave or zigzag. I remained focused and made it happen. But it's only if you do the kinds of things I've talked about that it can happen. It's mostly perspiration and tenacity. In the movie business I learned this expression called "relentless patience." You have to have patience, knowing that certain things you want to get done will take a lot longer than you think they ought to, but if you persist and are tenacious and don't let go, it can pay off. You have to need it more than anything. You have to sacrifice many aspects of your life. And it can affect your personal life seriously. It can affect everything else that matters to you. That's why it comes back to need.

TC: And many times you don't realize you're paying that cost. You just do what you do.

MB: Sure. I was lucky because along the way my former second wife wanted to be a mother. I was busy but, we became parents and I have two wonderful kids—thirty and thirty-two and now a granddaughter. That wouldn't have happened if it had been just left to me. As you know, so many people in this business are single, divorced, itinerant, or whatever. . . .

TC: What direction do you see theater going as we enter the twenty-first century?

MB: The direction it's going and the way it's evolved—we're talking about regional or noncommercial theater—you have to be very resourceful because of the ever-expanding economics. I've spent my entire adult life in the arts, and I guess I felt that my mission was to bring more culture or whatever to American society. To my despair, it didn't happen that way. Look at what's happened to the National Endowment and grants and everything else—it's all being reduced drastically. So anyone who wants to be in this business can't think of getting rich. You've got to know about how to raise money, how to keep the company running economically. It hasn't changed in my lifetime and I doubt it will. The cultivation of America isn't growing, it's declining. Movies are getting dumber, television is making everyone dumber, so what is the future of the theater?

There'll always be creative people. All too many creative writers, because it is so tough to get plays on, go to Hollywood and keep going there because they can make money writing sitcoms or films. In the theater what does a playwright get? A small option on a play. Only if it runs does he make any money. If it runs a week he gets nothing. If it runs a year, he makes money, but that happens very infrequently. Those are the exceptions. Many are called but few are chosen—that old cliché. There will be periods when the theater rises up, but look what saved Broadway—the English musicals. What on earth did we deliver? [Stephen] Sondheim is very special. There are high periods in any of the arts—in painting there was Impressionism, Post-Impressionism, and then there were the great musicals, musicians, and composers, Berlin and Cole Porter and the Gershwins and all those people, Jerome Kern, but where are their equivalents today? It isn't like turning cars out at a factory, it's just sheer luck. Look what happened to great music—who came after Beethoven, after Mozart? It just doesn't happen that they're going to be there forever. So you want to bear that in mind if you choose the arts—not just theater, but arts management or whatever. The audience for serious music is declining. Where will the next generation come from? Modern music doesn't seem to make much of an impression. Modern operas—they're trying to promote modern operas but I don't know if it's going to work. The culture keeps changing. Who knows what will happen?

GORDON G. FORBES

Gordon G. Forbes is the secretary-treasurer of the Association of Theatrical Press Agents and Managers (ATPAM) and has worked as a manager on and off Broadway for the past twenty-five years. He has been a union member since 1981.

TC: One of the frequent issues that comes up for unionized workers is the belief that if you're management, then how can you belong to a union? What is your response to such a question?
GF: Many Americans have preconceived notions about what unions are and what their function is. When you say "union" to most people, it conjures up an image of factory workers on an assembly line or farm workers bent over in a field. Many people fail to realize that the area of fastest growth for unions today is "white collar" workers. This includes a broad range of professionals including doctors, lawyers, computer programmers, and people who work at various levels of middle management in such industries as publishing, the arts and entertainment, airlines, high technology, etc. As a result, there are different types of unions. There are traditional trade and craft unions which represent blue collar workers in industry. But there are also unions and guilds which function as hybrids of trade unions and professional associations.

ATPAM is a union whose members walk a fine line between being employees and confidential supervisory personnel. In the theater industry as we have known it for many decades, this has not been a problem because of the "mom and pop" size of companies. However, as large corporations (such as Disney) have entered the live theater field there is a reluctance of their part to allow unionization of midmanagement personnel, because they view it to be a conflict and at odds with their company culture. However, while "supervisory personnel" are not protected under the National Labor Relations Act, every American is entitled to organize and belong to a union. My prediction is that the next century will see many people who would never have gone near a union in different times seeking membership and representation as competition for existing jobs becomes more intense.
TC: In 1994, ATPAM affiliated itself with IATSE. Do you expect this affiliation to continue and if so, in what ways do you think it benefits the union and its membership?
GF: In 1994 ATPAM affiliated with the IATSE because the handwriting was on the wall. The League of American Theatres and Producers, the main employer group, was threatening to seek "unit clarification" with regard to ATPAM and "supervisory personnel" status with the NLRB. If they had carried out that threat it would have lead to the decertification and death of ATPAM. A small union of less than 1,000 members in the

United States and Canada would not be able to stand up to such an attack. However, IATSE president [Thomas] Short[6] has made a commitment to ATPAM that as part of the IATSE, ATPAM will always have a contract with the League. And he has the strength of nearly 100,000 members to put behind that promise. While there are many ancillary benefits to the affiliations, that one alone is worth the $100,000.00 a year ATPAM pays in dues to the IATSE.

TC: In what ways do you see the nature of theatrical work changing?

GF: Not much. Technological changes will have an impact on the product, but most of the job titles will remain the same—with the exception of a few areas, such as box office, which technology will eventually reduce to one or two employees per venue.

TC: Some critics argue that unions have become parental, resulting in employees not taking responsibility for themselves or their actions, and expecting employment to be their right. Can you respond to this criticism?

GF: I think that is an old mantra still being chanted by traditional anti-union forces. What truth there is to it is probably more evident in public sector unions, where a bureaucratic, civil service mentality would continue to exist, with or without unions because of the nature of the work.

TC: What is your response to a person who faces the choice of working for a nonunion production or maintaining union membership?

GF: There is no easy answer. People have to support themselves. If a union forbids a member to take nonunion employment in an attempt to police jurisdiction, I believe the union has an obligation to help the member find comparable employment, or at least to offer short-term financial aid.

TC: What do you see as the true benefits of union membership and the downside of union membership?

GF: There are many, many benefits to union membership, including networking and being able to share a community of interest with others who work in your field. Traditionally, the main advantage has been benefits. Unions have structured funds to offer pension, health, annuity, continuing education, etc. These benefits are usually portable and travel with the member from job to job. Nonunion employers often have little or no benefits and they usually cease the moment the employee leaves employment. The only downside is paying dues. Nobody likes to do that.

TC: What is the best career path for someone wanting to become a manager?

GF: Apprentice to the best working manager you can find and try to get a wide variety of experience.

TC: How are the issues of today's union different from the issues of previous decades?

GF: Many of the things the old labor movement fought to get for workers, such as an eight-hour workday and overtime after forty hours have either become law or just accepted practice. The next era of unions will have to expand the range of services they offer members, and deal with the growing pains of the global economy by leading the fight to maintain the quality of life American workers have achieved in this century. ATPAM will have to deal with the accelerating move to corporate structure of producers and theater owners.

TC: How has your union work changed you personally?

GF: Even in the darkest days of trying to rebuild a local union that had totally disintegrated, I have found it tremendously rewarding to be able to do things that improve the quality of life of ATPAM members and others who work in our industry.

TC: What kind of union do you expect ATPAM to be in the twenty-first century?

GF: Bigger, smarter, and a respected force in the entertainment industry.

EDWARD C. POWELL

Edward C. Powell is a second and senior vice president of the International Alliance of Theatrical Stage Employees (IATSE). In a career that spans over fifty years, he has played a unique role in the growth and development of the San Francisco Bay Area theatrical, film, and video industry. He served as the business agent for San Francisco's Theatrical Stagehand Employees Union, IATSE Local 16 for thirty-one years. In that capacity he oversaw a multifaceted jurisdiction that included virtually every category of craft and production technicians, from grips and gaffers to set decorators and makeup artists. Beginning his career as a teenager, he has worked in nearly every backstage position including carpenter, property, electrics, pryrotechnics, flyman, and rigger.

TC: How did you start working in this industry?

EP: My grandfather came from Swansea, Wales, on a square-rigger sailing ship when he was fourteen years old. He and his brother landed in San Francisco and eventually got into show business, then my granddad joined the Spanish-American War, I think in '97, '98. When he came back to San Francisco he joined Local 16[7] in 1900. So I have family association with the industry. In my early years, living with my grandparents as I did, I was familiar with backstage since I was about three years old. I always had the feeling I would walk in my grandfather's footsteps and become a stagehand—little knowing I would end up being the executive officer of my local [chapter] and an International officer as well. I just wanted to be a good stagehand.

TC: So you worked mostly through the union local as a stagehand and then became involved with the International?

EP: In high school I took stagecraft. When I was seventeen the union needed some extra people right away and I was one of the lucky ones who got chosen. Then I worked intermittently through the local until I got my apprenticeship in the latter part of 1951. In those days the business was very, very slow—extremely sporadic. Most of the stage jobs were not in legitimate theater but in other areas of the industry. We had a number of what were called maintenance employees who were a holdover from the vaudevillian days in motion picture exhibition houses. The maintenance people would work two shifts a day, seven days a week, and maintain the house, open and close the curtain, lower the lights—do anything necessary such as plumbing, electrical, carpentry, broken seats—things like that. They were a productive force in the exhibition theater because they kept the theaters looking first class. Those were the main jobs back then. Legit theater was only open twenty to thirty-five weeks a year, if that much. Light operas were only operating three weeks apiece in the 1940s and 1950s. The Los Angeles and San Francisco Light Operas had a twelve- to a fourteen-week season consisting of four productions.

TC: So from stagehand work, you ended up going toward union administrative jobs, which are more political?

EP: I worked over seventeen years in the industry before I wound up as the business agent of the local. I did just about everything within the framework of our jurisdiction. I was a carpenter, electrician, a flyman, a rigger. I worked pyrotechnics. I worked on motion picture locations as a gaffer, a grip, and a camera assistant. It so happened that I was also one of the officers of the local. I served as a vice president, on the executive board, and held different offices on the examining board, which is the educational body of our new apprentices. While doing these duties the business agent retired and the president, Lyle Anderson, asked me if I would take the job. . . . That was in the latter part of 1963.

TC: So you were business agent of Local 16 from 1963 to about 1991?

EP: 1994.

TC: Is there a lot of difference working for a local then jumping to International work?

EP: I became an International officer in the late '60s. I received my vice presidency in 1971, so I did both. There was never a conflict between one job and the other. The International position gave me a much broader view of the industry than I received as a business agent, and one worked with the other.

TC: Weren't you recently in Las Vegas organizing hotels?

EP: I went not to organize hotels, but to restore the stability of the local union. I spent the year 1996 down there.

TC: How do you respond to management guru Tom Peters' statement that the courts are making labor unions irrelevant, and his belief that unions will "continue to atrophy."[8] I'm sure you must have an opinion on that.

EP: I do. I think he's incorrect. There have been many transitional changes in the labor movement. Technological changes alone have diminished the work that used to be done. The shrinking of industry in middle America by having tax advantages given to industries that go into third world countries has cut the labor force down tremendously. I could sit here for the next half hour and give you all kinds of reasons why Peters is wrong. However, if you want to paint with a broad brush as he has done, I would say that he's correct in his numbers—the AFL-CIO has shrunk from about 17 million to 14 million people mainly because certain industries no longer prevail. The maritime industry, for instance, used to be a very, very strong industry and one that had a very large membership. They're shrinking because there are no American ships on the high seas carrying passengers. The teamsters had a very large union at one time. The entrepreneurial and wildcat truckers defected from the union and competition has made it so tough for teamsters to exist. No union contracts prevail in that section of the industry. Most of the overland companies that the teamster's union used to have contracts with were forced to go out of business because they were competing with the wildcat truckers. United Parcel Service, however, is still under contract with the teamsters. We could zero in on each individual aspect—building trades, for instance. They've diminished in numbers over the years, partly because of technological change, partly because a number of their people have opened up their own business and competed with the union.

The service unions, on the other hand, prospered. The American Federation of State, County, and Municipal employees, commonly known as AFSCME, have well over a million people. Postal employees—the same. So in the service area, the unions have grown, and in many craft areas—the maritime and the construction trades—they have shrunk, but that doesn't mean they're no longer viable. They're still viable, they're just going through a transitional period.

TC: The entertainment unions seem to be strong.

EP: Entertainment unions are exceptionally strong. Our union in particular has gone up in numbers. We are a craft union. The International used to represent fifty to fifty-five thousand people between the United States and Canada. We're bordering on one hundred thousand now. We have increased.

TC: Including ATPAM.[9]

EP: That's right. Including ATPAM. That was my recommendation, by the way.

TC: Yes, I remember that. At one time the League of American Theatres negotiated Broadway contracts that set the standard for the rest of the country. With Disney never joining the League and Livent deciding to negotiate their own CBAs, is this good or bad for union labor? And how do you think theatrical unions will respond to this situation?

EP: The League of New York Theatres preceded the American League and they negotiated all of the bargaining contracts for the unions—the stagehands, musician's union, the actor's union, and the ancillary unions that work in the legitimate theater. Then, later on the bargaining unit for the employers became the American League. When Garth Drabinsky[10] came into New York as well as Disney, they wanted to walk to the beat of their own drum. They sat down with the unions and went through a long protracted negotiation, but the end result was that they came out with contracts which were in parity with those contracts with the American League. It makes it more difficult to negotiate outside of a master contract. It's much better for the employers to be part of a master contract, but on the other hand, if that's the way an individual employer or producer wants to deal with it, it can be reckoned with.

TC: Very often, it's reported in *Variety* that work rules, and not wages, are key sticking points in negotiations.

EP: First of all, you have to ask yourself—why do we have work rules? There are work rules because there were abuses in the workplace. There was a meeting of the minds across the bargaining table as to what can and cannot happen. I don't think work rules are a problem. Work rules are a good guideline for both sides to adhere to. They promote safety. There are circumstances where people have to eat within a certain period of time, have to have a certain amount of rest between calls so that they don't work thirty, forty, and fifty hours at a stretch, like I did years ago where you'd literally fall asleep on your feet. So when we say work rules, let's examine the rules, what they are, and then form a judgment based on that.

TC: How do you advise someone wanting to work in theater to break into areas that are under union jurisdiction?

EP: It would depend on what part of the theater they wanted to break into. But I think the best way to answer your question is to tell you a story about a time when I was asked to deliver a speech to some students at DeAnza College. One of our men had taught a class down there and asked me to talk to them. I based my speech on *A Chorus Line*. It'd just opened at the Curran Theater. I asked how many in the group had had the opportunity to see it. Almost every hand went up. Then I asked about the theme of the show, which is that there are a hundred people after six jobs. I told the group the same thing happens in the technical side of the industry. We have a surplus of people wanting to get in to an industry which has stardust, spangles, dreams, and grease paint, and they want to hear the roar of the crowd. They want to be part of showbiz, but the business can only assimilate so many people, so my advice is—learn your lessons, take stagecraft in college or study a specialty. Today we have such great numbers in our industry, most people fall into special categories—there are electricians, carpenters, property people, and fabricators, audio/visual technicians, pyrotechnic technicians—all different kinds of categories. When an individual has the potential and the criteria, then somewhere along the line they'll find the means to get into the industry.

TC: Do you think negotiations between unions and employers will get tougher in the future?

EP: I don't know that they'll get tougher. I think they're tough now and always have been because it's a question of how you split up the dollar. There's only so many dollars that come through the box office, and everybody's got their hand out to get their fair share. That's why we have collective bargaining agreements. I think that if you find that one union is passive, the other union will be more aggressive because they will see that they can get that much more. We've seen this happen between the actors, the musicians, and the technical unions over the years. Each person in live theater is a very special individual because the show could rest on their merits and how well they're doing their job.

TC: When union members are at odds with management and their own unions, the result can often be lengthy legal procedures (from NLRB and EEOC filings to individual lawsuits), and expensive attorney's fees. Why do you think this kind of activity is on the rise and what do you think is the best response to it? Are union members negating the efforts of their own union when they proceed in this manner?

EP: I don't know if I can really answer that—let me say that years ago, the union and the employer used to have continuous dialog, and a lot of the problems that would ensue in a theater could be resolved mutually to the satisfaction of the grievant. The legal profession has entered into the scene and has become a very influential part of the industry. Employers now have the unions negotiate with an attorney. That protracts the negotiations, and it's very costly for the employer because attorneys don't come cheap. Attorneys are entering more and more into the workplace. Recently because of the O.J. Simpson situation, and now President Clinton's situation,[11] we've become a litigious society. People know more about the law now than they ever have in the history of mankind, and as a result, there are literally tens of thousands of attorneys in the state looking for ways to make a fee. So where you get into these grievances—if the union does not grieve an issue on behalf of an employee, the employee can turn around, get an attorney, go after the union and say that the union has unfairly represented that individual. So the union is forced to take action that it would never have taken years ago. I really can't answer the direction that we're going [in] because I'm not happy at all with it. But if I had my druthers I'd keep the attorneys out of the picture, and let the union and the employer sit down and commonly come to a mutual resolution on situations that require their attention.

TC: What has been the highlight of your union work?

EP: The highlights have been the rapport that I have had with the employers in San Francisco. The honesty that has prevailed between us over the thirty years that I was the executive officer has produced the highest quality contracts with the least problems. We haven't had one work stoppage. We haven't had one strike. We have had minor disagreements, but ironically, we've not had one single case with any of the employers I've dealt with in the theatrical field that has gone to arbitration. So that's quite a record. Second, I believe that through the collective bargaining process we were able to put together the best health and welfare fund, which we did in 1965, and the best pension plan, which we put together in 1967, that exist in the entire field of unionized labor in the United State and Canada.

TC: What changes lie in store for union members in the twenty-first century?

EP: Let's talk about the entertainment industry first. I still believe that technological change will have a great impact because each year that goes by gives us new ways to do things. It doesn't necessarily mean, nor has it in the past, that it will diminish manpower because the manpower that is diminished on the work end of the performance is usually made up in the setting up or the taking down of the attraction. Very similar to *Phantom of the Opera* where it takes two or three months to set the show up, and maybe a month to restore the house. Years ago we used to do a light opera that employed thirty-five or more people backstage that we would bring in on a Sunday morning. We'd work around the clock and have it ready for show time at 8:30 P.M. on Monday night. Today, you can't do that with an ordinary show unless it's a one-set show. You can't do it with a musical or a multi-set show. So I see more technology coming where it's going to change the way that we wire, the way that we amplify sound, the way we hang lights—things of that nature. All in all show business is show business and people still want to see a live person and hear a live voice, and I think as time goes on it won't be that great of a change in the industry.

In organized labor, on the other hand, there will be changes because people—even though they're getting what they believe are good deals with an employer—401K plans, and in some cases, the plans may be portable from employer to employer—the fact is that when they have any kind of a problem, they can't address it any other way than sitting down with a supervisor whose job it is to protect the employer. So sooner or later, the union comes into focus where the person thinks—well, if I join a union, I can be represented, I can be part of a group, I don't have to bargain for myself, I don't have to grieve for myself, I can have somebody else do that for me and there's a safety net factor involved with that. I think as time goes on you're going to see more and more people look favorably toward the union. The pendulum will certainly swing the other way, as it always does, and the union will be in the upswing.

NOTES

1. Tony (H. Anthony Reilly III) is a lifelong friend who later became the general manager of San Francisco's Shorenstein Hays*Nederlander Organization, which operates the Curran, Golden Gate, and Orpheum Theaters.

2. At the time of this interview, New York's state attorney general had launched an investigation of ticket-scalping. This practice is discussed in chapter 11.

3. At the time of the interview the Bill Clinton/Monica Lewinsky scandal was full, blown with the Starr report coming out a day later. It was impossible to avoid the subject in almost any conversation. In that honesty was a topic in this interview, what was happening on governmental levels seemed topical.

4. Barbara Boxer is one of California's State Senators up for reelection the year this interview was conducted (1998).

5. First Lady, Hillary Clinton.

6. Thomas C. Short, international president of International Alliance of Theatrical Stage Employees, Moving Picture Technicians, Artists, and Allied Crafts of the United States and Canada.

7. Theatrical Stage Employees Local Number 16.

8. Peters, Tom. 1997. "SoundOff!" *Fast Forward*, September 12.

9. ATPAM represents press agents and theater mangers and became affiliated with the International Alliance of Theatrical Stage Employees in 1994.

10. Garth Drabinsky was a cofounder of the producing company Livent, which filed for bankruptcy in 1998.

11. Mr. Powell refers to the Bill Clinton/Monica Lewinsky scandal that dominated the news in 1998.

Chapter 18

Manager Topics:
In Our Own Words

The situations managers find themselves in each day can range from the upsetting to the hilarious. At times we are certain we must be on *Candid Camera* because it seems that certain incidents couldn't possibly really happen. At other times we wonder if an aggressive consumer affairs reporter is going to step out of the shadows and push a microphone in our face. At the same time, we are simply employees who have our own job concerns. We wonder if there will be enough shows to provide us with work; if a new management change will keep us on; if our union will go on strike. We are like anybody else. This chapter was opened up for managers to speak on any issue or topic they wanted to share—in their own words.

About Managing: "The worst thing I ever did to myself as a manager was believing I could never make a mistake. There were always so many people around me complaining—customers, employees, bosses—that I thought I had to be perfect; more was expected of me than of anybody else in the company. I held myself to a standard that was impossible to meet. If you don't make mistakes, you don't learn or grow. I wish employers gave a little leeway for this, but it's not an idea for which they have very much sympathy. It's easier to blame the manager."

A Customer: "We had a customer who continually jumped across the ropes that blocked access into the auditorium. After the third time of asking him to go through the ticket-takers he jumped the ropes again. This time his foot landed on the rope causing him to lose his balance and pitch forward. The two stanchions jerked inward and conked him on both sides of the head. If only we'd had a camera it would have been great for *America's Funniest Home Videos*."

Local Conditions: "It's part of my job to inform show personnel of any union-related procedures. In our town one rule is that you inform the unions when you bring in TV cameras and press to opening night, and assure the unions that all guidelines will be followed. One press agent assured me this didn't need to be done, that she'd been part of the New York negotiating committee that had done away with all those archaic rules. I explained to her that the local unions didn't care what she'd done in New York and that she'd have to tell the local business agents that there'd be press, especially TV cameras on certain performances. About ten minutes before opening night, the musician's business agent was instructing the TV cameras to break down their crew because they had no authority to tape the show. And they're doing it! We almost lost all the press for an opening night! The press agent was standing in the background not knowing what to do. I had to scream at the business agent as he argued that I couldn't tape the show without telling him. I finally told him to go sit down and we'd straighten it out tomorrow. He did, but basically because I'd yelled at him. The TV crews got their tape, but the press agent never said a word to me about being sorry she hadn't done it the way I told her to. She left town the next day."

Reality: "Let's get this straight right up front—managers are not putting on the show. You won't be watching rehearsals to give the stage manager and director your opinion, or talking on a regular basis with the star performers. However, you will hear from all of these people if it is too hot, too cold, too medium or there's not enough toilet paper in the bathroom."

My Worst Experience in Theater: "My worst night in a theater was early in the first frenzied run of *Cats*. A sold-out house five minutes before intermission: a fourteen-year-old boy stood up in the middle of a balcony row and announced he was about to be sick. As he inched out of the packed row, he vomited on the heads and shoulders of the people in front of him—all the way to the aisle. The panicked ushers warned me to get to the balcony. In the lobby, I confronted what looked to be atomic bomb victims: people holding their clothes at arms length, staggering about with arms outstretched, hair, faces and shoulders covered with debris. The first [two people] I spoke to were both lawyers. It went downhill from there. My first coherent thought was: I must find who did this and get them out of the theater. I followed the debris trail to the balcony men's room, back out and down the stairs to the mezzanine lobby and into the mezzanine's men's room. Inside I find a puking kid and his worried father. The father says to me, 'I just don't know what happened. We were all excited about coming to see the show, so we went out to celebrate before hand and had a huge shellfish dinner.' The father wants to go up to the balcony and apologize to the crowd. I suggest he and his son leave before they are torn limb from limb. I hustle them out the door and into a cab. How we got through the rest of the evening I will never know. Despite a heroic effort by the staff, there were many empty seats in the balcony during the second act. Months later, I was still reseating patrons who left, and getting endless dry cleaning bills. The worst thing about it was how everyone blamed me personally for ruining their evening, as if I had anything to do with that boy and his shellfish dinner."

Don't Look Behind That Curtain: "My theater has these rather elaborate boxes on the side of the auditorium. Entrance halls behind the boxes are curtained off but light can leak through the curtains so the ushers must constantly check them to make sure they are properly closed. One night during a show an usher finds two customers having sex in the hallway. They quickly returned to their seats and the stunned usher repeats his story to others in the front-of-house. After the story had circulated for a while, a box office person remembers the woman buying the tickets and insisting on that particular box. Other staff remembered them as having come to the theater more than once. We all figured this wasn't their first time doing 'the deed' in the theater."

A Union Yarn: "The best story I heard was about a New York GM who had also been a stage tenor. As a GM for a big New York firm, he found himself in a union negotiation across the table from the producer-wildman David Merrick. Merrick, eyeing the GM, made a loud aside to the effect he wasn't used to negotiating with 'chorus boys.' The GM reached across the table, pulled Merrick up, and said, 'You will with this chorus boy, or he's going to throw you out that window!'"

A Bad Settlement: "The worst settlement I saw was between an assistant general manager for a local venue and the major production of Broadway's then hottest director. The assistant was known for her temper and disorganization. She overwhelmed her adversaries with chaos and a raised voice. No one, including the show's GM and even the venue staff, could figure out her settlements; the holding figures—in the millions—were held onto for months, mostly because no one could figure out who owed what. A victory for the theater perhaps, as it held onto lots of money, but future contracts had clauses that put a stop to this."

Settlement Woes: "An interesting settlement I did was between my theater and a major production with a superstar actor. The deal was inherited when my company bought the theater, and the deal made the theater bleed. The previous owner had been desperate for a booking. The producer offered the new owner a take-it-or-leave-it option, but we needed the booking, too. Early on in the engagement I raised a big fuss about a minor issue, which drove the show's GM nuts, but it showed I meant business. There was enough vague language in the contract for me to charge the show everything under the sun—pencils, envelopes, whatever I could find. When the run was over, I had recovered over $150,000 in general expenses, enough to make us a small profit."

A Customer: "A manager told me about a woman who accused an usher of cleaning during intermission and taking her $10 souvenir program and umbrella. When informed that the ushers don't clean at intermission she said the usher stole the items. The house manager asked if she saw an usher steal it and she said 'No.' Then the manager asked if another patron might have stolen her things. The woman said, 'A customer would never do that.' To which the house manager responded, 'But an usher would?'"

ADA: "One thing I am never prepared for is able-bodied people who complain that disabled people are ruining their enjoyment of the show. To people who complain about the hard of hearing person next to them who is wearing a headset, I say, 'Isn't it wonderful technology gives them a chance to hear a show just like you,' and then I ignore their complaint. To people who complain that a wheelchair is in their way, I will gladly refund or move them, but I will not tolerate any blaming of the other party. I'll get frosty and make it clear I will not listen to discriminatory talk. My worst experience was a signed performance for deaf people. Hearing customers, in nearby seats, complained the signers were a distraction. One loud and irate man complaining in front of the deaf patrons was shouted down by me (the word "Stop!" delivered with all the force my lungs could muster did the trick). I then quickly invited him to leave, promising a hand-delivered refund check the next day if he would keep his mouth shut and leave quickly. He was escorted to the door by my assistant to insure no further disruptions."

Change: "New management comes in waves. Some of it will be effective and other times you'll just roll your eyes, ride it out, and hope it falls by the wayside. We once had an overseer who referred to everyone in the theater as 'you people.' New management's intentions may be good, but the result can sometimes be disastrous on morale. What the manager has to deal with in every case is change. Not many people are comfortable with it, but it does keep coming. Remember that new management's goal is to improve business for the owner, not necessarily respond to the needs of the workers. And this is okay because new policies should serve the business, but all too often they only serve the higher-ups. The other problem is when the people who are sent in to 'fix' things are clueless. I've watched a number of them go nuts or burn out. The ones that come in crazy to begin with must be dealt with. Remember that when engaged in battle—never negotiate with a madman, instead plan your way around them."

Back Then: "If you are well prepared for disabled people, you won't have too many problems. Of course the age of the facility is the major factor, but just having some helpful staff who move in when asked (or when obviously needed) can smooth things over. When blamed about any condition, I laugh it off with something like, 'Well if I had been born when the architect of this building drew up the plans, I certainly would have made some changes.' Any rough stuff or threats are dismissed with, 'Let's leave that to lawyers. My job is to get you in and make you comfortable.'"

Just Deserts: "Customers are always accusing the staff of embarrassing them. Sometimes they deserve to be embarrassed, like after they've taken pictures or videos of the performance, and when we ask them to stop and they agree, but then continue. They're usually sitting in the middle of a row where we have to disturb other customers to get to them. When confronted at the end of the show, they deny they've done anything and complain loudly about how much you've embarrassed them."

Disability Unfriendly: "This woman wanted to move two chairs behind her mother's wheelchair. She claimed to work in customer service and said she would work it out herself, and shooed me away. I asked her how she would do that and she said 'Don't challenge me!' She ended the conversation by saying she didn't like how I was handling this, that I was not being professional and wasn't going to do anything for her, but she would be calling to complain. Then she walked away. First of all managers are not customer service representatives. You are a manager, of which customer service is one aspect of your job. Any customer service representative who would put a customer in a dangerous situation, such as blocking a wheelchair in with another chair, is not only stupid but is putting his company in a position of extreme liability. In the event of a disaster where that setup caused harm or injury, that manager may face criminal charges. The customer who thanks you for 'working out the problem' will not remember your kindness when she [is] filing her wrongful death suit because of your incompetence of letting her block her own mother's wheelchair. The next issue you need to deal with is what to do when your employer gets these letters about you. It is an unfortunate reality that they will probably side with the customer and reprimand you."

Don't Forget to Duck: "Customers that go berserk or ballistic are customers that you don't need. The airlines have been more supportive of their crews, but that has not followed in theater where the management is not supportive of their own staff against customers. On an airplane the captain is in command. Disruptive passengers can be restrained or even handcuffed. Assaulting or interfering with a flight crew is a federal offense. For some theater customers who go out of control it is a shame that this is not also a federal offense. There may even be a crime involved, such as assault or battery. But often theater employees tolerate this kind of behavior from customers."

Union Negotiations: "One of the problems with the union/theater relationships is that there is nowhere to escape to should negotiations bog down. Management does not have the ability to move its theater to another place the way a manufacturing company might move its work to another state or country."

Manager Techniques: "Sharing problems—find someone who can do the things you're bad at, and at a later time you can return to favor. One manager I know was not good at dealing with female patrons and I, occasionally, would call them for him. I, on the other hand, had an awful relationship with a particular vendor we often had to deal with, and he'd make those calls for me."

Concluding Thoughts

I began this book with a story about a bullet. A bullet that ended a life. Throughout this book I have tried to demonstrate ways to dodge, side-step, or direct the path of the metaphorical bullet. In the case of Hewlett Tarr there was probably little he could have done to avoid his fate. I am ending with the story of another bullet, equally as tragic, but one that I hope all those who work in the entertainment industry strive to avoid. It is not a foregone conclusion that any of us will escape the real bullet. One sort of bullet is the one that took the life of Mr. Tarr. There is also another kind.

When I was twenty-one years old, beginning my career and working as the assistant manager of the Golden Gate Theater, I met a press agent named Horace Greeley MacNab. He is best described as an old-timer, a character whose first words were usually, "How are you? I'm peachy-keen."

On opening night of *A Chorus Line* he strolled up to me and asked in a high-pitched nasal tone, "What's a pretty girl like you doing in a business like this?" At first, I thought he was flirting, as Horace's girlfriend was only slightly older than me. Then, his face changed. The crusty jowls and crinkled skin hardened, and the only life in him was the twinkling eyes, concentrated in thought. He said to me, "Get out of this business. Get out of it before it kills you."

I stood there, saying nothing, not knowing what to say. He smiled a sad, bittersweet smile, turned, and walked away. Months later, Horace committed suicide. Horace had had more than a career; he had a life in show business. Perhaps his life had ceased to have meaning; perhaps he saw his career fading to a new generation of press agents where he was a caricature of himself, not a "passer-on of knowledge." Perhaps he lost his hold on choice. His earlier advice that day in the lobby of the Golden Gate has always disturbed me. No one should stay in a business that kills you. Everyone talked about Horace for a while. Some mourned him, all speculated on how many years he had planned his dramatic death, but then, they went on. . . . Act II.

When I first began working on this book, part of my goal was to provide information to those who come after me, a stepping-stone, so to speak, so that beginning managers might not be thrown into situations for which they are unprepared. Its contents reflect areas that are important to me, incidents that have happened to me, the experiences of other managers and colleagues who work in this business. They may not provide conclusions that are popularly thought of as good management, but instead it is practical management based on what happens in the real world. Often this counsel will be contrary to popular management theory. Instead I am seeking information that works.

Much of this book is concerned with the problems of managing a theater. Beginning managers are often ill prepared to handle the uniqueness of these incidents. They are the kinds of situations most likely to cut a career short. I remember when I first started working in theater, a coworker told me, "don't bring the general manager the problem, bring him the solution." There are enough cheerleaders in this industry who will tell you how to make it in Hollywood. They will inspire, coach, and point the way. You are the only one who will walk the path.

Fifth row center orchestra is two seats. On any one night they cannot be filled with the ten people who are absolutely certain they purchased them. Experts who write books on management theory and customer service are usually at home having dinner with their families at 8 P.M. They are not there as backup when a customer waving theater tickets in your face is screaming and calling you every name in the book.

Yet this path has a different side as well. After several years of working as a theater manager, a young man walked up to me in the lobby of the Curran Theatre and handed me his resume. "I just can't work a normal job anymore," he said. "I've had it with nine-to-five." We had no positions open.

Like the dancers in *A Chorus Line*, many people want the few jobs available in theater. Once we have these jobs, we fall in love with them. We adjust to the things we do not like and accommodate the idiosyncrasies just like we might with a partner. No matter how much overtime goes unpaid, we begin to realize how lucky we are to work in an industry where we have fun. Our job becomes more than something we do during the day or night. It becomes our life.

I have described and quoted some of the people that a house manager will interact with during the course of a week. While I have taken the viewpoint of the theater manager I would like to reiterate that all of these people have complex and exacting jobs. However, there is a multitude of books on producing, directing, acting, stagecraft, stage managing, publicity, and production design. Theater management often warrants no more than a paragraph in a few of these books. I have tried to expand on these meager descriptions and draw a full portrait of the breadth of the job as well as the details associated with it. Perhaps of all the definitions, the one that encompasses all our duties is, "The theater manager is the only person in contact with all the elements of a production—onstage, backstage, and front-of-house. It is your job to bring all those elements together, and no matter what, remember, the show must go on" (Schneider and Ford 1993, 191).

Appendix A
Specs Package: Advance Information and Backstage Information

Advance Information

The Renaissance Theater
1221 Main Street
Midtown, USA

Telephone Numbers

Staff	Position	Telephone Number
Joshua Jones	Owner	555-5555
		fax: 555-5555
Eric Edwards	General Manager	555-5555
		fax: 555-5555
Tess Collins	House Manager	555-5555
		fax: 555-5555
Sally Smith	Box Office Treasurer	555-5555
		fax: 555-5555
Adam Alridge	Subscription Manager	555-5555
		fax: 555-5555
Connie Conway	Group Sales	555-5555
		fax: 555-5555
Frank Finn	Head Carpenter	555-5555
		fax: 555-5555
George Grant	Head Electrician	555-5555
		fax: 555-5555

Isis Ingram	Head Propertyman	555-5555
		fax: 555-5555
Karen Kombs	Head Sound	555-5555
		fax: 555-5555
Luke Lufkin	Stagedoor	555-5555
		fax: 555-5555
Martin Mendez	Head Usher	555-5555
		fax: 555-5555
Nathan North	Head of Security	555-5555
		fax: 555-5555

Auditorium Capacity

	Orchestra	1,500
	Mezzanine	700
	Balcony	300
	Total Capacity	2,500

Please notify theater management if you expect the set to obstruct the view of any seat in the auditorium, or if you intend to take out seats for a sound or electric board.

The sound booth is located in the balcony and measures 15′ × 6′. If you do not intend on using it and plan on taking out seats in the auditorium to accommodate your soundboard, you must have the permission of general manager prior to the show moving into the theater.

Banking Information

The following procedures have been set up with a local bank so that your company members may cash production paychecks and per diem checks.

1. The show's bank must send a letter guaranteeing certain moneys per week with the stipulation that no individual check will exceed $_____ amount.

2. The company manager will send the local bank a list of names and signatures of all personnel employed by the show who will be cashing checks.

3. Each person listed should be provided with an identification card or letter confirming his or her credibility.

4. The company manager should provide a sample of payroll and per diem checks to the bank.

The above information should be sent to the attention of:

Joe Banker
Bank of Midtown

201 Main Street
Midtown, USA
phone: 555-5555

Things to Know about the Theater and Midtown, USA

1. State Tax: All money paid to the show is subject to a 10% state tax. At times this tax can be lowered by having your accountant or financial advisor talk to the tax board. The address is:

State Tax Board
P.O. Box 5555
State Capitol, USA
(555) 555-5555

2. Unions: Copies of union contracts are available in the manager's office upon request. We recommend that you familiarize yourself with the contracts to avoid any misunderstandings or situations that will cost the company money.

Stagehands Union
Opal Owens, Business Agent
1414 Maple Street
Midtown, USA
(555) 555-5555

Wardrobe Union
Peter Parker, Business Agent
1512 Oak Street
Midtown, USA
(555) 555-5555

Musicians Union
Ruth Rowen, Business Agent
2214 Tulip Street
Midtown, USA
(555) 555-5555

Teamsters: Sam Sinclair, Sinclair Moving & Storage
(555) 555-5555

3. Taxes: For company managers needing information on taxes for out of state employees, contact:

Employment Tax District Office
1215 Maple Street

Midtown, USA
(555) 555-5555

4. Pets Backstage: No pets of any kind are allowed in the backstage areas of the theater. This rule has been instituted due to health, safety, and
space and noise considerations. In addition, the safety of the pets themselves requires they not be brought to the theater because of rodent control devices and bait traps.

5. Minors Employed by Show: Minors must get a state theatrical work
permit. Employer must show proof of Worker's Compensation coverage,
the minor's birth certificate, and last school report. For information call:

Superintendent of Schools
Midtown, USA
(555) 555-5555

General Information

ASPCA	For shows traveling with animals	555-5555
Body Work:	Grady's Health Club: Swedish, deep tissue massage, acupressure Medical Massage	
	67 11th Street	555-5555
Charter Buses:	Midtown Bus Service	555-5555
	Shuttle Transportation	555-5555
	Visitor's Bus Lines	555-5555
For Individuals:	Rocket Shuttle	555-5555
	Midtown Taxi	555-5555
Child Care:	Dora's Daycare	555-5555
	The Playpen	555-5555
Computer/Typewriters:	Compu-rent	555-5555
	784 12th Street	
Dry Cleaners:	Day & Nite Dry Cleaning	555-5555
	188 Main Street	
Dry Ice:	Midtown Ice Company	555-5555
Fire Department:	For permits	555-5555
Health Club:	Grady's Health Club	555-5555
	6578 Reggaes Road	
	Midtown Hotel ($120 per month)	555-5555
	One Main Square	555-5555
Limousine Service:	King's Sedan Service	555-5555
	Midtown Limousines	555-5555
Notary Public:	Midtown Secretarial Services	555-5555
	789 16th Street	

Oxygen:	Midtown Medical	555-5555
Refrigerators:	ABC Rentals	555-5555
	1256 Green Street	
Salons:	Gina's Salon (facial, waxing,	555-5555
	manicures)	
	123 North Oak	
	Jeffrey's Hair Design	555-5555
	Midtown Mall	
	Macy's Spa	555-5555
	154 Gray Street	
Shoe Repair:	Bill's Shoe Service	555-5555
	12 Main Street	
Veterinarian:	Midtown Animal Hospital	555-5555
	145 South Street	

Local Doctors This list of doctors has been compiled from recommendations by other performing companies and theater employees. They are not affiliated with the theater and there is no guarantee they will be able to accommodate your needs. For special services the best solution is to call Physicians Access.

General Practice:	Midtown Physicians Access	555-5555
	Dr. Sam Sarris	555-5555
	45 Down Street	
Chiropractic:	Dr. Barry Chin	555-5555
	100 Bush Street	
	Dr. Claudia Callandaer	555-5555
	27 Southern Street	
Orthopedic:	Dr. David Ross	555-5555
	898 Bush Street	
	Midtown Orthopedic Center	555-5555
	2845 Main Street	
Ear/Nose/Throat:	Dr. Baron Douglas	555-5555
	3546 13th Avenue	
	(used by Midtown Opera)	
	Dr. Brian Post	555-5555
	4736 Green Street	
Ob/Gyn:	Dr. Susan Jones	555-5555
	1245 6th Avenue	
	Dr. Bruce Taylor	555-5555
	467 Spruce Street	
Sports Injuries:	Center for Athletic Medicine	555-5555
	Midtown General	
Dermatologist:	Dr. Robert Warren	555-5555
	876 15th Avenue	
Dentist:	Dental Referral Service	555-5555

	Dr. Bill Hyde	555-5555
	78 Pine Street	
Nearest Hospital:	Midtown General	555-5555
	1253 Jaynes Street	
	Emergency Room	555-5555
	1255 Jaynes Street	

For Police, Fire, and Ambulance Emergencies Only, Dial 911

Housing Information   The places listed below are the most frequently used housing in the area of the Renaissance Theater. Please call for rates. Others are on file in the manager's office if the places below cannot accommodate your company's needs.

Hamlet House
124 Bush Street (about 6 blocks from theater)
555-5555

Midtown Towers
1528 Main Street (about 2 blocks from theater)
555-5555

Post Plaza
3553 Post Street (about 1 mile from theater)
555-5555

Trinity Courtyard
845 12th Avenue (about 5 blocks from theater)
555-5555

Hotel Information

Expensive

Broadway Gardens, 253 12th Street, 555-555
Midtown Hotel, 1343 Main Street, 555-5555
Shannon Spa, 45 Spruce Street, 555-5555

Moderately Priced

Billingsly Hotel, 345 Main Street, 555-5555
Brewer's Hotel, 35 Green Street, 555-5555
Lindsay Place, 34 5th Street, 555-5555
For additional information please speak with the house manager.

Also Include in Advance Information

Letters of reference from companies interested in doing business with traveling shows; information on local restaurants; emergency instructions on whatever local disaster occasionally hits your area—earthquakes, floods, tornadoes, hurricanes; and other information pertinent to your city or facility.

Backstage Information

The Renaissance Theater
1221 Main Street
Midtown, USA

Stage

Stage: Proscenium
Width of Proscenium Opening: 45 ft
Height of Proscenium Opening: 35 ft
Center Front Stage to Back Wall: 47 ft
House Curtain: Guillotine
House Rigging System: Counter Weight, 62 sets
First Working Set: 2 ft
Flying Height to Grid: Sets 1–20: 58 ft
                        Sets 21–62: 69 ft
Width of Stage Area:
   Wall to Wall: 112 ft
   Center Line to Stage Right: 62 ft
   Center Line to Stage Left: 50 ft
Stage to Fly Floor: 25 ft
Pin Rail from Deck: 32 ft
First Working Set to Edge of Pit: 4 ft
Distance between Sets: 6 in.
Number of Sets with Short Travel: 15
Distance from stage Floor to House Floor: 4 ft 2 in.
Stage Floor is Softwood with Masonite Deck

Orchestra Pit

Front of Orchestra Pit to Apron at Center Line: 10 ft
Orchestra Pit Side to Side at Apron: 45 ft
Height: 7 ft
Orchestra Pit Rail: 36 in.
Pit accommodates approximately twenty to twenty-six people, depending on instrumentation. We have available: one conductor's podium with light, thirty-two music stands with lights, electrical outlets, and changing room. If you do not use the pit, it can be disassembled and covered over

with a floor and two rows of theater seats. We do not have a stage extension over the pit. Communication equipment between conductor and stage manager must be supplied by show.

Loading Door

Access to the loading door is in the rear parking lot. The door measures 8 ft wide and 12 ft high. To bring items through the front of the theater you must secure permission from the house manager. All rugs must be covered in order to prevent damage from road boxes.

Dressing Rooms

Basement: Two chorus rooms measuring 20′ × 20′, usually accommodating up to twenty-five people. Each has shower, bathroom, mirrors with makeup lights, and three quad box outlets. The basement level also has two men's and women's bathrooms on the east end of the building with additional showers.

Stage Level: Two star dressing rooms, 15′ × 15′, dressing area and guest area. Each has its own bathroom and shower, a single line phone outlet, refrigerator, and air conditioner. Sometimes these rooms are used as the stage manager's office or a quick change room.

Principle Dressing Rooms: Twenty rooms (8′ × 8′) on two levels, stage right. There is one shower and bathroom on each floor.

Offices

The company manager's office is in the front-of-house beside the box office. It measures 8 × 8 and is furnished with two desks, bookcase, filing cabinet, and two tables. There are two rollover phone lines and a separate fax line.

The stage manager's office is in the basement, on the east end of the building. It measures 8′ × 6′ and is furnished with two desks and file cabinets. There is a single phone line with call-waiting.

Wardrobe

A 30 × 20 open section underneath the stage is used as the wardrobe area. It has fluorescent lighting, twelve wardrobe racks, and additional hanging pipes. There are four industrial washer/dryers and a row of sinks for hand washing. Please see wardrobe head for local dry cleaning vendors.

Electrics

Power:

A.C. Only. Company racks can be on the deck or the stage right fly floor, which is 30 ft high. Six 400 amp. Legs 2 phase 2,000 amps on fly floor; 80 ft feeders needed if racks are on stage. House light control is at stage level on stage right, 5 ft off stage.

Hanging Position:

Front-of-House: Mezzanine and Balcony rails

Width: 35 ft

Distance from Plaster Line: Mezzanine: 50 ft
Balcony: 70 ft

Number of House Circuits: 30 each level

Capacity per Circuit: 2,000 watts

Type of Connector: Pin

Box Booms: Four on each side of theater, eighteen house circuits per side, 2,000 watts per circuit, pin connectors

Spot Booth: Located in rear of Balcony, 120 ft from stage; 180 amps available for four spotlights. The house owns two spotlights that are available for rent.

There is no house sound system. If soundboard is to be located in the house, please inform house manager of locations so these seats can be taken off sale. Rear balcony often requires supplemental speakers.

If your show has extensive pyrotechnics, we need to inform the local fire department at least one month in advance. A state licensed pyrotechnic must travel with the show or be hired locally. Please contact the house manager well in advance to make arrangements.

City Theatrical Vendors

JB Productions, 333 James Street, 555-5555
Midtown Theatrical Lighting, 533 2nd Avenue, 555-5555
Davis Sound, 53 Battery, 555-555
Gina's Pianos, 345 James Street, 555-5555
For additional vendors, please talk to department heads or house manager.

Copyright Infringement

In order to protect the copyright of the production, the Renaissance Theater has brass signs posted on each level of the theater and a prohibitive warning on the ticket and in the program. We encourage every company to make an announcement prior to the start of the show reiterating that picture taking, video, and sound recording are not allowed.

If our staff sees a patron recording the show, they will ask the person to stop. We are unable to confiscate a customer's personal property, and we have no law in this state allowing us to do this. We will request that any film, video, or tape be given to us with the promise of reimbursement to the customer at the show's expense. In the event that the patron refuses, we will ask for their name, address, and phone number and turn this information over to you. It is then up to the show to proceed in civil court against the offending party.

Also Include in Backstage Specs

Plot line with measurements and weight capacity; drawing or computer layout of house showing sound position, spot booth, disabled seating; drawing or computer layout of backstage showing offices, wardrobe, dressing rooms, and loading door; drawing or computer layout of orchestra pit. Seating chart. Map of city; map of state.

Any other information pertinent to your facility.

Appendix B
Emergency and Security Procedures

These procedures were reviewed and added to by security consultant, Louis Ligouri of Ligouri Associates, Napa, CA 94558.

The Renaissance Theater
Emergency Procedures
Revised 6/03

Introduction

The Renaissance Theater's policy is to manage its activities with the goal of promoting the safety and health of its employees, customers, and show personnel. In the event of an emergency, the staff will need to act quickly and calmly to assist in whatever way necessary. With education, training, and coordinated effort, we will be able to eliminate panic and confusion. Please let your department head or the house manager know immediately of any unsafe conditions or emergency situations.

Emergency Telephone Numbers

Police, Fire Dept., Paramedics: 911
Theater Manager's Office: 555-5555, intercom 21
    cell phone: 555-5555
Administrative Office: 555-5555
Head of Security: 555-5555
        pager: 555-5555

Building Overview and Safety Features

The Renaissance Theater is equipped with fire extinguishers, manual pull stations, stage fire curtain, sprinkler system, stand pipes and hoses, fire pump, emergency lights, neon exit signs, and a building-wide public address system.

When the life safety system is activated, the emergency system will engage by notifying the fire department via telegraphic signal. An audible building alarm will sound and strobe lights over each exit will flash. The fire department will respond to the emergency alarm. Listen for announcements over the public address system as to whether the emergency is actual or a false alarm. Until you know, you should proceed as if there is an emergency and begin evacuation procedures.

This plan is divided into four segments:

I. Preemergency

II. Emergency

III. Postemergency

IV. Specialized: bomb threats, earthquake, civil and individual violence, stalkers, disabled patrons, box office robbery.

Part I: Preemergency   Upon arriving to work, each employee should take a few minutes to inspect his or her work site. Correct and report any unsafe conditions so that action may be taken to ensure against reoccurrence. Report any condition you are unable to correct to the house manager.

Front-of-House
House Manager

1. Will schedule life safety training for employees as needed.
2. Will respond to any unsafe condition reported by an employee and report to the owner if the condition is not immediately correctable.
3. Will conduct weekly safety inspections of the theater.
4. Will conduct or provide for violence-in-the-workplace training and education.

Ushers/Ticket-Takers

1. Inspect your assigned areas to ensure exit doors work, no lights are burned out, stairwells are clear of obstructions and trip hazards.
2. Make note of disabled patron's locations so they can be assisted in the event of an evacuation.
3. Any unsafe condition should be reported to the head usher or house manager.

Box Office

1. Turn on box office alarm when office is unattended.
2. All employees should know how to activate silent alarm in the event of robbery.
3. Inspect your assigned areas to ensure exit doors work, no lights are burned out, stairwells are clear of obstructions and trip hazards.
4. An unsafe condition should be reported to the house manager.

Housekeeping

1. Keep interior and exterior sidewalks, pathways, stairs, aisles, and exits clean and clear of trip hazards.

Security

1. Keep front of theater clear for emergency vehicles.

Backstage
Stagedoor

1. Check that hallways and staircases are clear of obstructions and trip hazards.
2. Check to ensure serviceability of locks, door, lights, etc.
3. Report hazards or failed equipment/hardware.

Stagehands/Wardrobe

1. Respond according to your department: Carpentry—maintenance on doors, maintain fire curtain; Props—check carpet for trip hazards; Electrics—check nightly for burned out light bulbs, other faulty equipment or conditions.

Engineer

1. Weekly inspections and test of fire and life safety monitoring system.
2. Weekly inspection of fire pump.
3. Daily inspection of emergency lighting system.

Fire Prevention Measures
Do not accumulate discarded files and paper trash in your office. Pay special attention to housekeeping in areas that produce any amount of

trash. Keep electrical appliances and cords in good repair. Inspect all electrical cords for damage and do not overload outlets or use extension cords unless authorized by house manager or house electrician.

Emergency Equipment
The theater is equipped with an emergency system that alerts the fire department when a pull station or sprinkler system is activated. In addition, fire extinguishers are located throughout the building. A paging system is in the front-of-house in the event an evacuation is necessary. Department heads are to carry their walkie-talkies at least one hour prior to show time and afterwards until the auditorium is empty. All ushers must have a flashlight when on duty.

Part II: Emergency
Evacuation
In the event of an evacuation the goal is to empty the building of audience and staff, locate them to a safe area, and make the building accessible to emergency response teams (fire, police, swat team, bomb squad).

During Evacuation: Keep talking to a minimum. Listen for instructions over the public address system. Advise customers to remove platform or high heel shoes until they arrive at street level. Walk down exit staircases. Do not use elevators. Staff assigned to outside the theater should direct patrons away from the theater. If possible after evacuation, ushers, stage-door, and security should search for stragglers, people hiding, disabled people, and anyone else in need of assistance.

After Evacuation: All employees should check in with their department heads. Department heads should survey employees to confirm everyone is out of the building and report any missing people to the house manager, as well as any conditions relevant to the situation. In the event that the house manager is incapacitated and you have relevant information, report to the head of the emergency response team. Await instructions from the house manager or the ranking head of the emergency response team.

Department Head Instructions:
Upon hearing through the public address system that the theater will be evacuated:
The house lights will be turned on by house electrician.
Ushers should open exit doors and direct customers. Use a flashlight in the event of power failure. Aid any disabled person who is still in the theater. If you are unable to evacuate them, place them as close to the exit as possible and report their position to the house manager and the emergency response team.

If You Discover A Fire:
Alert house manager and other occupants by pulling fire alarm pull station and calling 911. Attempt to contain or stop a small trashcan or ash-

tray fire with a fire extinguisher or water. Leave the building if the fire is anything other than a small ashtray/trashcan fire. Take whatever measures are possible to protect property. CLOSE ALL DOORS ALONG THE EXIT ROUTE.

Do NOT break windows to vent smoke. Falling glass is a serious threat to people and fire fighters below. DO NOT OPEN HOT DOORS. Before opening any door, touch it near the top to see if it is hot. A fire on the other side will blast through the slightest opening with tremendous force and heat. Wait outside the building and inform the fire department of the status and location of the fire when you call in the alarm.

Part III: Postemergency   When the ranking head of the emergency response team has approved returning to the building, each department head should assess his/her department, take actions necessary to protect property, and report to the house manager.

Part IV: Specialized   With all emergencies, be prepared for panic.

Earthquake: In the event of a major earthquake, the safest thing to do is remain inside the theater. Patrons and staff should be encouraged to remain seated until after the shaking stops. Take cover under tables, desks, and under strong doorways. Keep clear of file cabinets, shelves, and materials stacked over a foot high. Check for any injured persons and administer first aid as necessary.

Bomb Threat: In the event of a bomb threat or bomb incident, all situations are not identical and must be approached by employees with good judgment and cooperation. In the event a call is received, all employees informed to do so should conduct a search of their areas. In case a suspicious item is located, the finder should not touch it, but immediately notify the proper authorities.

Civil Disturbances: Stay in the building, away from windows. If the windows are in danger of being broken, they can be boarded up using plywood from backstage or blocked with furniture or curtains. Taking further action will depend on conditions.

Stalkers: If you see any person who has previously been identified as stalking a performer or individual, alert house and company manager, stagedoor, and security immediately. Do not engage the individual. Note description, race, sex, height, weight, color of hair and eyes, facial hair, clothing, car license number.

Individual Violence: Notify security. If an individual becomes violent, irrational, or threatening, extract yourself from the situation and report the incident to the house manager. In the case of extreme violence, such as use of a weapon that has caused injury, call 911 and request police.

Disabled Patrons: When seating disabled patrons, point out to them and their guest, if any, the nearest exit if it is not in view. If during an evacuation you are unable to assist a disabled person out of the building, locate them to the nearest exit, then report their position to the emergency response team.

Box Office Robbery: Do not try to stop a robbery. Give robbers whatever cash you have and wait for them to leave. Hit the silent alarm if or when you can do it without being noticed. Get out of the robber's sightline as soon as you are able. While the robbery is in progress, note robber's appearance, demeanor, voice, and in what direction he flees. After the robbery, do not attempt to follow the robber. Wait for police and give them all information you can.

The Renaissance Theater Security Procedures
Introduction

The policy of the Renaissance Theater is to manage its activities in a manner that protects and promotes the safety and health of its employees, patrons, and visiting shows. It is an unfortunate sign of our times that buildings, events, performers, and even individuals are targets for disruption and mayhem.

While no certain or correct response can be advocated for security-related situations, we advise caution and safety first. The following information is offered to assist you in your employment and in your personal life. The intention of the following information is to provide you with knowledge in hope that it will prepare you for an unforeseen emergency or event.

Emergencies

For emergencies, call 911

For nonemergency information, call Police Department: 555-5555

Other emergency numbers:

    Poison control: 555-5555

    Nonemergency ambulance service: 555-5555

    Suicide prevention: 555-5555

    Midtown Water Emergencies: 555-5555

    Midtown Electrical Services: 555-5555

Building Overview and Features

Locks on doors in the Renaissance Theater are keyed to a security system. Keys cannot be legally duplicated except by those managers whose names are on file with the security company. Keys must be signed out in the manager's office and are not transferable between employees.

Exit doors outfitted with panic bars also have lime-colored security bars on the inside as an additional precaution. At the bottom of the main staircase is a rolling metal door fastened with a padlock. Doors into the auditorium have interior bolt locks that can only be opened from the inside.

Box office entry is equipped with video system and voice monitor. Only after you have confirmed the identity of the person at the door should they be allowed entry. If you do not recognize the person, ask them to step to the box office window and state their business. Code words are assigned to each employee to be used to signal "a distress situation." If an employee uses the code word, do not open the door but do activate the silent alarm. Box office windows are constructed of bulletproof glass, and seller stations are equipped with silent alarms that when activated alert the police department that a robbery is in progress.

The telephone intercom system is located on every level near the top of the staircase and at various places backstage. Each phone can be used to call the police in the event of an emergency by dialing 9-911.

General Instructions for Entry into the Building

Prior to entering the building, particularly if you are alone, survey the surrounding area for unsafe situations. If anyone suspicious is watching you or the door, do not attempt access—continue past the building and wait until the person is gone or other employees arrive. Call the police, if necessary. If the situation is such that you cannot get access to the building, such as a person sleeping in the doorway, or an individual acting in a threatening manner, go to a nearby phone or business and call the police.

When entering the theater, it is always a good idea to look behind you to ensure that no one is too close and might have the opportunity to force his or her way in after you. Often vendors making deliveries do not take the precaution of locking doors behind them. After a delivery, check that doors have been secured. If you are unable to do so, let the manager know that there may be an unlocked door so that they can secure the premises.

General Instructions for Performances

Four security guards are on duty during the performance. Prior to the performance they are stationed outside the theater and around the building. As soon as patrons are off the street, one guard will report to the box office area, but will not intervene in any dispute between customers and box office personnel unless physical violence occurs. During performance, guards will remain in the outer lobby and make periodic checks of the outside of the building. In nonemergency situations, notify the theater manager of the incident prior to engaging security. In emergency situations, seek security's assistance immediately, then notify the manager.

A stagedoor person is located at the stagedoor. He will determine who goes into the backstage area based on instructions given to him by the theater manager. You must check in with him before proceeding past the stagedoor.

General Instructions for Exiting the Building

Box office: When box office personnel are locking up, you should leave lights on and have at least one other person with you to check the restrooms in the main lobby. Customers have access to these areas during the day and could be hiding or be unaware that the theater is closing. Check the main doors to the auditorium and make sure they are locked. Check locks to ensure they are not taped or jammed. If you find one open, report to the house manager. If you see an unauthorized person an any area, your safety should be foremost in your mind. For instance, if customers are wandering around trying to find their seats, they can be told they are in an unauthorized area and asked to leave. If the individual is indigent, seems mentally unsound, or is hiding for unknown purposes, then you should leave the building and call security and the police. Do your best to inform any other people in the building of the situation. If you are unsure who you are dealing with, leave the building and call the police. Use common sense, but act on the side of caution.

Before leaving the building, survey the area outside to see if it is safe for you to exit. Be especially cautious when turning around to lock the door.

Ushering and Stagedoor Lock-Up: For instruction in this area, see the head usher and stagedoor department head. If neither of these department heads are available, see the house manager. Security guards will stay until the premises are secure.

Special Circumstances

We cannot tell you how to respond in an emergency situation that is beyond our control. The primary objective is the preservation of life and safety of all employees and patrons. The information below is meant to support that premise.

Box Office Window Robbery: Robbery is the felonious taking of personal property in the possession of another, from his/her person or immediate presence, and against his will. It is accomplished by means of force or fear. Robberies are mainly crimes of opportunity enhanced by the belief that substantial monetary gain will result. Occasional news stories of large ticket sales can lead individuals to assume that large amounts of cash may be available at a theater.

Box office employees must utilize caution at all times and always be alert for a possible robbery. The off-street locations of many box offices afford a would-be robber concealment from police patrols and witnesses. A degree of protection is presently in place; the hardened undersiding (cement and marble) of the box office wall and the bulletproof glass shields employees and serve as a deterrent to crimes since a potential robber's ability to threaten and/or injure is minimized.

Box office employees are less apt to be subjected to a robbery attempt when two or more employees are present. This is particularly true because of the makeup of the facility and the inability of a robber to control all employees inside the box office. Employees should be especially alert for a robbery attempt at times when pedestrian traffic in and about the box office is minimal or absent.

If a robbery does occur, employees are asked to take the following steps to increase the possibility of later apprehension and conviction:

> Observe the robber's physical features, voice, accent, mannerisms, dress, the kind of weapons he has, and any other characteristics that would be useful for identification purposes. Protect and do not disturb any evidence left by the robber. Do not handle it. Show it to police when they arrive. Refrain from touching and prevent others from touching articles or places the robber may have touched or evidence he may have left, in order that fingerprints may be obtained. Give the robber no more money than the amount he demands. If possible, observe the direction of escape. Call the police. Never resist the demands or instructions of a robber, especially if he is armed, unless such resistance may be accomplished without any possible risk of injury to yourself and/or other employees.

Note opportunities: If the third window is being robbed, the person at the first window may be able to touch the hold-up alarm, but only if you can do so unobserved by the robber.

Box Office Invasive Robbery: If armed robbers ever gain entry to the box office, employees are instructed to comply with all instructions and/or demands. This situation obviously presents the greatest risk of harm to employees since the robbers have both access and the ability to injure anyone who is uncooperative as well as the advantage of being able to proceed outside the view of potential witnesses or passing police patrols. Employees should surrender any moneys demanded. While cooperating fully, they are also urged to make observations and take the actions described in the box office robbery paragraph.

Denial of entry into the box office area is the obvious key for preventing any box office invasion robbery. Employees are instructed to insure that they always know who they are letting into the box office area before doing so. A knock at the door is not enough. They should not let anyone in until they are certain of the person's identity via the intercom. Code words can be used to indicate a distress situation. Any unknown person asking for entry should be directed to the ticket sale window and be recognized by someone before being allowed into the box office.

Gunfire: If gunfire erupts on the property of the theater, or along the perimeter sidewalk area, employees should take every precaution to ensure their own safety. This means seeking out a position of cover out of the line of fire, or of any stray bullets. From a cover position, the employee should yell a warning to any other person in the area who may be in danger. Any situation involving guns is a police matter, and employees are instructed to refrain from any involvement other than calling for police, and making whatever observations are possible for use as a witness at a later time. Employees are also reminded that security personnel are armed. If any security personnel are available, they should immediately be notified of the situation. The theater manager should be notified as well, but only when it is safe to do so.

Hostage Situation: Theater personnel are instructed to avoid any involvement in any hostage situation on or near the property of the theater. Hostage situations are police matters and require very special treatment by trained negotiators and other law enforcement personnel. Improper actions by an untrained individual could risk the well-being of the person(s) held hostage. Any employee having knowledge of a hostage situation, or one about to occur, should notify security personnel, the theater manager, and the police department. All other employees should be directed away from the scene in order to avoid the chance of additional hostages being taken. Employees may set up at some safe distance to ward off entry into the hostage area by an unknowing employee, customer or other citizen, vendor, etc. Security personnel, if available, will attempt to cut off any potential avenue of escape by the hostage-taker until the police arrive. Employees set up on a perimeter at a determined safe distance should watch for the police or other emergency units, and be able to guide them to the precise location of the hostage scene.

Make notes of assailants: note appearance, demeanor, voice, and in what direction she/he flees. Do not attempt to follow them. Wait for police and give all information that you can.

Additional information regarding the Renaissance Theater can be found in the theater's emergency procedures. These materials and additional copies can be obtained from the theater manager.

Appendix C

Building Forms

The Renaissance Theater • Accident/Incident Form

Date:_____

Name of Injured Party:_____

Address:_____

_____ Phone Number:_____

Injured Party's Seating Location: _____

Time of Accident:_____

Time You Were Notified:_____

Accident/Incident Details:

(Use Additional Paper If Necessary)

_____

_____

_____

Was an Ambulance Called? _____Yes _____No

If Not, Was This at the Party's Request? ____Yes ____No

Witnesses:

Name:_____

Address:_____

_____

Phone:_____

Name and Position of Employee Completing this Form:

_____

The Renaissance Theater   •   Lost And Found

Show: _____
Performance Date: _____
Matinee: _____ Evening: _____
Name: _____
Address: _____
City: _____
State: _____ Zip: _____
Phone: (Home) _____ (Work) _____
Detailed Description of Article:

_____

_____
_____

Location in Theater Where Article Was Lost/Found:

_____

Report Taken by: _____
Date: _____
Follow-Up Action: _____

The Renaissance Theater   •   Inspection Report

Show that just closed: _____ Date: _____
Inspected by: _____
Main Lobby:
Main Auditorium:
Mezzanine:
Balcony:
Back Stage:
Stage Level:
Principal Dressing Rooms:
Chorus Rooms:
Also check: Lights, seats, walls and doors, banisters and steps, carpet and
floors, plumbing, exits and alleys, marquee and 3-sheets, telephones

The Renaissance Theater   •   Lost and Found

Date: _____
Dear _____,
We have received a report that you lost

_____

_____

in the theater during the run of _____.

Unfortunately, at this time we have not recovered an item matching the description. If it should be located at some future date, we will contact you. I am sorry we cannot be of greater assistance. We highly recommend you contact the appropriate authorities if you lost credit cards or important identification, and take action to prevent unauthorized use.

Please note: For lost prescription eyeglasses, it is sometimes difficult to tell whether or not we have them by the customer's description. This is by far the most common lost item. Please feel free to come by the theater during show hours and ask to look through the lost and found box for eyeglasses.

Thank you.

The Renaissance Theater • Problem Form

To: Theater Manager   Date:_____
From: _____   RE: Problem in Theater
Problem:

Diagram Drawing: (if necessary)

Report made by:_____
- -
To be filled out by Manager's Office
Directed to:
_____ Box Office
_____ Backstage   Specify: _____
_____ Front-of-House
_____ Janitorial
_____ Phone Room
_____ Subscriptions
_____ Other   Specify: _____
Instructions:

_____

To be filled out by appropriate department or person, and directed as indicated above. Return to Manager's office on same day received.
Action Taken:

Date completed:

Remarks:

Signed: _____ Date: _____

The Renaissance Theater • Weekly Inspection Report

Month: _____
Show: _____

Week Ending:	6/6/03	6/13/03	6/20/03	6/27/03
Lights:				
Walls and Doors:				
Banisters and Steps:				
Carpet and Floors:				
Plumbing:				
Exits and Alleys:				
Marquee and 3-Sheets:				
Telephone:				
Other:				

Checked By: _____

The Renaissance Theater • Standard Cancellation Form
The Renaissance Theater
1221 Main Street
Midtown, USA
Date: _____
Dear _____,
Please accept this letter as notice of discontinuation of service for the Renaissance Theater until further notice. Specifically, we would like to discontinue:

_____

_____

Our last billing period should be: _____
We anticipate reopening in _____, and my office
will inform you as to the exact date.

Thank you.

_____
Of the Theater Manager's Office
555-5555

The Renaissance Theater • **Standard Authorization Form**

The Renaissance Theater
1221 Main Street
Midtown, USA
Date: _____

Please accept this letter as authorization for the following services to be provided by your company:

_____

_____

_____

Thank you, and should you have any questions, please do not hesitate to call us at the number below.

Sincerely,

_____

Theater Manager's Office
(555) 555-5555

Appendix D

Show and Performance Forms

These are sample forms and memos that may be helpful and can be modeled for your own venue.

The Renaissance Theater
1221 Main Street
Midtown, USA

Information Sheet
Thank you for your interest in our theater. The following shows are currently scheduled for the time period you asked about. Tickets go on sale approximately two weeks to one month before the show opens. Please check local newspapers regarding ticket prices and firmness of dates, or call our information line to hear a recording at 1-800-555-5555.

_____
_____
_____
_____
_____

You may order tickets by phone for any of the above shows by calling the ticket agency at the following number: 1-800-555-5555
Or, you may order by mail from the theater. Please include your name, address, phone, credit card number and expiration date, and at least two dates on which you can attend the show.

Company Manager Information Form

To: Company Manager[1]
Date: _____
From: Theater Manager
RE: Renaissance Theater Information

Welcome to the Renaissance Theater. Listed below are some specifics about the theater intended to make the transition to our city easier. If you have any questions, please contact the house manager.

Office Equipment: There is a copier, typewriter, and fax machine available for company use in the house manager's office. If you want to rent your own typewriter they are available from Smith Office Supplies (555-5555). We request that only one or two people from the company do all the copying to avoid machinery breakdown. Please use the sign-up sheet beside the copier to indicate how many copies were made. The copier is generally not available for company use on Saturdays.

Offices: All company offices are located on the third level of dressing rooms. There are two active phone lines in each office. The company manager's office also has a dedicated line that can be used for a fax line or e-mail. Phone numbers are listed on the jack. If you do not travel with phones, they can be checked out at the house manager's office. Dressing Rooms 1, 2, 8, and 12 also have active phone jacks.

If you are planning to use the offices during the day, you will need to arrange for a stagedoor person to open the theater. The backstage area is generally closed during the day unless you have work calls scheduled.

Rehearsal/Work Calls: At least one house department head must be in the theater for rehearsals. Work calls can be arranged by the stage manager with the house carpenter. The stagedoor person generally reports a half hour prior to the call time unless other arrangements are made through the house manager's office. Company members should enter the theater by the stagedoor. Stagedoor personnel will be on duty two hours prior to show time. If cast members need access to the backstage at any other time, arrangements should be made as there is not always someone available to let them in. The box office will not be able to admit company members inside the theater on a regular basis, and for security reasons, they will not let in anyone they do not know. Anyone who needs access to the theater during nonperformance times on a regular basis (such as wardrobe) should check out keys with the approval of the company manager.

Keys: Keys can be checked out from the theater manager. Our keys are on a security system and are quite expensive to duplicate, so be sure to

---

1. Usually I will give this memo to the company and stage managers on the first day they arrive at the theater. It covers some of the same information that is in the specs package, but often those files are locked in road boxes and company management may not have immediate access to them.

turn them in at the end of the run. Any lost keys may result in charges to the company for replacing both keys and cylinders. For this reason, we highly recommend that you do not carry theater keys on a key chain that will identify them as belonging to a show.

Mail: Mail arrives at the theater between 11 A.M. and 2 P.M. It is sorted by the box office and put in the company basket. It can be picked up by the company or stage manager only. We will not release mail to anyone else unless given instructions by either of these people. Other company documents such as wraps, statements, etc. are also in this basket.

Pets: No dogs, cats, or pets of any kind are allowed in the backstage area of the theater. This rule has been instituted because of health, safety, space, and noise considerations. In addition, the safety of the pets themselves requires they not be brought into the theater because of the presence of rodent control devices and bait trays.

Smoking: There is no smoking in the theater by ordinance of the State Fire Marshall.

Payroll: All theater payrolls must go through the theater's accounting office. If a local man replaces a roadman, this arrangement must be approved by the theatrical union with jurisdiction and at authorized rates. There can be no exchange of cash between road and theater personnel.

Copyright Infringement: The Renaissance Theater does all that is in its power to protect the copyright of the production. We have "Cameras and Recording Prohibited" signs posted in every lobby as well as printed in the program. We encourage each company to make an announcement at the beginning of the show as an added measure to discourage picture taking, video, and sound recording.

While the company is the owner of the copyright and the theater personnel in the position to protect it, we do not have any law backing us when it comes to confiscating a customer's personal property. We would be subjecting ourselves to a lawsuit. This threat has made it impossible to confiscate personal effect from customers. Over the years, we have found that a procedure which works the best to obtain the actual film and/or recordings. We will leave it up to you to decide whether you want us to follow it. The steps are:

1. We ask the customer for their film, telling them we will get the negatives developed and return any negatives that are not of the show. Most times, they agree. The company would reimburse the theater for this cost, usually around $15.00 per roll of film.
2. If the customer refuses to turn over their film, we ask for their name and address, fill out a report and give it to the company manager. It is then up to the company to pursue the matter in civil court.

Closing Memo

The Renaissance Theater
To: Company and Stage Manager
From: House Manager
Date:
RE: Reminder list for closing
----

1. Turn in keys before you leave. Keys checked out by your company are as follows:

_____

_____

2. Turn in phones to manager's office.
3. Leave us a list of items to be picked up after you have left.
   a. They must be left in the lobby.
   b. You have to call for the pickup.
   c. Describe for the manager's office:
      1.) Name of item to be picked up.
      2.) Name of company.
      3.) Company's phone number.
      4.) Time schedule for pickup (between 11 A.M. and 4 P.M.)
   d. Give the company the manager's phone number (555-5555) because often our front door is locked.
   e. If you do not call or bring items to the front-of-house, this may result in extra charges to you.
4. If you have items to be delivered to the theater that have not arrived prior to your departure, let us know so we can watch for them and forward them to you.
5. Mail is forwarded to whatever address is given to us by the company manager.

These cards can be useful to stuff into ticket envelopes, or given to customers as needed.

```
Be Our Guest!
Two Complimentary Beverages
at the Renaissance Theater
```

```
For updated recorded information
on shows at
the Renaissance Theater
please call 555-555-5555
```

If you are planning on seeing
The Time of My Life
during the holiday season, please allow extra time for parking.
Increased traffic as well as limited parking availability may add
time to your commute.
Public Transportation Is Highly Recommended.

The Renaissance Theater • Front-of-House Policies

Revised 6/1/03

The following behavior is banned. Violations are just cause for immediate termination:

Drunkenness, drug usage, theft, gross insubordination, rudeness to customers or coworkers, using foul language, physical or verbal abuse of patrons or coworkers, leaving one's post (except in an emergency), admitting people without a ticket into the theater.

Additionally, all staff members are required to observe the following rules. Continued disregard of these policies can lead to disciplinary action and/or termination.

1. No eating, smoking, drinking, or gum-chewing in public areas or in view of patrons.
2. No sitting on stairs, garbage cans, railings, or the floor in public areas or in view of the patrons.
3. Arrive on time.
4. When finished working, leave the premises. Do not remain to socialize.
5. Do not come to the theater on your time off unless on business.
6. Keep talking to an absolute minimum in all areas during performances.
7. No card or game playing, radios, TVs, or tape recorders in public areas or in view of patrons. Books or periodicals are allowed, but must not interfere with job duties.
8. Employees must work in uniform and have a flashlight.
9. Inform management of any condition related to safety such as burned out lights, broken seats, torn carpets.
10. Friends are not allowed to visit during work time and you may not allow friends into the theater without a ticket.

Below are some typical situations that front-of-house employees may encounter. While every case is different, these are the suggested ways to handle them.

Double Seating:

- Check both sets of tickets for date, location, and show.
- If one party is here on the wrong night, send them to the box office.
- Leave the tickets in the customer's possession. It is too easy to get the tickets mixed up or for a customer to accuse you of switching tickets.
- If it is a true double sale, bring both parties with both sets of tickets to the box office, if possible. If the performance has begun, you may only be able to bring back the latecomers.
- If there is a seating pass and tickets, check the seating pass to see if the box office has noted that it has precedence over the tickets. If so, seat the pass and bring the ticketed people to the box office. If there is no notation, bring both sets of people to the box office.
- If the show has begun and you cannot check the tickets of the seated party (particularly if they are in the middle of the row), reseat the latecomers in available seats and try to straighten it out at intermission. If the theater is sold-out, bring the party to your supervisor who will put them in standing room or available seating. If the customers object, the manager may offer to reschedule or refund them.
- If a patron refuses to go the box office, let your supervisor know at once. It will be too late to rectify a situation after the show has started.

Picture Taking:

- Ask the audience member to stop.
- If they are in the middle of a row, you may need to wait between songs before calling out to them.
- Inform the head usher or manager of the situation.
- Note that the firmness of this policy can vary from show to show, so check with your supervisor to see if it has changed.
- Do not physically touch a person or their property. They often perceive this as an attack, and you can be charged with battery.

Talking during the Show:

- If you can speak to the people, tell them that they are disturbing others and to please be quiet.
- If they are in the middle of a row, wait for a break in the show's scene and say "Shhhh."
- If the talking continues, sit in the row or on the steps where they can see you, and at intermission, speak with them directly.
- Inform your supervisor of the problem, as perhaps the people will be asked to leave, or moved to another location.

Seating Dissatisfaction:

- Patrons can return to the box office to see if they can upgrade to another location.
- If the box office is closed, bring the patron to the head usher or manager. If seats are available a supervisor can arrange for the upgrade.
- On sold-out performances where an upgrade is not possible, tell them they can write a letter of complaint to the theater, give them the address, and show them where they can find the appropriate names in the program.
- With permission of your supervisor, you may move patrons to different seats within their same price range.

Children:

- Children making noise should be treated similarly to adults who are talking.
- If the noise continues, you will have to speak to the parent or guardian at intermission. Inform your supervisor or the house manager if the problem does not resolve itself.
- If the noise still continues, tell the supervisor that you have some people who should be removed from the theater.

In cases where you need a supervisor's attention, but for various reasons are unable to find anyone, you can tell the customer to write a letter to the manager. We do respond to every letter, and often, a customer with a legitimate complaint will receive some adjustment or gratuity.

These are just some of the ways to deal with various situations that involve audience members. There may be others. It is always a good idea to discuss how to handle customer problems with your supervisor or manager. They can give you the best advice as to whether your ideas are ones that the theater management wants to incorporate into their customer service policy.

The Renaissance Theater • Pre-Show Information

Show: _____ Playing Dates: _____

Load-in: _____ Start: _____ End: _____

Wardrobe: _____ Start: _____ End: _____

Pyrotech:

(candles, cigarettes, special effects)

Recorded Music:

(number of minutes, name of music, how used)

Rehearsals:
Papering:
Tech Rider Up-to-Date:
Special Needs:

The Renaissance Theater • Show Summary Sheet

Show: _____ Number of Weeks Played: _____
Weekly Gross Receipts: Ticket Discounts:
w/e: _____
w/e: _____   Statement:
w/e: _____   Subs: _____
w/e: _____   Groups: _____
w/e: _____   Other: _____
Total:
==========
Ticket Prices:
Orchestra $ _____   First Day and Date of Sales: _____
Mezzanine $ _____   Total Wrap: _____
Balcony $ _____   First Week's Total Wrap: _____
   Total Show Advance: _____
Advertising consisted of:
Prints, TV, Radio
Other:
Any holidays or special situations during the run of show:
(Ex: fires, earthquake, canceled shows)
Contract Terms:
Loss or Profit:

Appendix E

Sample Budget

<table>
<tr><td colspan="4">The Renaissance Theater
Estimated Show Expenses
Tentative Date: June 2003</td></tr>
<tr><td>Estimated Theater Expenses</td><td colspan="3">Show: *The Time of My Life*</td></tr>
<tr><td>*Payrolls*</td><td>*Weekly Cost*</td><td>*One-Time Cost*</td><td>*Tech Rider*</td></tr>
<tr><td>1. Stagehands</td><td>47,536.25</td><td></td><td>4,500.00</td></tr>
<tr><td>2. Musicians</td><td>36,430.00</td><td>3,358.08</td><td></td></tr>
<tr><td>3. Wardrobe (incl. est. work calls)</td><td>23,303.83</td><td></td><td></td></tr>
<tr><td>4. Box Office (2nd col. = prelim.)</td><td>6,767.46</td><td>11,444.16</td><td></td></tr>
<tr><td>5. Engineer</td><td>2,780.00</td><td></td><td></td></tr>
<tr><td>6. Stagedoor</td><td>660.24</td><td></td><td></td></tr>
<tr><td>7. Security</td><td>4,216.32</td><td></td><td></td></tr>
<tr><td>8. Ushers</td><td>9,265.37</td><td></td><td></td></tr>
<tr><td>9. Load-in</td><td></td><td>24,760.05</td><td></td></tr>
<tr><td>10. Theater Manager</td><td>3,243.00</td><td></td><td></td></tr>
<tr><td>11. Load-out</td><td></td><td>17,066.37</td><td></td></tr>
<tr><td>Total Payrolls:</td><td>134,202.47</td><td>56,628.66</td><td>4,500.00</td></tr>
<tr><td></td><td>========</td><td>=========</td><td>======</td></tr>
</table>

(continued)

265

Bills	Weekly Cost	One-Time Cost	Tech Rider
1. Advertising	43,750.00		
2. Insurance	2,500.00		
3. Housekeeping	3,000.00		
4. General Bills	5,000.00		
5. Administrative Fee	5,000.00		
6. Theater Rent	20,000.00		
7. Other (Tech Rider)			3,500.00
8. Other (Cushion)		10,000.00	
Total Bills:	79,250.00	10,000.00	3,500.00
Total Payrolls:	134,202.47	56,628.66	4,500.00
Total Bills:	79,250.00	10,000.00	3,500.00
Total Expenses:	213,452.47	66,628.66	8,000.00

The Renaissance Theater
Budget
Show: *The Time of My Life*
Approximate Dates: June 2003
Number of Performances: 32, 4 weeks
Prepared by: Tess Collins

Stagehands	Shows/ Hours	Crew	Rates	Vacation 8%	Subtotal	Total
Heads	8	4	$210.00	$16.80	$226.80	$7,257.60
S.T.			$32.00	$2.56	$34.56	
O.T.	1	4	$48.00	$3.84	$51.84	$207.36
Flyman	8	6	$150.00	$12.00	$162.00	$7,776.00
S.T.			$30.00	$2.40	$32.40	
O.T.	1	6	$45.00	$3.60	$48.60	$291.60
Extra Crew	8	18	$120.00	$9.60	$129.60	$18,662.40
S.T.			$26.00	$2.08	$28.08	
O.T.	1	18	$39.00	$3.12	$42.12	$758.16
				Subtotal	$34,953.12	
				14% Benefits	$4,893.44	
				22% Taxes	$7,689.69	
				TOTAL:	$47,536.25	

The Renaissance Theater
Budget
Show: *The Time of My Life*
Approximate Dates: June 2003
Number of Performances: 32, 4 weeks
Prepared by: Tess Collins

Load-In	Shows/ Hours	Crew	Rates	Vacation 8%	Subtotal	Total
Heads-S.T.	8	4	$32.00	$2.56	$34.56	$1,105.92
Heads-O.T.	2	4	$48.00	$3.84	$51.84	$414.72
Flyman						
S.T.	8	1	$30.00	$2.40	$32.40	$259.20
O.T.	2	1	$45.00	$3.60	$48.60	$97.20
Extra Crew						
S.T.	8	44	$26.00	$2.08	$28.08	$9,884.16
O.T.	2	44	$39.00	$3.12	$42.12	$3,706.56

Subtotal	$15,467.76
14% Benefits	$2,165.49
22% Taxes	$3,402.91
TOTAL:	$21,036.16
	=========

The Renaissance Theater
Budget
Show: *The Time of My Life*
Approximate Dates: June 2003
Number of Performances: 32, 4 weeks
Prepared by: Tess Collins

Load-Out	Shows/ Hours	Crew	Rates	Vacation 8%	Subtotal	Total
Heads-S.T.			$32.00	$2.56	$34.56	
Heads-O.T.	5	4	$48.00	$3.84	$51.84	$1,036.80
Flyman						
S.T.			$30.00	$2.40	$32.40	
O.T.	5	1	$45.00	$3.60	$48.60	$243.00
Extra Crew						
S.T.			$26.00	$2.08	$28.08	
O.T.	5	44	$39.00	$3.12	$42.12	$9,266.40

Subtotal	$10,546.20
14% Benefits	$1,476.47
22% Taxes	$2,320.16
TOTAL:	$14,342.83
	=========

Performance Week						
Box Office	Hours	Crew	Rates	Vacation 5%	Subtotal	Total
Treasurer	40	1	$25.00	$1.25	$26.25	$1,050.00
Asst. Treasurer	40	1	$22.00	$1.10	$23.10	$924.00
Window	40	4	$19.00	$0.95	$19.95	$3,192.00
				Subtotal		$5,166.00
				9% Benefits		$464.94
				22% Taxes		$1,136.52
				TOTAL:		$6,767.46
						========

Preliminary Box Office (2 weeks)						
Box Office	Hours	Crew	Rates	Vacation 5%	Subtotal	Total
Treasurer	80	1	$25.00	$1.25	$26.25	$2,100.00
Asst. Treasurer	80	1	$22.00	$1.10	$23.10	$1,848.00
Window	80	3	$19.00	$0.95	$19.95	$4,788.00
				Subtotal		$8,736.00
				9% Benefits		$786.24
				22% Taxes		$1,921.92
				TOTAL:		$11,444.16
						========

Ushers	Shows	Crew	Rates	Vacation 5%	Subtotal	Total
Early Ushers	8	14	$20.00	$1.00	$21.00	$2,352.00
Late Ushers	8	10	$35.00	$1.75	$36.75	$2,940.00
Ticket-Takers	8	6	$25.00	$1.25	$26.25	$1,260.00
Head Usher	8	1	$62.00	$3.10	$65.10	$520.80
				Subtotal		$7,072.80
				9% Benefits		$636.55
				22% Taxes		$1,556.02
				TOTAL:		$9,265.37
						========

Stagedoor	Shows	Crew	Rates	Vacation 5%	Subtotal	Total
Door Person	40	1	$12.00	$0.65	$12.60	$504.00
				Subtotal		$504.00
				9% Benefits		$45.36
				22% Taxes		$110.88
				TOTAL:		$660.24
						======

Stagedoor Load-In	Shows	Crew	Rates	Vacation 5%	Subtotal	Total
S.T.	8	1	$12.00	$0.60	$12.60	$100.80
O.T.	3	1	$18.00	$0.90	$18.90	$56.70
				Subtotal		$157.50
				9% Benefits		$14.18
				22% Taxes		$34.65
				TOTAL:		$206.33
						======

Stagedoor Load-Out	Shows	Crew	Rates	Vacation 5%	Subtotal	Total
S.T.			$12.00	$0.60	$12.60	
O.T.	5	1	$18.00	$0.90	$18.90	$94.50
				Subtotal		$94.50
				9% Benefits		$8.51
				22% Taxes		$20.79
				TOTAL:		$123.80
						======

Security	Hours	Crew	Rates	Subtotal	Total
Performance	32	6	$18.00	$18.00	$3,456.00
				Subtotal	$3,456.00
				22% Taxes	$760.32
				TOTAL:	$4,216.32
					=======

Security Load-In	Hours	Crew	Rates	Subtotal	Total
Load-In	9	1	$18.00	$18.00	$162.00
				Subtotal	$162.00
				22% Taxes	$35.64
				TOTAL:	$197.64
					======

Security Load-Out	Hours	Crew	Rates	Subtotal	Total
Load-Out	5	1	$18.00	$18.00	$90.00
				Subtotal	$90.00
				22% Taxes	$19.80
				TOTAL:	$109.80
					======

House Manager	Weekly	Time	Subtotal	Total
Manager	$1,600	1	$1,600.00	$1,600.00
Asst. Manager	$750	1	$750.00	$750.00
			Subtotal	$2,350.00
			16% Benefits	$376.00
			22% Taxes	$517.00
			TOTAL:	$3,243.00
				=======

Engineer	Hours	Crew	Rates	Subtotal	Total
Chief	40	1	$50.00	$50.00	$2,000.00
O.T.			$75.00	$75.00	
				Subtotal	$2,000.00
				17% Benefits	$340.00
				22% Taxes	$440.00
				TOTAL:	$2,780.00
					=======

Wardrobe	Shows/ Hours	Crew	Rates	Vacation 6%	Subtotal	Total
Supervisor	7	1	$75.00	$4.50	$79.50	$556.50
Sun. Show	1	1	$100.00	$6.00	$106.00	$106.00
S.T.	12	1	$20.00	$1.20	$21.20	$254.40
O.T.	8	1	$30.00	$1.80	$31.80	$254.40
Dressers	7	15	$70.00	$4.20	$74.20	$7,791.00
Sun. Show	1	15	$90.00	$5.40	$95.40	$1,431.00
S.T.	12	15	$18.00	$1.08	$19.08	$3,434.40
O.T.	8	15	$27.00	$1.62	$28.62	$3,434.40
				Subtotal		$17,262.10
				13% Benefits		$2,244.07
				22% Taxes		$3,797.66
				TOTAL:		$23,303.83
						========

Wardrobe Load-In	Hours	Crew	Rates	Vacation 6%	Subtotal	Total
Supervisor	8	1	$20.00	$1.20	$21.20	$169.60
Extra Crew	8	15	$18.00	$1.08	$19.08	$2,289.60
				Subtotal		$2,459.20
				13% Benefits		$319.70
				22% Taxes		$541.02
				TOTAL:		$3,319.92
						=======

Wardrobe Load-Out	Hours	Crew	Rates	Vacation 6%	Subtotal	Total
Supervisor	4	1	$30.00	$1.80	$31.80	$127.20
Extra Crew	4	15	$27.00	$1.62	$28.62	$1,717.20
				Subtotal		$1,844.40
				13% Benefits		$239.77
				22% Taxes		$405.77
				TOTAL:		$2,489.94
						=======

Orchestra	Shows	Crew	Rates	Vacation 6%	Subtotal	Total
Musicians	8	24	$115.00	$6.90	$121.90	$23,404.80
extra/10%	8	10	$11.50	$0.69	$12.19	$975.20
extra/20%			$23.00	$1.38	$24.38	
extra/35%	8	8	$40.25	$2.42	$42.67	$2,730.88
Contractor/50%	8	1	$57.50	$3.45	$60.95	$487.60
					Subtotal	$27,598.48
					10% Benefits	$2,759.85
					22% Taxes	$6,071.67
					TOTAL:	$36,430.00
						========

Orchestra	Hours	Crew	Rates	Vacation 6%	Subtotal	Total
Rehearsal	4	24	$25.00	$1.50	$26.50	$2,544.00
					Subtotal	$2,544.00
					10% Benefits	$254.40
					22% Taxes	$559.68
					TOTAL:	$3,358.08
						=======

Works Cited

The Actors' Fund of America. Brochure. No date.

Adams, James L. 1986. *Conceptual Blockbusting*. 3rd ed. Reading, Pa.: Addison-Wesley.

Allen, Teresa. 1986. "Infamous Cons Lie in Peace." *Marin Independent Journal*, 26 June.

American Federation of Musicians. 1998. "AFM History." At www.afm.org (access date May 1998).

Aronson, Arnold. 1993. "Architecture, Theatre." In *Cambridge Guide to American Theatre*, edited by Don B. Wilmeth and Tice L. Miller. Cambridge: Cambridge University Press.

Atkinson, Brooks. 1985. Revised Edition. *Broadway*. New York: Limelight Editions. Original edition, New York: Macmillan, 1974.

Barreca, Regina. 1995. *Sweet Revenge*. New York: Harmony Books.

Bell, Marty. 1993. *Broadway Stories: A Backstage Journey through Musical Theatre*. New York: Limelight Editions.

Bennis, Warren. 1989. *On Becoming a Leader*. New York: Addison-Wesley.

———. 1994. *An Invented Life*. Reading, Mass.: Addison-Wesley.

Bing, Stanley. 1992. *Crazy Bosses*. New York: William Morrow.

Block, Peter. 1991. *The Empowered Manager: Positive Political Skills at Work*. San Francisco: Jossey-Bass.

Botto, Louis. 1984. *At This Theater*. New York: Dodd Mead.

Botto, Peter. 1998. Personal interview. September 10, 1998.

Broadway Cares/Equity Fights Aids. 1998. "About Broadway Cares/Equity Fights AIDS." At http://www.bcefa.org/about/index.htm (access date August 1998).

"Broadway's Ticket-Selling Practices Investigated." 1998. *San Francisco Chronicle*, 28 July, D5.

Brockett, Oscar G. 1995. *History of Theatre.* 7th ed. Boston: Allyn and Bacon.

Brower, Mitchell. 1998. Personal interview. August 31, 1998.

Carroll, Jerry. 1997. "Fire in a Crowded Theater." *San Francisco Chronicle* , 18 December, E2.

Carter, Jay. 1989. *Nasty People.* New York: Dorset Press.

"Crowds See Robber Kill Theater Man." 1933. *San Francisco Chronicle,* 20 November, 1.

Curry, Jane Kathleen. 1994. *Nineteenth-Century American Women Theatre Managers.* Westport-London: Greenwood Press.

De Becker, Gavin. 1997. *The Gift of Fear.* Boston: Little, Brown.

Department of Justice ADA Business Connection Page. 2002. "The Americans with Disabilities Act." At http://www.usdoj.gov/crt/ada/business.htm (access date June 2002).

Dilts, Robert B. 1994. *Strategies of Genius.* Vol. 1. Capitola: Meta Publications.

———. 1996. *Visionary Leadership Skills.* Capitola: Meta Publications.

Dilts, Robert B., with Gino Bonissone. 1993. *Skills for the Future: Managing Creativity and Innovation.* Cupertino: Meta Publications.

Dmytryk, Edward. 1984. *On Screen Directing.* Boston: Focal Press.

Douglas, John, and Mark Olshaker. 1995. *Mind Hunter: Inside the FBI's Elite Serial Crime Unit.* New York: Scribner.

DuBoff, Leonard. 1996. *The Performing Arts Business Encyclopedia.* New York: Allworth Press.

Egan, Gerard. 1994. *Working the Shadow Side.* San Francisco: Jossey-Bass.

Evans, Greg. 1994a. "Tommy Tour Tunes Up." *Variety,* 6 February, 71.

———. 1994b. "Shuberts Fire Philly Five." *Variety,* 24 April, 67.

———. 1995. "Broadway League Faces a Long Hot Summer." *Variety,* 26 June, 87.

Faber, Donald C. 1981. *Producing Theatre: A Comprehensive Legal and Business Guide.* New York: Limelight Editions.

———. 1993. *From Option to Opening.* 2nd ed. New York: Limelight Editions.

FEMA California Flood News. 1998. "News Releases." At www.fema.gov/home (access date August 1998).

Forbes, Gordon. 1998. Written interview. August 19, 1998.

Gerard, Jeremy. 1994a. "Ice Fishing in Gotham: Deja Vu All Over Again." *Variety,* 15 May, 193.

———. 1994b. "Scandal Aftermath: Buried Treasurers." *Variety,* 14 August, 67.

———. 1995. "Scalping Probe Ends AMEX Tix Service." *Variety,* 8 January, 80.

———. 1996. "Two Sacked in 'Smokey' B.O. Scam." *Variety,* 19 May, 71.

Ghiselin, Brewster, ed. 1985. Reprint. *The Creative Process.* Berkeley: University of California Press. Original edition, 1952.

Gold, Michael Evan. 1989. *An Introduction to Labor Law.* Ithaca: ILR Press.

Goldman, William. 1984. Reprint. *The Season.* New York: Limelight Editions. Original edition, New York: Harcourt, 1969.

Greenberg, Jan, comp., and Sandy Manley, ed. 1993. *Association of Theatrical Press Agents and Managers: A History of Its Founding.* New York: ATPAM.

Hamlin, Jesse. 1993. "The Opening-Night Crunch." *San Francisco Chronicle,* 14 October, D1.

Hanff, Helene. 1989. *Underfoot in Show Business.* New York: Moyer Bell.

Harris, Andrew B. 1994. *Broadway Theatre*. London/New York: Routledge.

Herman, Edward E., Joshua L. Schwarz, and Alfred Kuhn. 1992. *Collective Bargaining and Labor Relations*. Englewood, N.J.: Prentice Hall.

Hochschild, Arlie Russell. 1983. *The Managed Heart*. Berkeley/Los Angeles: University of California Press.

Ionazzi, Daniel A. 1996. *The Stage Craft Handbook*. Cincinnati, Ohio: Betterway Books.

Jackall, Robert. 1988. *Moral Mazes*. Oxford: Oxford University Press.

"Jury Brings Verdict after Long Battle." 1933. *San Francisco Chronicle*, 27 December, 1.

Karayannakos, Elias. 2002. "Description of an Ancient Theater." *Ancient Greek Theatre*. At http://users.panafonet.gr/ekar/index.html (access date February 2003).

King, Patricia. 1987. *Never Work for a Jerk!* New York: Barnes & Noble by arrangement with Franklin Watts, Inc.

Kissel, Howard. 1993. *David Merrick: The Abominable Showman, The Unauthorized Biography*. New York: Applause Books.

Koestler, Arthur. 1989. Reprint. *The Act of Creation*. New York: Arkana Penguin Books. Original edition, 1964. Hutchinson.

Landrum, Gene N. 1993. *Profiles of Genius: Thirteen Creative Men Who Changed the World*. Buffalo, N.Y.: Prometheus Books.

———. 1994. *Profiles of Female Genius: Thirteen Creative Women Who Changed the World*. Amherst, N.Y.: Prometheus Books.

Langley, Stephen. 1990. *Theatre Management and Production in America*. New York: Drama Book Publishers.

Law, Jonathan, et al. 1994. *Brewer's Theater*. U.S. ed. Great Britain: Market House Books Limited. New York: HarperCollins.

Lazzara, Robert. 1998. Written interview. November 24, 1998.

The League of American Theatres and Producers, Inc. 1998. "Live Broadway." At www.broadway.org (access date July 1998).

"Loma Prieta Facts." *Quake of '89*. At www.kron.com/specials/89 quake (access date August 1998).

MacDonald, Bob. 1998. Written interview. November 20, 1998.

McCarthy, E. Jerome, and William D. Perreault Jr. 1993. *Basic Marketing*. 11th ed. Boston: Irwin.

McDermott, Douglas. 1993. "Unions, Theatrical." In *Cambridge Guide to American Theatre*, edited by Don B. Wilmeth and Tice L. Miller. Cambridge: Cambridge University Press.

Menear, Pauline, and Terry Hawkins. 1989. *Stage Management and Theatre Administration*. Schirmer Books Theatre Manuals. New York: Schirmer Books.

Miller, Milt. 1997. "History of Tickets." *INTRIX, The International Ticketing Association Newsletter*. September 10.

Mintzberg, Henry. 1990. "The Manager's Job: Folklore and Fact." *Harvard Business Review*, No. 2 (March/April): 163–76.

Morgan, Gareth. 1986. *Images of Organization*. Beverly Hills, Calif.: Sage Publications.

Morse, Sally Campbell. 1996. "President Morse Addresses IA Convention." *ATPAM HI-LITES* 59: 7.

Mowen, John C. 1993. *Judgment Calls*. New York: Simon.

NASA. "Oakland Hills Fire Storm: Remote Sensing and Emergency Management." At www.nasa.gov (access date August 1998).

Neilson, Carol. 1998. Written interview. September 23, 1998.

O'Steen, Kathleen. 1994. "Troubles Sink H'wood Blvd.'s Fortunes." *Variety*, 13 November, 7.

Peters, Tom. 1994. *The Tom Peters Seminar: Crazy Times Call for Crazy Organizations*. New York: Vintage Books.

———. 1997. "SoundOff!" *Fast Forward*, September, 12.

Pfeffer, Jeffrey. 1992. *Managing with Power*. Boston: Harvard Business School Press.

Pickering, Jerry V. 1975. *Theater: A Contemporary Introduction*. New York: West Publishing.

Poincaré, Henri. 1985. Reprint. "Mathematical Creation." In *The Creative Process*, edited by Brewster Ghiselin. Translated by George Bruce Halsted. Berkeley: University of California Press. Original edition, 1952.

Powell, Edward C. 1998. Personal interview. September 22, 1998.

Richardson, Jerry. 1987. *The Magic of Rapport*. Cupertino: Meta Publications, 1987.

Schneider, Richard E., and Mary Jo Ford. 1993. *The Well-Run Theater*. New York: Drama Publishers.

Scott-Morgan, Peter. 1994. *The Unwritten Rules of the Game*. New York: McGraw.

Senge, Peter. 1990. *The Fifth Discipline: The Art and Practice of the Learning Organizations*. New York: Currency.

Shekerjian, Denise. 1991. *Uncommon Genius*. New York: Penguin Books.

Sinetar, Marsha. 1991. *Developing a 21st Century Mind*. Villard ed. New York: Ballantine Books.

"Slayer of Curran Cashier Caught in Holdup, Confesses." 1933. *San Francisco Chronicle*, 19 December, 1.

"Slayer Tells Own Story of Crimes Here." 1933. *San Francisco Chronicle*, 19 December, 1.

Spence, Gerry. 1995. *How to Argue and Win Every Time*. New York: St. Martin's.

Taylor, Markland. 1994. "Heads Hunted in Mass. Scalp Sting." *Variety*, 27 November, 42.

"Thanks for the Memories." 1993. *Variety*, 19 July, 59.

Tjosvold, Dean. 1993. *Teamwork for Customers*. San Francisco: Jossey-Bass.

Traina, Joe. 1998. Written interviews. October 27 and 15, November, 1998.

Vega, Jose. 1994. Personal interview. June 22, 1994.

Walton, Richard E., and Robert B. McKersie. 1991. *A Behavioral Theory of Labor Negotiations*. 2nd ed. Ithaca: ILR Press. Original edition, New York: McGraw, 1965.

Ward, Thomas B., Ronald A. Finke, and Steven M. Smith. 1995. *Creativity and the Mind*. New York: Plenum Press.

Whiting, Sam. 1995. "Sneezy, Chatty, & Fidgety." *S.F. Chronicle Datebook* , 3 September, 28.

Williams, Montel, with Daniel Paisner. *Mountain, Get Out of My Way*. New York: Warner, 1996, paperback 1997.

Wilmeth, Don B. 1993. "Fires." In *Cambridge Guide to American Theatre*, edited by Don B. Wilmeth and Tice L. Miller. Cambridge: Cambridge University Press.

Witt, Scott. 1983. *How to Be Twice As Smart*. West Nyack, N.Y.: Parker.

Ziegler, Dolores. 1996. "Dismissals Denied in Shooting Case." *San Francisco Daily Journal*, 20 December, 2.

Index

About the Author

Tess Collins has worked over twenty years in theater management for the Shorenstein Hays * Nederlander Organization. She has managed the Golden Gate, Orpheum, and Curran Theaters, major Broadway show venues in San Francisco. She received a B.A. from the University of Kentucky and a Ph.D. from The Union Institute. She is the author of *The Law of Revenge*, *The Law of the Dead*, and *The Law of Betrayal* thrillers set in Appalachia, and three plays *Tossing Monte*, *Barbarians*, and *Helen of Troy*. Access her web site at www.tesscollins.com.